HOW DIVINE IMAGES
BECAME ART

Dr. Oleg Tarasov is an independent scholar (Rome). The author of numerous publications on cultural history and art, his books include *Icon and Devotion: Sacred Spaces in Imperial Russia*, transl. and ed. by R.-M. Gulland (London: Reaktion Books, 2002), *Framing Russian Art: From Early Icons to Malevich*, transl. by R.-M. Gulland and A. Wood (London: Reaktion Books, 2011), *Russian Art Nouveau and Ancient Icons* (Moscow: Indrik, 2016) (in Russian) and others. Tarasov obtained a Ph.D. in History at the Institute of Slavic Studies of the Russian Academy of Sciences and in Art History at Department of History and Theory of Arts of the State Moscow University. He held posts at the State Moscow University, Department of History, and at the Department of Cultural History of the Institute of Slavic Studies of the Russian Academy of Sciences (Senior Research Fellow).

Stella Rock (the translator of this volume) is Honorary Associate at the Faculty of Arts and Social Sciences, School of Social Sciences and Global Studies, Religious Studies at the Open university (UK).

How Divine Images Became Art

Essays on the Rediscovery, Study and Collecting of Medieval Icons in the *Belle Époque*

Oleg Tarasov

Translated by Stella Rock

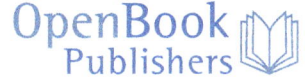

https://www.openbookpublishers.com

©2024 Oleg Tarasov

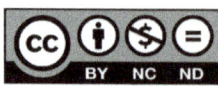

This work is licensed under a Creative Commons Attribution-NonCommercial-NoDerivatives 4.0 International license (CC BY-NC-ND 4.0). This license allows you to share, copy, distribute and transmit the work for non-commercial purposes, providing attribution is made to the author (but not in any way that suggests that he endorses you or your use of the work). Attribution should include the following information:

Oleg Tarasov, *How Divine Images Became Art: Essays on the Rediscovery, Study and Collecting of Medieval Icons in the Belle Époque*. Cambridge, UK: Open Book Publishers, 2024, https://doi.org/10.11647/OBP.0378

Copyright and permissions for the reuse of many of the images included in this publication differ from the above. This information is provided in the captions and in the list of illustrations. Every effort has been made to identify and contact copyright holders and any omission or error will be corrected if notification is made to the publisher.

Further details about CC BY-NC-ND licenses are available at
http://creativecommons.org/licenses/by-nc-nd/4.0/

All external links were active at the time of publication unless otherwise stated and have been archived via the Internet Archive Wayback Machine at https://archive.org/web

Any digital material and resources associated with this volume may be available at https://doi.org/10.11647/OBP.0378#resources

ISBN Paperback: 978-1-80511-158-0
ISBN Hardback: 978-1-80511-159-7
ISBN Digital (PDF): 978-1-80511-160-3
ISBN Digital eBook (EPUB): 978-1-80511-161-0
ISBN XML: 978-1-80511-162-7
ISBN HTML: 978-1-80511-163-4

DOI: 10.11647/OBP.0378

Cover image: Icon of Archangel Michael (fourteenth century). Novgorod School. Tempera on wood, 86 x 63 cm. From the collection of Stepan Riabushinskii in Moscow. Tretyakov Gallery, Moscow. Wikimedia, public domain, https://commons.wikimedia.org/wiki/File:The_archangle_Michael_(Novgorod).jpg
Cover design: Jeevanjot Kaur Nagpal

Contents

Acknowledgements	vii
Introduction	1
1. Fashion, Taste and Form	11
2. From Images of Italy to Early Russian Art	45
3. The New Museum of Medieval Icons	67
4. Florenskii, Metaphysics and Reverse Perspective	117
Conclusion	171
Bibliography	177
List of Figures	199
Index	205

Acknowledgements

While working on this book, I had the unwavering support of many of my friends and colleagues. Above all, I would like to express my special and deep gratitude to Boris Uspenskii, whose long-term and friendly relations have always stimulated me to search for new topics and scientific approaches. Uspenskii is credited with the discovery and first publication in 1967 of Pavel Florenskii's article 'Obratnaia perspektiva' ['Reverse Perspective']. Therefore, it is no coincidence that our numerous discussions about the term 'reverse perspective' and the origin of the semiotics of the medieval image inspired me to continue searching for new documents in this field, and to write an essay exploring Florenskii's metaphysics of the icon. Uspenskii also kindly agreed to read the manuscript at the stage of its preparation for publication and made a number of very valuable comments.

Engaging in discussions and the exchange of ideas with Ksenia Muratova, Valentino Pace and Rita Giuliani within the framework of the Pavel Muratov International Center of Studies in Rome once again allowed me to clarify certain features of Muratov's biography, and enabled me to incorporate additional relevant literature into my research on this topic.

Anna Maria de Strobel kindly helped me become acquainted in detail with the collection of Greek and Russian icons in the Vatican Museums, and Giovanni Pagliarulo introduced me to the collection of Italian 'primitives' and the archive of Bernard Berenson at the Villa I Tatti near Florence. With their assistance, I managed to discover a number of little-known historical facts.

Of course, I am deeply grateful to Stella Rock for her very professional work: she undertook the task of translating the manuscript from Russian into English and checked the English quotations from the original sources.

My final thanks are to the staff at Open Book Publishers and, above all, Alessandra Tosi, Adèle Kreager, Cameron Craig and Jeevanjot Nagpal.

Introduction

This book introduces to the western reader a major topic which has, so far, attracted little attention: the simultaneous perception of medieval Russian icons and of Early Renaissance painting as *pure art* in the cultural context of pre-war Europe. There is a fairly substantial literature addressing the discovery of the Italian 'primitives', and likewise a string of significant publications providing an overview of Byzantine and post-Byzantine icons.[1] Consequently, the reader will welcome acquaintance

---

1 Italian scholarship reveals that the Italians were the first to become interested in collecting 'primitives'. While the occasional scholar paid attention to them during the Reformation era, others examined them during the Enlightenment and Romantic eras. See F. Zeri, 'Qualche appunto sul Daddi', in F. Zeri, *Giorno per giorno nella pittura. Scritti sull arte Toscana dal Trecento al primo Cinquecento* (Turin: Allemandi, 1991), pp. 19–23; L. Venturi, *Il gusto dei primitivi* (Bologna: Zanichelli, 1926); G. Previtali, *La fortuna dei primitivi: dal Vasari al Neoclassicismo* (Turin: Einaudi, 1964). Analysing Previtali's book, Mario Praz highlighted the significance of eighteenth-century anti-Baroque polemics for the study of 'primitives', and of Romantic interest in folklife and folk religion (M. Praz, *Il patto col serpent* (Milan: Adelphi, 2013), pp. 131–39). These ideas were reflected in the landmark catalogue of an exhibition on the 'primitives' in Italy during the eighteenth and nineteenth centuries, held in 2014 at the Gallery of the Academy of Fine Arts in Florence (A. Tartuferi and G. Tormen, *La fortuna dei primitivi. Tesori d'arte dalle collezioni italiane fra Sette e Ottocento. Firenze, Galleria dell'Academia, 24 giugno–8 dicembre 2014* (Florence: Giunti, 2014)). For their part, English authors argue that historical interest in Italian 'primitives' may be observed primarily from the mid-nineteenth century onwards (see F. Haskell, *Rediscoveries in Art. Some Aspects of Taste, Fashion and Collecting in England and France* (Ithaca, NY: Cornell University Press, 1976), pp. 21, 82; see also E. H. Gombrich, *The Preference for the Primitive. Episodes in the History of Western Taste and Art* (London: Phaidon, 2002), pp. 154–55). Further works of relevance include K. M. Muratova, 'Ital'ianskoe iskusstvo XIII i XIV vekov v russkoi kritike: sviazi, vzaimovliianiia, sud"by', in *In Christo. Vo Khriste. Obmen khudozhestvennymi i dukhovnymi shedevrami mezhdu Rossiei i Italiei*, ed. A. Melloni (Rome: Treccani, 2011), pp. 521–68; S. Moretti, *Roma bizantina. Opere d'arte dall' impero di Costantinopoli nelle collezioni romane* (Rome: Campisano, 2014). Among other general works, see V. Lazarev, *L'arte russa delle icone dalle origini all'inizio del XVI secolo*, ed. G. I. Vzdornov (Milan: Jaca Book, 1996); T. Velmans, ed., *L'arte dell'icona* (Milan: Jaca Book, 2013); T. Velmans, ed., *Icone. Il grande viaggio* (Milan: Jaca Book, 2015).

©2024 Oleg Tarasov, CC BY-NC-ND 4.0   https://doi.org/10.11647/OBP.0378.00

with the history of the rediscovery and study of medieval Russian icons, which represent a significant branch of Byzantine and post-Byzantine painting. An understanding of medieval icons and 'primitives' as a special type of art was finally affirmed in the key era of the *Belle Époque* (c. 1871–1914) – but, to this day, this perspective is still, occasionally, questioned. This work aims, therefore, to demonstrate that the creative output of Byzantine, medieval Russian and early Italian masters is genuine art, based on its own rhetorical schemas and the specificities of the creative imagination.

The book consists of four essays, written for a broad audience. Their shared theme is the Formalist theory of art, connoisseurship and the influence these had on the study and collection of medieval Russian icons and the works of Early Renaissance artists in the years of the *Belle Époque*. Art history took shape as an independent academic discipline only in the middle of the nineteenth century. However, it is precisely on the threshold between the nineteenth and twentieth centuries that the artistic form of an artwork is singled out from other questions of aesthetics, and becomes a separate topic pondered by scholars, art critics and artists. The main personages on our stage, then, are those art historians and collectors famous in their day: Bernard Berenson (1865–1959), Pavel Muratov (1881–1950), Ilya Ostroukhov (1858–1929), Pavel Florenskii (1882–1937) and several others. They will appear before us together with their different fates, their diverse interests and their, at times, diametrically opposed academic predilections. However, we will easily identify that which unites them – a previously unseen interest in painting 'on golden backgrounds' and, more precisely, in the artistic forms of medieval icons and early Italian art of the fourteenth and fifteenth centuries. In their eyes, that which had long been considered 'primitive' and unskilled suddenly acquired the status of unique artwork.

The term 'primitive', which arose in the Enlightenment era and became widespread in nineteenth-century art criticism, was clearly connected with determining the boundaries of art from the very beginning. All the art of the 'primitive', colonized peoples of Asia, Africa and America lay beyond these bounds, due to the Eurocentrism of the times, while the works of Byzantine, early Rus' and Western European artists of the thirteenth and fourteenth centuries provided the classic models of the 'primitive'. Occasionally, artists of the *Belle Époque* themselves were deemed 'primitives'. From the end of the 1890s, the term 'primitive' began to lose its original meaning, although it continued to be used to describe Early Renaissance art. Up until the birth of Cubism in 1907, any divergence from the rules of linear perspective was viewed as incompetence. The discovery, in that same year, of reverse perspective as an independent system for the composition of artistic space prompted an aesthetic re-evaluation of early icons ('primitives') by analogy with Renaissance painting. The orientation of linear perspective on the external viewer's point of view was called into question. The ancient, 'primitive' image, a construction of artistic space that suggested several viewpoints simultaneously, was put forward for consideration in place of the Renaissance painting. This is why artists of the Russian and European avant-garde, together with scholars, may rightly be considered pioneers of the new aesthetic knowledge of medieval art. In other words, Byzantine and medieval Russian icons, Italian 'primitives' of the thirteenth, fourteenth and fifteenth centuries, Gothic stained glass and African sculpture were all incorporated into the orbit of the highest artistic values and reinterpreted in both new works on the history and theory of art, and in the new developments of avant-garde painting, beginning with Cubism, Futurism and Neoprimitivism.

Moreover, it was not only a new style of art that was consolidated in the *Belle Époque*. A new way of understanding the world connected with the cult of art – that last flowering of the religion of beauty which brought significant shifts in Western European and Russian culture – was also established. Aestheticism and the Nietzschean 'death of God' led to affirmation of a multiplicity of points of view on the world. It would therefore hardly be an exaggeration to say that the particular worldview which, to this day, determines the basic dimensions of our picture of the world was, to a great extent, shaped in those very years of the *Belle Époque*.

A fair amount has been written about Berenson and his activity as an art critic and private art dealer, as well as his connections with major scholars, museums and collectors. This famous American researcher and connoisseur was distinguished by his brilliant literary language and compared the icons of Duccio (c. 1255/60–c. 1318/19) with the works of Raphael (1483–1520) in their magnificence of colour and 'feeling' of space. Genuine art 'produces life-enhancement' according to his theories, which were grounded in the psychology of vision.[2] After Berenson settled in the Villa I Tatti near Florence in 1901, his house became a meeting place for American millionaires, major international antiquarians and also the owners of local antiquarian-restoration establishments frequented by middlemen in search of masterpieces of Italian painting. Isabella Stewart Gardner (1840–1924), Frederick Mason Perkins (1874–1955), Philip Lehman (1861–1947) and Robert Lehman (1891–1969), Robert Langton Douglas (1864–1951), Helen Clay Frick (1888–1984), Sir Joseph Duveen (1869–1939), Stefano Bardini (1836–1922) and many others visited the villa on more than one occasion. Today, the villa houses the Harvard University Center for Italian Renaissance Studies (I Tatti), which has recently prepared a seminal catalogue of the scholar's collection.[3]

Meanwhile, the Russian art historian and writer Muratov is comparatively less well known to a western audience, although it was in fact Muratov who laid the foundations for the stylistic analysis of medieval Russian icons and wrote a great deal on the Italian 'primitives'. Nevertheless, his contribution to introducing the western reader to the aesthetics of early Russian painting is unquestionable.[4] It is appropriate

---

2   B. Berenson, *The Italian Painters in the Renaissance* (Oxford: Oxford University Press, 1952), p. 199.
3   See *The Bernard and Mary Berenson Collection of European Paintings at I Tatti*, ed. C. D. Strehlke and M. B. Israels (Florence: Villa I Tatti, 2015). See also the overviews by E. Samuels, *Bernard Berenson. The Making of a Connoisseur* (Cambridge, MA: Harvard University Press, 1979); E. Samuels, *Bernard Berenson. The Making of a Legend* (Cambridge, MA: Harvard University Press, 1979); W. Weaver, *A Legacy of Excellence: The Story of Villa I Tatti* (New York: Harry N. Abrams, 1997); R. Cohen, *Bernhard Berenson: A Life in the Picture Trade* (New Haven, CT: Yale University Press, 2013); for an Italian translation of this book, see R. Cohen, *Bernard Berenson: da Boston a Firenze*, trans. M. Gini (Milan: Adelphi, 2017).
4   P. Deotto, 'Pavel Muratov', in *Dictionary of Literary Biography: Russian Émigré Writers of the Twentieth Century*, ed. M. Rubins (Washington, DC: Thomson Gale, 2005), pp. 237–47. Muratov's new approaches to the study of medieval Russian painting are touched upon in Ivan Foletti's book on the famous Russian Byzantinist Nikodim Kondakov: I. Foletti, *From Byzantium to Holy Russia. Nikodim Kondakov (1844–1925) and the Invention of the Icon*, trans. S. Melker (Rome: Viella, 2011). See also K. M. Muratova, 'Pavel Muratov historien d'art en Occident', in *La Russie et l'Occident. Relations intellectuelles et artistiques au temps des révolutions russes*, ed. I. Foletti (Rome: Viella, 2010), pp. 65–95. Muratov's important work, *Obrazy Italii*, has recently appeared in Italian translation: P. Muratov, *Immagini dell'Italia*, ed. R. Giuliani, trans. A. Romano, 2 vols. (Milan: Adelphi, 2019–21).

to note, too, the influence of Berenson's works on Muratov, with whom he was personally acquainted.⁵ Federico Zeri (1921–98) once highlighted the significance of Henri Matisse's (1869–1954) perspective on the Russian icons he encountered during his 1911 trip to Moscow:

> It is necessary to emphasize one single thing. Matisse was a big fan of icon-painting from his youth. Icon-painting in the West as a whole is not perceived as art, so in Italy there has long been a tradition to consider icons not as works of painting, but only as 'a semblance of art'. However, Matisse thought differently: his passion for pure color, of course, to some extent comes from icons, which sometimes have dazzling coloristic intonations. This explains the artist's rapid success in the Russian cultural environment.⁶

Muratov continued the work of Matisse in acquainting the western observer with the aesthetics of early Russian icons. His 1925 monograph, *Drevnerusskaia zhivopis'* [*Russian Medieval Painting*], was first published in Western Europe in Italian.⁷ In short, this was the first book in which the new methods of stylistic analysis of medieval Russian icons were employed. Recalling this translation, the Italian Slavicist Ettore Lo Gatto (1890–1983) said: 'My most important meeting with Pavel Pavlovich [Muratov] was related to "La pittura russa antica" – at that point the fashion for icons, which was followed by the publication of a series of superbly produced works in various European languages, had not yet arrived in the West'.⁸ Muratov's book was next translated into French, with the inclusion of new material.⁹ 'His French book on the Russian icon', as a contemporary wrote about the publication of *Les icones russes* [*Russian Icons*],

---

5   At the beginning of the 1920s, Muratov translated Berenson's essays on Florentine Renaissance paintings (published as a stand-alone edition) from English into Russian. He also translated a large extract from the American researcher's book *Critical Essays on Italian Art*, published in the first issue of the journal *Sofiia*, of which he was the chief editor. See B. Berenson, *Florentiiskie zhivopistsy Vozrozhdeniia*, trans. with an introduction by P. P. Muratov (Moscow: S. I. Sakharov, 1923); B. Berenson, 'Osnovy khudozhestvennogo raspoznavaniia', *Sofiia*, 1 (1914), 40–69.
6   F. Zeri, *Abecedario pittorico* (Milan: Longanesi, 2008), p. 142.
7   P. P. Muratov, *La pittura russa antica*, trans. E. Lo Gatto (Rome: A. Stock, 1925).
8   E. Lo Gatto, *I miei incontri con la Russia* (Milan: Mursia, 1976), pp. 56–59.
9   P. P. Muratov, *Les icones russes* (Paris: Schiffrin, 1927).

became something of an event [...] a whole sphere of art, which had remained not only undervalued but simply unknown, was revealed to the foreign reader. In those days, who had heard the name of Andrei Rublev, or Theophanes the Greek? What museum curator could distinguish an icon in the Novgorod tradition from others? The desire to collect icons, which continues to grow to this day, was largely generated thanks to Muratov.[10]

Alfred Barr (1902–81), the founder and first director of the Museum of Modern Art in New York, noted in his diary that, in Moscow in January 1928, he read Muratov's book *Les icones russes* in French, which had been lent him by the artist and collector Ostroukhov. After visiting Ostroukhov's Museum of Medieval Russian Painting, he was 'finally conquered by Russian icons', as Matisse had been earlier.[11] At the same time, Barr was studying medieval art and comparing early icons with Russian and western Modernist compositions. In other words, Muratov's books in Italian and French may be seen as the first serious attempt in the West to interpret the Russian icon as a distinct world of artistic forms. After Muratov emigrated to the West in 1922, his name was erased in Soviet Russia. His scholarly works on the history of Italian culture and medieval Russian painting were not republished until the arrival of perestroika in the USSR in the 1980s, alongside increased interest in his intellectual legacy.[12]

---

10 A. Bakhrakh, '"Evropeets" s Arbata', in *Vozvrashchenie Muratova. Ot 'Obrazov Italii' do 'Istorii kavkazskikh voin'. Po materialam vystavki 'Pavel Muratov – chelovek Serebrianogo veka' v Gos. Muzee izovrazitel'nykh iskusstv imeni A. S. Pushkina 3 marta–20 aprelia 2008 goda*, ed. G. I. Vzdornov and K. M. Muratova (Moscow: Indrik, 2008), pp. 158–59 (p. 159).

11 See S. G. Kantor, *Alfred H. Barr, Jr. and the Intellectual Origins of the Museum of Modern Art* (Cambridge, MA: MIT Press 2002), p. 165.

12 In 2008, the first exhibition of its kind, 'Pavel Muratov – A Man of the Silver Age', was held in the Museum of Fine Arts in Moscow. See *Vozvrashchenie Muratova. Ot 'Obrazov Italii' do 'Istorii kavkazskikh voin'*, ed. Vzdornov and Muratova. Art historian Ksenia Muratova created the International 'Pavel Muratov' Study Centre in Rome in 2012 (Centro Internazionale di Studi Paolo Muratov, https://www.pavelmuratovcentre.org/it), which welcomes European and American writers, artists, art historians and patrons with the aim of preserving and disseminating Muratov's artistic and intellectual heritage. The third international conference organized by the Centre was held in Naples in September 2017. See *Letture Muratoviane III. Atti del Colloquio Internazionale (Napoli, 28–30 settembre 2017). Studi in memoria di Xenia Muratova*, ed. R. Giuliani (Rome: Lithos, 2021). See also O. Tarasov, 'Pavel Muratov, i "primitivi" italiani e le icone russe antiche', in *Letture Muratoviane III*, ed. Giuliani, pp. 247–55; M. Bernabo, 'Pavel Muratov sull'arte

The collection of the artist and social activist Ostroukhov, considered in Russia a pioneer of the new collecting of early icons as masterpieces of painting, offers insights into important general trends in both the study of the artistic forms of icons and 'primitives', and in their collection and the reshaping of the art market. Entirely in the spirit of *Belle Époque* aestheticism, Prince Sergei Shcherbatov (1874–1962) – an active figure in the art world at the start of the twentieth century – spoke of Ostroukhov as a collector who created 'the atmosphere of an icon cult' in Moscow of the 1910s, while Ostroukhov's new private Museum of Medieval Russian Painting called to mind a new church of the 'aesthetic religion'.[13] In essence, it was this same taste for 'primitives on golden backgrounds' that was instilled in the American millionaire Berenson from at least the end of the nineteenth century.

If Muratov examined the icon from the point of view of the development of style, the Russian philosopher and theologian Florenskii was the first to explore the medieval icon's profound philosophical meaning and how it is constructed within a system of reverse perspective. Since Florenskii paid particular attention to the construction of the religious image's artistic space, analysis of his texts is key in establishing the icon as a work of high art. In this regard, Florenskii's view on the metaphysics of the icon may be of particular interest to the reader. For Berenson, for example, real art should produce 'a sense of heightened vitality'.[14] For Florenskii, in contrast, genuine art must direct the gaze beyond the bounds of the reality that surrounds us. It always creates a special aura and a sensation of distance. In this respect, the ideas of the Russian philosopher to some extent corresponded with the thinking of members of the Russian and western avant-garde. In essence, the complex language of the icon, distinguished by unusual expressiveness, is far from 'Primitivism' and is explained by the epoch's characteristic

---

bizantina e russa e sui primitivi italiani (1924–1928)', in *Letture Muratoviane III*, ed. Giuliani, pp. 257–69.

13 S. Shcherbatov, *Khudozhnik v ushedshei Rossii* (Moscow: Soglasie 2000), pp. 210–11. Shcherbatov was a well-known Moscow patron, artist and collector. He emigrated in 1919 and lived in France (in his Cannes villa), the United States of America and Italy. In 1927, he became one of the founders of the Icon Society in Paris. He moved to Rome in 1953 and is buried in the Testaccio cemetery.

14 B. Berenson, *The Italian Painters of the Renaissance* (London: Phaidon, 1959), p. 54.

worldview rather than by 'mistakes' in the construction of linear perspective.

Florenskii's name, and his works on the icon, remained unknown for many years. Italian researcher Elémire Zolla (1926–2002) laid the foundations for their study in Western Europe back in 1977, publishing 'Ikonostas' ['*Iconostasis*'] – Florenskii's most famous essay on the icon – in Italian. Since then, interest in the works of the 'Russian Leonardo' has only grown, with conferences and a large body of literature dedicated to Florenskii, and his works republished and translated into foreign languages.[15] A portrait of Florenskii appeared in the papal Redemptoris Mater Chapel, in the Vatican, in 1999.

---

15 See P. A. Florenskii, *Le porte regali. Saggio sull' icona*, ed. E. Zolla (Milan: Adelphi, 1977); an English abridged translation of *Iconostasis* edited with a foreword by J. L. Opie was published in 1976. See P. A. Florenskii, 'On the Icon', *Eastern Churches Review*, 8.1 (1976), 11–37. For a full English translation, see P. A. Florenskii, *Iconostasis*, trans. D. Sheehan and O. Andrejev (Crestwood, NY: St. Vladimir's Seminary Press, 1996). Works in English on Florenskii of particular note include: R. Slesinski, *Pavel Florensky: A Metaphysics of Love* (Crestwood, NY: St. Vladimir's Seminary Press,1984); V. Bychkov, *The Aesthetic Face of Being: Art in the Theology of Pavel Florensky* (Crestwood, NY: St. Vladimir's Seminary Press, 1993); C. Antonova, *Visual Thought in Russian Religious Philosophy. Pavel Florensky's Theory of the Icon* (New York: Routledge, 2020). For a bibliography of works in Italian on Florenskii, see N. Valentini, 'Bibliografia', in P. A. Florenskii, *La mistica e l'anima russa*, ed. N. Valentini and L. Zak (Milan: Edizioni San Paolo, 2006), pp. 51–54. On early studies of Florenskii's works on the icon, see J. L. Opie, *Nel mondo delle icone. Dall'India a Bisanzio* (Milan: Jaca Book, 2014), pp. 167–72; *P. A. Florenskij e la cultura della sua epoca*, ed. N. Kauchtschischwili and M. Hagemeister (Marburg: Blaue Hörner Verlag, 1995). Florenskii's article 'Reverse Perspective' was first published in Russian in 1967 by Boris Uspenskii, the renowned representative of the Moscow-Tartu Semiotic School (P. A. Florenskii, 'Obratnaia perspektiva', *Trudy po znakovym sistemam*, 3 (1967), 381–416). The first English translation of this text (together with several of Florenskii's articles on art) was published in 2002. See P. A. Florenskii, *Beyond Vision. Essays on the Perception of Art*, ed. N. Misler, trans. W. Salmond (London: Reaktion, 2002). See also O. Tarasov, 'Florensky and "Reverse Perspective": Investigating the History of a Term', *Sobornost/Eastern Churches Review*, 43.1 (2021), 7–37. Archival materials relating to the 'Analysis of Perspective', the lecture cycle that Florenskii delivered in Moscow in 1921–24, have also recently been published in Russian. See P. A. Florenskii, *Istoriia i filosofiia iskusstva. Sbornik tekstov*, ed. A. Trubachev et al. (Moscow: Akademicheskij proekt, 2017). This volume brings together, for the first time, corrected and supplemented texts in Russian of works such as 'Ikonostas' (1919–22), 'Obratnaia perspektiva' (1919), 'Analiz prostranstvennosti i vremeni v khudozhestvenno-izobrazitel'nykh proizvedeniiakh' (1924), and also articles on art from 1918–25. I draw primarily on this volume (henceforth Florenskii, *Istoriia i filosofiia iskusstva*) when quoting these works. Florenskii's family, and above all the hegumen Andronik (Aleksandr)

Today, significant museum collections of Byzantine, Italo-Greek and Russian icons, not to mention collections of the works of early Italian artists, may be found in Western Europe and the USA. These are all exhibited, discussed by respected scholars and presented in seminal catalogues.[16] This evolution highlights how the foundations of many contemporary historico-cultural practices were laid in the years of the *Belle Époque*. The displaying of these early icons began to change the perception of them as works of art, leading to new illustrations, advertisements and to a new design of books and magazines, placing the compositions of Byzantine and post-Byzantine masters on a par with the works of modern European artists.

Trubachev and Mariia Trubacheva played a key role in preserving and promoting Florenskii's creative legacy.

16 See, in particular, J. Durand, ed., *Byzance. L'art byzantine dans les collections publiques françaises* (Paris: Éditions de la Réunion des musées nationaux, 1992); N. Chatzidakis, *Icons. The Velimezis Collection. Catalogue raisonne* (Thessaloniki: The Benaki Museum, 1997); A. A. Karakatsanis, ed., *Treasures of Mount Athos* (Thessaloniki: Museum of Byzantine Culture, 1999); M. Acheimastou-Potamianou, *Icons of the Byzantine Museum of Athens* (Athens: Ministry of Culture, Archaeological Receipts Fund, 1998); E. Haustein-Bartsch and I. Bentchev, *Ikonen-Museum Recklinghausen* (Moscow: Ikonen-Museum Recklinghausen, 2008); P. Zachauk, ed., *Icons. Icon Museum Frankfurt am Main* (Frankfurt: Ikonenmuseum der Stadt Frankfurt am Main, 2005); R. Cormack, ed., *Icons* (London: The British Museum Press, 2007); W. Salmond, *Russian Icons at Hillwood* (Washington, DC: Hillwood Museum and Gardens, 1998); A. W. Carr, ed., *Imprinting the Divine: Byzantine and Russian Icons from the Menil Collection* (New Haven, CT: Yale University Press, 2011). In Italy, there are significant collections of icons including at the Pinacoteca Vaticana, the Hellenic Institute of Byzantine and post-Byzantine Studies in Venice, the Florentine Academy of Arts, and the Intesa Bank's collection of Russian icons at the Palazzo Leoni Montanari in Vicenza. See G. Pavan, ed., *Icone dalle collezioni del Museo Nazionale di Ravenna* (Ravenna: Il Museo, 1979); M. F. Fiorin, *Catalogo della Pinacoteca Vaticana. Vol. 4: Icone della Pinacoteca Vaticana* (Vatican City: Edizioni Musei Vaticani, 1995); V. Conticelli and D. Parenti, eds., *Icone russe in mostra alla Galleria degli Uffizi. Catalogo. Galleria degli Uffizi* (Florence: Sillabe, 2014); C. Pirovano, *Icone russe. Collezione banca Intesa* (Milan: Electa, 2003). The major Italian exhibitions of early Russian icons and the accompanying catalogues edited by C. Pirovano are particularly noteworthy: Fondazione Giorgio Chini, *L'immagine dello spirito. Icone dalle terre russe, collezione Ambroveneto* (Milan: Electa, 1996); C. Pirovano, ed., *Icone russe. Gallerie di Palazzo Leoni Montanari* (Milan: Electa, 1999); C. Pirovano, ed., *Arte e Sacro Mistero. Tesori dal Museo Russo di San Pietroburgo* (Milan: Electa, 2000); M. Kazanaki-Lappa, ed., *Nasledie Vizantii: Muzei ikon Grecheskogo instituta vizantiiskikh i postvizantiiskikh issledovanii v Venetsii* (Moscow: Grand-Kholding, 2009).

1. Fashion, Taste and Form

> Seeing as such has its own history, and uncovering these 'optical strata' has to be considered the most elementary task of art history.
>
> —Heinrich Wölfflin (1864–1945)[17]

At the Intersection of Cultural Movements

Researchers and admirers of art long ago turned their attention to the discovery in Russia at the beginning of the twentieth century of the early icon's aesthetic significance. We are well aware of the key players involved in this discovery – the young art critics Pavel Muratov (1881–1950), Nikolai Shchekotov (1884–1945), Nikolai Punin (1888–1953) and the artist Aleksei Grishchenko (1883–1977). Details of the main icons of collections belonging to the artist Ilya Ostroukhov (1858–1929), the Old Believer banker-collector Stepan Riabushinskii (1874–1942), the scholar Nikolai Likhachev (1862–1936) and the major entrepreneurs Aleksei Morozov (1867–1934) and Pavel Kharitonenko (1852–1914) have come to light and been published in part. Much, too, has been written on the new restoration techniques which revealed the original layer of paint on early icons. This discovery, meanwhile, unfolded amidst the European genesis of new aesthetic theories, the development of novel approaches to the study of artworks, and ultimately within the glittering atmosphere of artistic life in the *Belle Époque* (c. 1871–1914). Our focus will therefore be on this context, with the aim of delineating the aesthetics of the early Russian icon against this backdrop of academic and artistic life unfolding in Russia and Western Europe at the end of the nineteenth

---

17 H. Wölfflin, *Principles of Art History: The Problem of the Development of Style in Early Modern Art*, trans. E. A. Levy and T. Weddigen (Los Angeles, CA: Getty Research Institute, 2015), p. 93.

and first decades of the twentieth centuries. 'The discovery of early Russian art was not, of course, happenstance', Muratov wrote in 1923,

> The spirit of the age brought to fruition recognition of its elevated artistic value. It could not have happened earlier than the first years of the current century precisely because of this. A European at the beginning of the twentieth century has access to immeasurably more artistic interests to aid comprehension than were available to people in the [18]60s and even the [18]80s. That we are indebted in this also to the painters of our recent and glittering past is not always acknowledged. Monet, the Impressionists, Cézanne were not only masters of their art but also great civilizers, in the sense of strengthening European humanity's connections, great reeducators of our sensibility. It is no coincidence that those who seemed to their contemporaries to be simply mad innovators, are for our generation the great traditionalists who revealed Velazquez, Poussin, Magnasco, Greek Antiquity, medieval sculpture, and Chinese painting.[18]

Indeed, the re-evaluation of early icons was furthered, one way or another, by German art criticism and formal-psychological aesthetics, a new wave of interest in Byzantine painting, the unprecedented discovery of the aesthetic significance of Italian and Flemish 'primitives', the work of English essayists and the famous Moscow collections of Impressionist and Modernist art owned by Russian industrialists Sergei Shchukin (1854–1936) and Ivan Morozov (1871–1921) (which will be further explored below). All this facilitated the discovery of the icon's aesthetic significance and its conception as an outstanding manifestation of art, heir to the traditions of Hellenistic and Byzantine culture.

It is significant that the early Russian icon's aesthetic importance was also discovered in the context of the Romantic *cult of art*, the development of that special 'aesthetic piety' which originated in the culture of the Enlightenment. We therefore find distinct internal interconnections in the academic and artistic life of Russia and Western Europe of the nineteenth and early twentieth centuries. It is no coincidence that the pioneers (including representatives of the Russian avant-garde) who revealed the aesthetic beauty of early icons sought to present the icon's history as connected to the history of Western European art, locating its

---

18 P. P. Muratov, 'Otkrytiia drevnego russkogo iskusstva', in P. P. Muratov, *Russkaia zhivopis' do serediny XVII veka. Istoriia otkrytiia i issledovaniia*, ed. A. M. Khitrov (St Petersburg: Bibliopolis, 2008), pp. 323–24.

origins in the intersection of cultural movements of the East and West. The enamoured gaze of scholars and collectors in Moscow, Rome and London upon Sienese Madonnas of the Trecento and Quattrocento and Novgorodian icons of the same period clearly took shape in parallel. If we look at the attitudes of connoisseurs and researchers to early icons and to the works of early Italian artists, this becomes obvious. Before these works were understood as artistic masterpieces, part of the highest levels of culture, their paths in the history of academia, fashion and taste were rather similar.

For the entire duration of the eighteenth century and for most of the nineteenth century, neither the Italian 'primitives' nor medieval Russian icons were regarded as works of *pure art* distinguished by the individuality of the artist. The lack of deep picture space and the two dimensionality of the image were entirely incomprehensible – viewed as curiosities and, when compared with Antique models, considered retrogressive. The culture of classicism excluded religious images on boards from the sphere of high art, and only Romanticism generated a little more interest in them, in its search for national identity and folk culture. It is for this reason that the first collectors of 'primitives' and icons in Italy were from the ranks of the clergy, and in Russia the first collectors were Old Believers,[19] who saw early icons as holy objects. The beauty of early icons and 'primitives' was perceived as integral to the ecclesiastical cult and a Christian worldview. Interest was accompanied by their renovation (often also their repainting), copying and placement in museums of Christian antiquities or private Catholic chapels.

Thus, Cardinal Stefano Borgia (1731–1804) was collecting Byzantine and post-Byzantine icons in the second half of the eighteenth century. His Museo Sacro, set up in Rome's Palazzo Altemps, was clearly based on the same model as the Museum of Christian Antiquities established in Rome by Abbé Giuseppe Lelli, Agostino Mariotti (1724–1806), a lawyer of the Sacra Congregazione, and Francesco Saverio de Zelada (1717–1801), who also served in the Vatican. Among the 'primitives' housed in this latter museum was Carlo Crivelli's (c. 1435–95) famous

---

19   The term 'Old Believers' refers to those who continued to follow the liturgical and ritual practices of the Russian Orthodox Church after the mid-seventeenth-century reforms of Patriarch Nikon – the so-called *raskol* [schism] which created a division that endures to the present day.

Saint Dominic (1476) polyptych, known in academia as the *Pala Demidov*, in reference to its later owner, Russian Anatole Demidov, Prince of San Donato (1813–70) (see Fig. 1.1).[20]

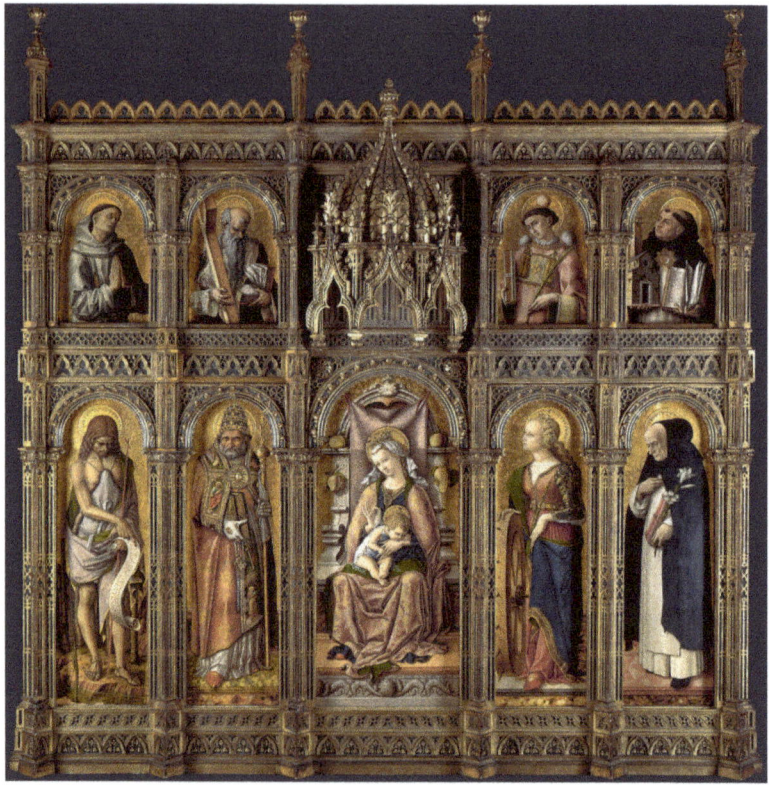

Fig. 1.1 Carlo Crivelli (c. 1435–95), *Poliptych of San Domenico (Pala Demidov)* (1476), tempera on wood. From the collection of Prince Anatole Demidov. National Gallery, London. Wikimedia, public domain.
https://commons.wikimedia.org/wiki/File:Carlo_Crivelli_005.jpg

The Vatican Library's Museum of Religious Art (Museo Sacro della Biblioteca Vaticana) took shape in the same period, with librarian Guiseppe Simone's (1687–1768) acquisition of Italian 'primitives' and icons. Francesco Vettori (1692–1770) presented Pope Clement XIII

---

20 Prince Demidov sold *Polittico di San Domenico (Pala Demidov)* in 1868 in Paris; it is currently housed in London's National Gallery. See G. Tormen, *Dipinti 'sull'asse d'oro': I primitivi nelle collezioni italiane tra Sette e Ottocento. Un itinerario*, in *Tesori d'arte dalle collezioni italiane fra Sette e Ottocento, Firenze, Galleria dell'Academia, 24 giugno–8 dicembre 2014* (Florence: Giunti, 2014), pp. 20–21.

(1693–1769) with a wonderful Russian icon of *Saint Nicholas with Scenes from his Life* (from the second half of the sixteenth century) in 1763, on the occasion of his first visit to the museum. On the reverse of the icon, he inscribed a dedication in Latin, supplementing an earlier donor inscription in Old Slavonic.[21] The Tuscan priest Angelo Maria Bandini (1726–1803) and the Jesuit Luigi Lanzi (1732–1810) began collecting paintings 'on golden backgrounds' in 1752. Bandini bought the old Oratorio di Sant'Ansano in Fiesole near Florence in 1795 and founded the first private museum of religious art in Tuscany there (*Museo Sacro di Sant'Ansano*), which still exists to this day. As well as appreciating the religious significance of the 'primitives', Abbé Lanzi – who features in every textbook on Italian painting – viewed them as works of art. Lanzi served as keeper of the Uffizi Galleries in Florence and, instructed to refurbish the display by the museum's director Giuseppe Bencivenni Pelli (1729–1808), began to purchase 'primitives' from local antiquarians in the second half of the 1770s. The resulting Cabinet of Early Paintings (*Gabinetto delle pitture antiche*) appeared in the Uffizi Galleries sometime around 1780, which included Russian icons as well as Byzantine and Italo-Greek exhibits displayed alongside the works of Cimabue (c. 1240–1302), Duccio (c. 1255/60–c. 1318/19) and Fra Angelico (c. 1395–1455). Since some of these works – in particular the *Beheading of John the Baptist*, an icon of the Stroganov School dating from the end of the sixteenth or beginning of the seventeenth century – came to the Uffizi from the Palazzo Pitti, they had evidently entered the Medici collection earlier. Icons and 'primitives' were viewed through the prism of Giorgio Vasari's (1511–74) evolutionary model, which was based on understandings of 'progress' and 'decline' in the history of art. This seems to have been the very first public display of Russian icons in Western Europe, which were then recognized as being on par with the examples of Byzantine and early Italian painting. Russian icons were fitted into the concept of *maniera bizantina* [Byzantine style] and ascribed to a period earlier

---

21   According to the Old Slavonic inscription, Princess Evdokiia, the daughter of Mikhail Andreevich Godunov, gave the icon to a Russian monastery in 1571 for the commemoration of the soul of her brother Ioann. The Latin inscription indicates that the first director of the Museo Sacro, Vettori, presented the icon to Pope Clement XIII on 2 April 1763, the occasion of his first visit to the museum. See M. F. Fiorin, *Catalogo della Pinacoteca Vaticana. Vol. 4: Icone della Pinacoteca Vaticana* (Vatican City: Edizioni Musei Vaticani, 1995), pp. 67–68, fig. 115.

than when they were actually painted.[22] Lanzi published the famous book *A History of Painting in Italy*, which distinguished the Florentine, Sienese, Neapolitan and other Schools for the first time and thus set a new direction in the history of painting. His Cabinet of Early Paintings aimed to show the stage that preceded the Florentine Renaissance in the development of art. Contributing his own perspective to the rehabilitation of the 'primitives', Lanzi also intended to distinguish the style and manner of each era and School.

Interestingly, famous artists also contributed to the discovery of Italian 'primitives' in the context of Romantic aesthetics. Proponents of the Nazarene movement and the Pre-Raphaelites, influenced by the ideas of Wilhelm Heinrich Wackenroder (1773–98) and John Ruskin (1819–1900), perceived a spiritual loftiness and original character of form in the 'naïve' representations of Sienese Madonnas and Tuscan Gothic art. Lord Alexander Lindsay (1812–80) also wrote on this in his famous *Sketches of the History of Christian Art* (1847). Lindsay, hailing from a famous aristocratic family, travelled extensively in Italy, collected 'primitives' and wrote on a wide range of topics. Byzantine and early Italian art, which he considered an important foundation for the revival and renewal of eastern culture, occupied a special place in his writings. In his day this was an unmistakeably novel point of view. In the section entitled 'Byzantine Art', he wrote:

> I can hardly doubt that the respect with which I have spoken of the arts of Byzantium, in the preceding pages, must have appeared rather strange to you. We are apt to think of the Byzantines as a race of dastards, effete and worn out in body and mind [...] But the fact is, that the influence of Christianity on Byzantium, and of Byzantium on modern Europe, has been much underrated.[23]

---

22 See V. Conticelli and D. Parenti, eds., *Icone russe in mostra alla Galleria degli Uffizi. Catalogo. Galleria degli Uffizzi* (Florence: Sillabe, 2014). These were mainly mass-produced Russian icons, reminiscent of the output by Italo-Cretan 'madonneri'. Cf. O. Tarasov, *Icon and Devotion. Sacred Spaces in Imperial Russia*, trans. R. Milner-Gulland (London: Reaktion, 2002), pp. 50–57; M. Chatzidakis, 'Le peintures des madonneri ou Veneto cretoise et sa destination', in *Venezia centro di mediazione tra Oriente e Occidente*, ed. H.-G. Beck, M. Manoussacs and A. Pertusi, 2 vols. (Florence: 1977), II, 675–90.

23 A. W. C. Lindsay, *Sketches of the History of Christian Art*, 3 vols. (London: John Murray, 1847), I, 59. see also J. Steegman, 'Lord Lindsay's "History of Christian Art"', *Journal of Warburg and Courtauld Institutes*, 10 (1947), 123–31.

Around the same time, the Ashmolean Museum in Oxford exhibited painting 'on gold backgrounds' to the broader public for the very first time. However, for almost the entire second half of the nineteenth century, the Italian 'primitives', and Byzantine and Italo-Greek icons, were more often viewed as religious objects or as handicrafts fashioned in the context of religious practice, attributed to an early stage in the development of painting, before the 'epoch of art'. English museums had no desire to exhibit the works of Giotto (c. 1267–1337) and Cimabue in the 1830s.[24] When it was suggested in the mid-nineteenth century that London's National Gallery might purchase a collection of early Italian paintings procured by a British antiquarian, the influential British magazine *Art Journal* made a characteristic comment: 'We do not need antiquities and curiosities of early Italian painters: they would only infect our school with a retrograding mania of disfiguring art'.[25] At the beginning of the 1870s, almost all American museums also rejected the 'primitives'. Art historian James Jackson Jarves (1818–88), the first American collector of early Italian painting, had lived in Florence in the 1850s and had there acquired a collection of 'primitives'; he was only able to sell his collection in the States to the Yale University Art Gallery in 1871, and, even then, only for a meagre sum. Other museums displayed no interest in his collection at all.

Old Believers and Their Oratories

The entire history of the collection of early Russian icons and Italian 'primitives' in Russia also testifies to the fact that they began to be perceived as works of *pure art* chiefly at the beginning of the twentieth century. Until then, their cultural role was entirely different. In Russia, early icons began to be collected and preserved within Old Believer communities as early as the second half of the seventeenth century, and this practice was flourishing in the middle and second half of the nineteenth century. In the genuinely religious gaze of the Old Believers,

---

24   E. Camporeale, 'On the Early Collections of Italian Primitives', in *Le stanze dei tesori. Collezionisti e antiquari a Firenze tra Ottocento e Novecento*, ed. L. Mannini (Florence: Polistampa, 2011), pp. 29–43 (p. 43).

25   Cited in F. Haskell, *Rediscoveries in Art. Some Aspects of Taste, Fashion and Collecting in England and France* (Ithaca, NY: Cornell University Press, 1976), p. 53.

however, the icon was not *pure art* but something infinitely higher. Its artistic aspect was valued to the extent to which it evoked religious sentiments and proximity to God. The artistic value of the devotional image was determined, above all, by its conformity with the medieval canon, as a visual form of the reality of the other world. From the point of view of the Old Believers, a purely aesthetic perception of the medieval icon was, in some ways, even blasphemous.

As almost all researchers have observed, Russian Old Believer collections were exclusively placed in prayer houses (*domovye molennye* [domestic oratories]), within a sacred space which had its own distinct characteristics. This space had largely inherited the furnishings of the 'home churches' that were built in the houses of the Russian nobility in the sixteenth and seventeenth centuries. The famous Russian historian Ivan Zabelin (1820–1908) provides us with a detailed description of a seventeenth-century prayer house: 'One of the walls', he writes, 'was entirely covered by an iconostasis of several rows, in which the icons were arranged as in a church iconostasis, beginning with the Deesis row or icons of the Saviour, Mother of God and John the Baptist'.[26] In other words, the space of the prayer house followed an ecclesiastical model of decoration, in which the iconostasis was the main feature. However, what distinguished this space was the personal devotional images, which reflected an individual's life path from birth to death. Especially venerated images (proskynetaria) – which hark back to the images decorating the tombs of early Christian saints – usually occupied the lower row of the iconostasis in a church. In prayer houses, this row was replaced by ancestral icons, those which blessed weddings, rewarded zealous service or were carried on feast days. *Votive icons* and crosses were ordered on the occasion of miraculous intervention in daily life. The *family icon*, which answered the family's collective prayers, was also located in the prayer house. This icon had Christ or the Mother of God at the centre, with the saints that family members were named after depicted nearby or around the icon's borders.

Pilgrim icons and reliquaries, brought back from monasteries and holy places, also occupied an important place in Old Believer prayer houses. It is worth recalling here Constantinople's Church of the Theotokos of

---

26 I. Zabelin, *Domashnii byt russkikh tsarei v XVI i XVII stoletiiakh*, 2 vols. (Moscow: V. Grachev and Komp., 1862), I, 193–94.

the Pharos, a church-reliquary that belonged to the Byzantine emperor. This provided the model for founding the design of the sacred space in both Orthodox churches and prayer houses on reliquaries. Saints' relics were, of course, always seen as vitally important sources of grace, highly valued in both the Catholic West and the Orthodox East. Relics therefore 'authenticated', as it were, the structure of sacred space in a prayer house. Moreover, for a believer, the saint was truly present on earth in both their relics and their icons, which made reliquaries and images closely aligned within the religious system. Consequently, those miracle-working icons which were especially venerated, all manner of reliquaries in the form of caskets and folding triptychs, enkolpion reliquary crosses and icons containing embedded relics, invariably took pride of place in a prayer house.

Stroganov icons, distinguished by their exquisite painting in miniature, began to appear in the chapels of the Russian nobility at the end of the sixteenth and first half of the seventeenth centuries. One of these Stroganov icons, as already noted, ended up in the Palazzo Pitti in Florence. 'Distinguished' members of the Stroganov family, of course, had their own icon workshops, but the Sovereign's iconographers also worked for them – Prokopii Chirin (d. c. 1627), Nikifor Savin (first half of the seventeenth century), Stefan Aref'ev (end of the sixteenth to the beginning of the seventeenth century) and several others. Their signed works were considered precious cult items, as well as highly valued investments and offerings.[27] In the future, it was precisely these 'Stroganov icons' that would take pride of place in the famous Old Believer icon collections of the Rakhmanovs, Riabushinskiis, Morozovs and other wealthy Russian families of the nineteenth and early twentieth centuries. Their sumptuous prayer houses, then, were often collections of medieval Russian and Greek icons (copies of wonderworking icons of the Mother of God, for example), or collections of all manner of reliquaries. However, the primary motivation for collecting and carefully preserving these icons stemmed from their symbolic significance within the rites of the Russian Church, until Patriarch Nikon's (1605–81) reforms and the decisions made at the Moscow Council of 1667. Thereafter, the primary artistic value of these early icons inhered in their canonicity;

---

27 For a general overview in English of Stroganov School icons, see J. Stuart, *Ikons* (London: Faber and Faber, 1975), pp. 119–27.

in other words, the specific semiotic system articulated by the sign of the cross made with two fingers, and by the abbreviated name of Christ (IC XC). To pray before icons with the abbreviation 'ИНС ХС' (i.e., those conventional after Patriarch Nikon's reforms and painted in a Western European style) was deemed blasphemous and associated with the veneration of the Antichrist.[28] The early image therefore became far more significant in the conception of salvation and in ritual practice. In preserving the medieval canon over centuries, Russian Old Believers not only followed the patristic tradition of icon veneration, but significantly enriched it, in their artistic practice and applied aesthetic outlooks.

Over the course of the eighteenth and nineteenth centuries, a unique system of expert folk knowledge concerning the stylistic manner of early Russian masters also developed within the Old Believer community. This was most fully formulated in an 1856 publication, *Obozrenie ikonopisaniia v Rossii do kontsa XVII veka* [*A Survey of Icon-Painting in Russia to the End of the Seventeenth century*], by the famous collector and expert on Russian folk art Dmitrii Rovinskii (1924–1895). On the basis of the Old Believer records, Rovinskii distinguished three main Schools of Russian icon-painting – the Moscow, Novgorod and Stroganov Schools, within which might be found multiple local styles of execution ('Romanov', 'Ustiug', 'Baronovskii' etc.).[29] The famous academic archaeologist Fyodor Buslaev (1818–97) observed in the mid-nineteenth century that Old Believers 'know the best masters of the Stroganov and Novgorod Schools by name and spare no expense in acquiring the icon of some renowned master or other and, while venerating it as a holy object, are also able to explain it and its artistic worth in such a way that their technical and archaeological observations may furnish useful material for the historiography of Russian ecclesiastical art'. Moreover, 'I have been able to visit many of the Moscow prayer houses and always come away with the most pleasing impression, full of the fresh artistic enthusiasm with which their pious owners relate to the treasures they have collected. They lift the icons from their places on the walls in order to better see all the detail of

---

28 See Tarasov, *Icon and Devotion*, trans. Milner-Gulland, pp. 144–67.
29 D. A. Rovinskii, *Obozrenie ikonopisaniia v Rossii do kontsa XVII veka* (St Petersburg: Izdatel'stvo A. S. Suvorina, 1856 [1903]).

execution or to discern an ancient inscription'.[30] One may also include the particularities of Old Believer restoration work on medieval icons in the aforementioned 'detail of execution'. Since the canonicity of a prayer house's image was paramount (that is, its conformity with the medieval canonical requirement that an icon be ordered according to reverse perspective and contain Christ's earlier title, 'IC XC'), after cleaning, Old Believers might repaint an icon according to their understanding of a particular School of early Russian painting.

Objects of Folk Religiosity or Artistic Antiquities?

Similarly, the museums and private individuals that began collecting icons in Russia in the second half of the nineteenth century did not accord the icon the status of a work of *pure art*; instead, the icon was regarded as an object of folk religiosity. Moreover, in the mid-nineteenth century, an emotional connection to the past took precedence over a structured approach to the study of the icon, and this characterized the nature of exhibitions of private repositories of rarities. The objects of such collections were united by the passion of the collector of antiquities, who had created an 'archaeological museum' with its roots in the European *Kunstkammer* [cabinets of curiosity] of the sixteenth century. This, in turn, had grown out of the Tuscan Duke Francesco de' Medici's (1541–87) famous *Cabinet of Rarities* in the Palazzo Vecchio in Florence, brought to fruition by Vasari in 1570–75. Cabinets of curiosity were inspired by Renaissance thought, and, in the era of Renaissance-Baroque Humanism and the Enlightenment, they reflected not only universal abilities of human understanding but also the very order of the surrounding world. These all-encompassing displays, organized like academic compendiums, would later be broken up and divided into collections of the natural sciences, picture galleries and also *cabinets of art* (comprehensive collections of artistic antiquities). In mid-nineteenth century Russia, one such cabinet belonged to Count Sergei Grigor'evich Stroganov (1794–1882). Among Russian aristocratic families (the Yusupovs, Galitsyns, Shuvalovs), the Stroganovs, of course, played

---

30 F. I. Buslaev, 'Moskovskie molel'ni', in F. I. Buslaev, *Sochineniia F. I. Buslaeva*, 3 vols. (St Petersburg: V Tipografii Tovarishchestva 'Obschestvennaia pol'za', 1908), I, 252–53.

a leading role in generating interest in early Russian and early Italian art. According to Buslaev's memoirs, the Count's Moscow 'cabinet' was a long room with walls entirely covered by bookcases and 'various rarities in pull-out drawers' that housed collections of Greek, Roman and Byzantine coins. A golden vase by Benvenuto Cellini (1500–71) stood out amidst cases full of valuable decorative sculptures, and above these hung paintings by Old Italian and Flemish masters. The Italian 'primitives' also found a home in this environment, as did Stroganov School icons from the end of the sixteenth to the beginning of the seventeenth century. The Count had acquired these as early as the 1840s, and aside from their belonging to the history of Christian antiquities, they evoked his famous ancestors who were proprietors of icon-painting workshops.[31] The collection included genuine masterpieces by the Russian iconographers Chirin, Nikifor and Nazarii Savin, Aref'ev and several others. The Count later donated nearly the entire collection of icons to the Russian Museum and the Theological Academy in St Petersburg.

Early Russian icons were viewed differently in state and private collections of national rarities, where they conveyed an image of an 'ancient' civilization and culture. The collection of the famous historian and Slavophile Mikhail Pogodin (1800–75) stands out amongst the wealth of private collections of the mid- to late nineteenth century. The special halls of Pogodin's famous 'Antiquities repository' in Moscow, visited by members of the imperial family, were literally crammed full of Russian antiquities. One might encounter here 'Scythian' jewellery and embroidery, portraits and wooden sculpture, and also genuine masterpieces of Russian painting, for example the famous fourteenth-century *vita* icon of St George, which today graces the Russian Museum in St Petersburg. These were all hung on the walls, stood on the floors, or kept in cupboards and in chests of drawers.[32] In 1852, Pogodin's entire collection was acquired by Emperor Nicholas I (1796–1855) for

---

31   F. I. Buslaev, *Moi vospominaniia* (Moscow: Tipografiia G. Lessnera i A. Geshel'ia, 1897), pp. 168–70.

32   For further detail on the history of Russian collections of medieval icons in the nineteenth century see G. I. Vzdornov, *The History of the Discovery and Study of Russian Medieval Painting*, ed. M. Sollins, trans. V. G. Dereviagin (Leiden: Brill, 2017), pp. 52–100, 251–320.

150,000 rubles; the collection, in almost its entirety, entered the Imperial Academy of Arts' Museum of Christian Antiquities in St Petersburg.

Italian 'Primitives' Arrive in Russia

The president of the Imperial Academy of Arts, Grand Princess Maria Nikolaevna (1819–70), was one of the first in Russia to show interest in the Italian 'primitives'. Maria Nikolaevna was captivated by the artists of the Nazarene School, particularly Peter von Cornelius (1783–1867) and Johann Friedrich Overbeck (1789–1869), who evidently opened her eyes to the value of this kind of art during her visit to Rome in the winter of 1842.[33] With her support, the Imperial Academy's Museum of Christian Antiquities was swiftly founded in St Petersburg, and included amongst its exhibits both Italian 'primitives' and Byzantine, Italo-Greek and Russian icons. Some of these were acquired and donated by the museum's *de facto* founder, Prince Grigorii Gagarin (1810–93), Vice-President of the Academy of Arts (1859–72). The *Madonna and Child Enthroned, with Attendant Angels* (1365–70, Museum of Fine Arts, Moscow), painted by Giovanni di Bartolomeo Cristiani (1340–96), entered the collection around 1860, having been acquired in Italy – probably in Florence – by Karl-August Beine (1815–58), a professor of architecture in the Academy of Arts. Notably, this work is the central panel of a folding composition, the side panels of which are the images of *Saint Bartholomew* and *Saint Dominic* in the Bandini Museum in Fiesole.

The Russian government also acquired Fra Angelico's fresco the *Madonna and Child with Saint Dominic and Saint Thomas Aquinas* (State Hermitage, St Petersburg), which once graced the monastery of St Dominic near Fiesole, from Florentine antiquarians in 1882. However, until the start of the twentieth century, Italian 'primitives' barely featured in the Hermitage's collection, as may be gauged from an article

---

33 Italian 'primitives' were to be found in Maria Nikolaevna's private collection and at her Villa Quatro near Florence; these included, notably, a work by Filippo Lippi (*The Vision of St Augustine* (c. 1465)). See T. K. Kustodieva, ed., *Sobranie zapadnoevropeiskoi zhivopisi. Katalog. Ital'ianskaia zhivopis' XIII–XVI vv* (Moscow: Gosudarstvennyi Ermitazh, 1994), pp. 234–35. On Princess Maria Nikolaevna's collection of paintings, see also E. Lipgart, 'Kak kollektsiionirovala Velikaia kniaginia Mariia Nikolaevna', in *Nasledie Velikoi Kniagini Marii Nikolaevny*, ed. Baron N. N. Vrangel (St Petersburg: n.p., 1913), pp. 8–11.

by the director of drawings and prints at the Hermitage, Baron Ernst von Liphart (1847–1932), which broaches the subject of the re-evaluation of early Italian painting. Addressing these new additions, the author underlined the significance of the 'primitives' for the Hermitage's collection and particularly for the teaching of art history, which would now start, he wrote, 'not with Fra Angelico but with the very genesis of Italian painting'.[34] In 1908 this Hermitage collection was further enlarged by works which had previously belonged to the Imperial Academy of Arts' Museum of Christian Antiquities, including the *Madonna and Child* by the circle of Ambrogio Lorenzetti (c. 1285/90–1348), and Cristiani's *Saint Romuald and Saint Andrew* (1365–70). According to Federico Zeri's (1921–98) reconstruction, these were the wings of the aforementioned folding work, the central panel of which is now in the Museum of Fine Arts in Moscow. The two side panels (*Saint Bartholomew* and *Saint Dominic*), however, are in the Bandini Museum in Fiesole.[35]

Early Italian paintings also became better known among private art enthusiasts in Russia from the second half of the nineteenth century onwards. This was due to visits to Italy, publications and personal connections with Italian collectors and antiquarians. It was the religiosity and historical-cultural value of the Italian 'primitives' that first attracted attention. Thus the Russian archaeologist Pyotr Sevast'ianov (1811–67) acquired the now famous icon *Madonna and Child Enthroned, with Scenes from the Life of Mary* (1275–80, Museum of Fine Arts, Moscow), from the circle of Coppo di Marcovaldo (1225–76), in Rome in 1863 (see Fig. 1.2).[36] In this same period, the writer Prince Pyotr Viazemskii (1820–88) brought the *Madonna and Child Enthroned, with Saints and Angels* (1370s, Museum of Fine Arts, Moscow) home from Italy to his Ostafyevo estate in the Moscow countryside. It was in Italy, too, that Dmitrii Khomiakov (1841–1919), son of the eminent Russian Slavophile Aleksei Khomiakov (1804–60), accumulated between 1886 and 1898 his small but extremely

---

34 E. Lipgart, 'Imperatorskii Ermitazh. Priobreteniia i pereveski', *Starye gody* (January 1910), 19.

35 C. Mavarelli, ed., *Museo Bandini di Fiesole. Guida* (Florence: Polistampa, 2011), pp. 50–51.

36 V. Lazarev, 'Un nuovo capolavoro della pittura fiorentina duecentesca', *Rivista d'arte*, 30 (1953), 3–63; A. Tartuferi, *La pittura a Firenze nel Duecento* (Florence: Alberto Bruschi, 1990), pp. 26–27, 77 (pp. 59–62); V. E. Markova, *Italiia VIII–XVI vekov. Sobranie zhivopisi Gos. Muzeia izobrazitel'nykh iskusstv im. A. S. Pushkina. Katalog*, 2 vols. (Moscow: Galart, 2002), I, 36–39.

valuable collection. This collection was donated to the Rumiantsev Museum in Moscow in 1901. Notably, it included Simone di Filippo Benvenuti's (c. 1300–99) 'per devozione privata' *Annunciation* icon (early 1380s, Museum of Fine Arts, Moscow) and Matteo di Giovanni's (1430–95) *Madonna and Child with Saints* (1490s, Museum of Fine Arts, Moscow). Finally, one of the most interesting collections of Italian 'primitives' in Russia was assembled by the Russian Consul General in Trieste, Mikhail Sergeevich Shchekin (1871–1920), who, while in Italy, managed to acquire the rarest works of Simone Martini (c. 1284–1344), Segna di Bonaventura (c. 1280–1331), Sano di Pietro (1405–81) and other artists. In 1909, these were all donated to the Museum of Fine Arts in Moscow, which will be discussed further below.

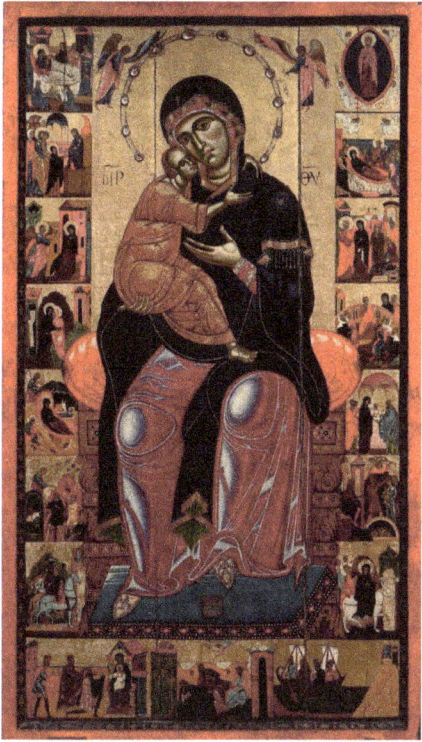

Fig. 1.2 Coppo di Marcovaldo (1225–76), *Madonna and Child Enthroned, with Scenes from the Life of Mary* (*Maestà*) (1275–80), tempera on wood, 246 x 138 cm. From the collection of Pyotr Sevast'anov. The Pushkin State Museum of Fine Arts, Moscow. Wikimedia, photograph by Sailko (2020), CC BY-SA 3.0, https://commons.wikimedia.org/wiki/File:Cerchia_di_coppo_di_marcovaldo,_maest%C3%A0.JPG

The creation of private house-museums in Russia, open to the public, also became fashionable in the last quarter of the nineteenth century. One may assume that Florence, with the special air of enthusiasm for early Italian art and the Renaissance era it generated in this period, was a particular influence here. The house-museums of amateur art enthusiasts Frederick Stibbert (1838–1906) and Herbert Percy Horne (1864–1916) appeared in precisely the last quarter of the nineteenth and start of the twentieth century, as did the showrooms in the elegant palaces of Stefano Bardini (1836–1922) and Elia Volpi (1858–1938), important dealers in Italian late medieval and Renaissance art. These supplied foreigners with valuable cult items procured from aristocratic collections and from Tuscany and Umbria's churches and monasteries. Florence, of course, becomes Europe's biggest antiquarian art market in the years of the *Belle Époque*, intrinsically linked with the new scholarship and cultural tourism of high society in England, Russia, Germany and America. We should not forget, too, that the grandiose collection of Western European painting owned by the Russian aristocratic family of the Demidovs was assembled and located on their estates near Florence. Part of the collection of Nikolai Demidov (1773–1828) was taken to Russia at the beginning of the nineteenth century, but representatives of the Demidov family in Tuscany continued to collect works of art in the second half of the nineteenth century, thus maintaining in Italy the tradition of creating large aristocratic collections.[37] Many items from the collection of the prominent Russian artist, philanthropist and wealthy collector Mikhail Botkin (1839–1914) also originated in Florence and Rome. Botkin set up an Italian Renaissance Hall in his St Petersburg house-museum, where Italian 'primitives', Greek and early Russian icons were to be found amidst the Renaissance pictures, furniture and maiolica (see Figs. 1.3 and 1.4).

---

37 For more information about the Demidov collections, see F. Haskell, ed., *Anatole Demidoff. Prince of San Donato (1812–1870)* (London: Trustees of the Wallace Collection, 1994); L. Tonini, *I Demidoff a Firenze e in Toscana, Atti del convegno* (Florence: Olschki, 1996); L. Tonini, 'Nicola Demidoff collezionista russo a Firenze all'inizio del XIX secolo', in *Il collezionismo in Russia da Pietro I all'Unione Sovietica*, ed. L. Tonini (Napoli: Artistic and Publishing Company, 2009), pp. 67–88.

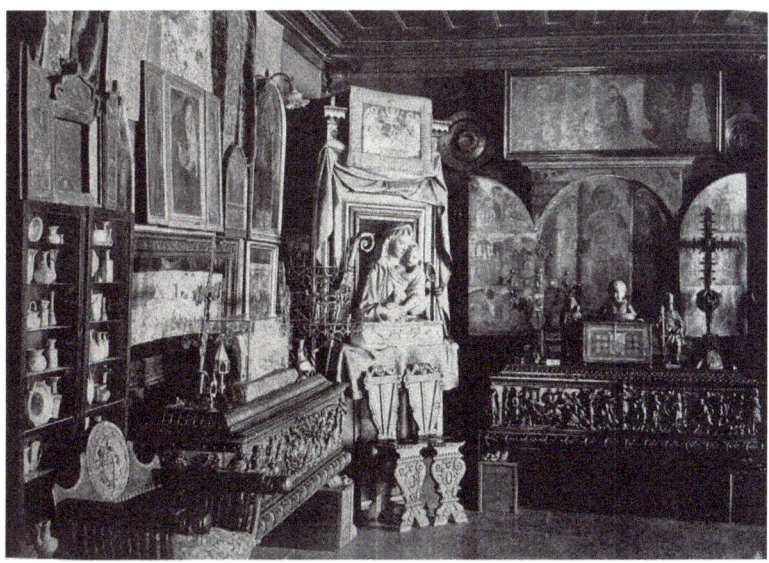

Fig. 1.3 The Italian Renaissance Hall: Italian 'primitives', medieval Greek and Russian Icons in the house-museum of Mikhail Botkin in St Petersburg. From the catalogue *Collection of M. P. Botkin* (St. Petersburg: R. Golike and A. Vilborg, 1911). Photograph by the author (2017), public domain.

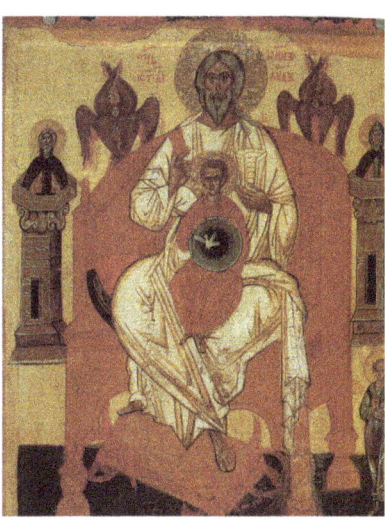

Fig. 1.4 Novgorod School, *The Trinity of the New Testament, With the Chosen Saints* (the second half of the fourteenth century), tempera on wood, 113 x 88 cm. From the collection of Mikhail Botkin in St Petersburg. Tretyakov Gallery, Moscow. Wikimedia, public domain.
https://commons.wikimedia.org/wiki/File:Otechestvo_ikona_Novgorod.jpg

In 1875, the Russian collector acquired one of the rare Greek icons of the first half of the sixteenth century, the triptych *Deesis and the Twelve Great Feasts* (c. 1540–49) with the coat of arms of Pope Paul III (1534–49), from the collection of Cardinal Andrea Altieri in Rome (see Fig. 1.5). This triptych was kept in Botkin's house-museum until 1914, and can be clearly seen in old photographs. The Soviet authorities sold it to Joseph Davies, the American ambassador in Moscow, in 1937. Davies later gave his collection to the University of Wisconsin–Madison.

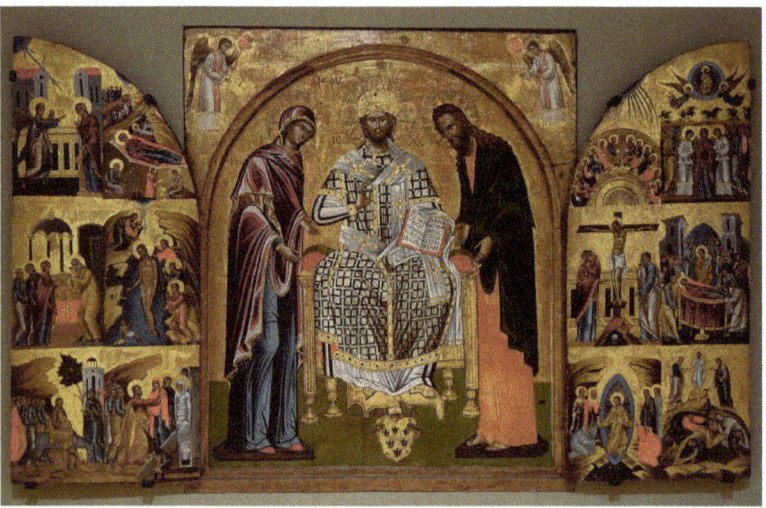

Fig. 1.5 Cretan School, *Deesis and the Twelve Great Feasts* (c. 1540–49), tempera on wood, 50 x 80 ¾ in. From the collection of Mikhail Botkin in St Petersburg. Chazen Museum of Art, University of Wisconsin–Madison, United States of America. Wikimedia, photograph by Daderot (2014), CC0.
https://commons.wikimedia.org/wiki/File:Great_Deesis_with_the_Twelve_Feasts_of_the_Church,_Greco-Byzantine,_c._1540-1549,_tempera_and_gilt_on_panel_-_Chazen_Museum_of_Art_-_DSC01943.JPG

Finally, the tradition of collecting Western European art by one of the richest Russian noble families, the Stroganovs, should once again be noted. Count Pavel Sergeevich Stroganov (1823–1911, son of the aforementioned Sergei Grigor'evich Stroganov), who served in the Russian Embassy in Rome from 1847 to 1862, stands out amid collectors of Italian 'primitives'. Intending to continue the family tradition of popularizing Western European painting in Russia, the Count focused especially on early Italian paintings 'on golden backgrounds'. According to contemporaries, the collection was arranged in Louis XV-style interiors, and his palace on Sergiev Street in St Petersburg was conceived as a collector's house, designed and built specially to house his unique collection.[38] The Count's study was decorated by, amongst other things, a favourite painting which his father had acquired back in 1856 for 20,000 francs; the *Lamentation over Christ with a Carmelite Monk* (c. 1510, Museum of Fine Arts, Moscow) by the brush of Cima da Conegliano (c. 1459–1517).

In Italy itself, individual masterpieces of early Italian art were to be found at the end of the nineteenth and beginning of the twentieth century in the collection of Pavel Sergeevich's brother, Count Grigorii Stroganov (1823–1910). The collection was housed in the Palazzo Stroganov, his personal palazzo in Rome, via Sistina 59. Most notably it included a painted tabernacle by Fra Angelico (the so-called *Stroganov Tabernacle*) (1425–30, State Hermitage, St Petersburg); the exceedingly rare *Madonna with the Christ Child Reading* (c. 1494–98, North Carolina Museum of Art, Raleigh), by Pinturicchio (1454–1513); the *Madonna and Child* (the so-called *Madonna Stroganov*) by Duccio (c. 1300, Metropolitan Museum, New York) (see Fig. 1.6), and the *Madonna from the Annunciation Scene* by Simone Martini (c. 1340–44, State Hermitage, St Petersburg) (see Fig. 1.7). Fra Angelico's tabernacle and the *Madonna* by Martini were purchased by the Count from the aforementioned antiquarian Bardini, whose house-museum in Florence had opened to the public back in 1883.[39] 'The Italian school of the Trecento and Quattrocento is very

---

38 D. V. Grigorovich, 'Dom P. S. Stroganov na Sergievskoi ulitse', *Pchela*, 1 (1875), 9. See also E. Lipgart, 'Dar grafa P. S. Stroganova Imperatorskomu Ermitazhu', *Starye gody* (April 1912), 33–45.

39 Stefano Bardini's *casa museo* in Florence was more a gallery-showroom, where clients were able to imagine pieces of art in their own urban residences and reconstructed villas in the neo-Renaissance style. Bardini's innovative installation had a considerable influence on museums and private exhibitions in Western Europe and the USA – in particular, in Berlin (Bode-Museum and Gemäldegalerie), Paris (Jacquemart-André Museum) and Boston (Isabella Stewart Gardner Museum). Bardini's main clients were British and American collectors. At the same time, research shows that 'a Bardini provenance' characterized countless objects in public and private collections throughout Europe, including imperial Russia. Bardini had a close business relationship with Wilhelm von Bode in particular. Initially, it was Bode who planned to acquire the tabernacle by Fra Angelico, but later it went to Count Stroganov and was transferred to the Hermitage by his daughter and heir Princess Maria Shcherbatova (Stroganov) (1857–1920) in 1912. See A. F. Moscowitz, *Stefano Bardini 'Principe degli Antiquari'. Prolegomenon to a Biography* (Florence: Centro Di, 2015), pp. 5–27, 49–53. See also V. Niemeyer Chini, *Stefano Bardini e Wilhelm Bode: mercanti e connaisseur fra Ottocento e Novecento* (Florence: Polistampa, 20090, pp. 109–18. For information about the

interesting', wrote Baron Nikolai Vrangel (1880–1915) and Aleksandr Trubnikov (1882–1966), the first to review this collection: 'the early Sienese works are especially worthy of note, including the works of rare masters such as Duccio, Simone Martini, Sano di Pietro. The earliest work in the collection is the fragment of fresco depicting the Madonna, painted by Margaritone (1236–1313), a master from Arezzo'. The authors highlighted a masterpiece by the hand of Duccio, in particular, in their article: 'A small Madonna represents [the work of] this rare master in the collection. She was exhibited in Siena and evoked rapture in art historians and lovers of the old masters'.[40]

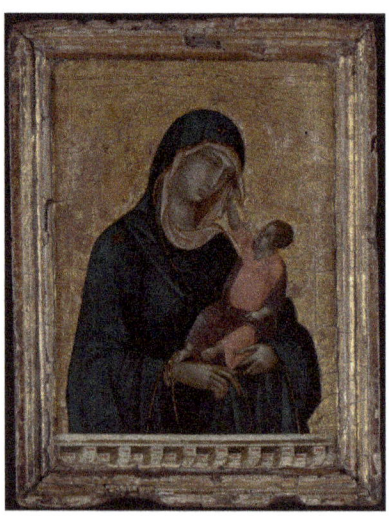

Fig. 1.6 Duccio (c. 1255/60–c. 1318/19), *Madonna and Child* ('*Madonna Stroganov*') (c. 1300), tempera on wood, 23.8 x 16.5 cm. From the collection of Count Grigorii Stroganov in Rome. The Metropolitan Museum, New York. Wikimedia, public domain. https://it.wikipedia.org/wiki/File:Duccio_Di_Buoninsegna_-_Madonna_col_Bambino.jpg

---

acquisition of Simone Martini's *Madonna* by Bardini, see the catalogue of Count Stroganov's collection: A. Muñoz and L. Pollak, *Pièces de choix de la collection du Comte Gregoire Stroganoff à Rome*, 2 vols. (Rome: Impr. de l'Unione editrice, 1912), II, 10. On the fate of the *Madonna* by Duccio and Grigorii Stroganov's Rome collection, see V. Chalpachcjan, 'Il destino della collezione romana del Conte Grigorij S. Stroganoff (1829–1910) dopo la scomparsa del collezionista', *Rivista d'arte*, 5.2 (2012), 446–73.

40 See N. N. Vrangel and A. Trubnikov, 'Kartiny sobraniia grafa G. S. Stroganova v Rime', *Starye gody* (March 1909), 115–17. See also Muñoz and Pollak, *Pièces de choix*, II, p. vii; A. Muñoz, 'La collezione Stroganoff', *Rassegna contemporanea*, 3.10 (1910), 9.

1. Fashion, Taste and Form

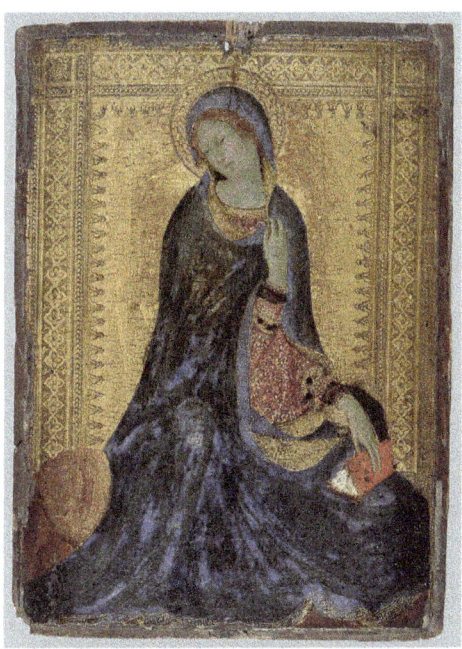

Fig. 1.7 Simone Martini (c. 1284–1344), *Madonna from the Annunciation Scene* (c. 1340–44), tempera on wood, 30.5 x 21.5 cm. From the collection of Count Grigorii Stroganov in Rome. State Hermitage, St Petersburg. Wikimedia, public domain, https://commons.wikimedia.org/wiki/File:Simone_Martini_076.jpg

Judging by the sumptuous catalogue of his collection of masterpieces, and by the artist Fyodor Reiman's (1842–1920) surviving watercolour interiors (c. 1905–10), the Count selected his favourite objects to decorate his 'art study'. It was here that he kept individual Italian 'primitives', a Quentin Matsys (1466–1530) portrait of *Erasmus of Rotterdam* (1517, Palazzo Barberini, Rome) brought from St Petersburg; a valuable tapestry, manufactured in Brussels in the sixteenth century; and decorated vases, antiques and Byzantine artefacts. Highlights among the Byzantine objects were the icons in enamel and inscribed on ivory, and especially an extremely rare enamel-inlaid icon-reliquary of *Saint Nicholas the Wonderworker*, dating from the sixth century and now located in the Hermitage collection in St Petersburg.[41] Moreover, there were individual Byzantine and Russian icons in the palace bedchamber,

---

41 For further details, see S. Moretti, *Roma bizantina. Opere d'arte dall'impero di Costantinopoli nelle collezioni romane* (Rome: Campisano, 2014), pp. 123–29, 134–52.

and the medieval and ancient sculptures that graced the galleries were accompanied by the works of Agnolo Gaddi (c. 1350–96), Matteo di Pacino (d. 1394) and Neri di Bicci (1419–91).

The Count was not seeking to replicate the Renaissance house-museum ambiance of the likes of Herbert Horne (1864–1916) in Florence, or Botkin in St Petersburg. His interiors were more reminiscent of the Roman nobility's palace-museums, and were permeated with that *Belle Époque* atmosphere of luxury and aestheticism reflected in famous literary works by Gabriele D'Annunzio (1863–1938) and Henry James (1843–1916). Count Grigorii Stroganov even features in D'Annunzio's *Child of Pleasure* (1889), buying various works of art in an antiquarian shop on Rome's via Sistina. The novel's literary hero resides on the Palazzo Zuccari, which was near the collector's house. Part of the Stroganov collection was also located in a specially constructed two-storey building on the via Gregoriana, the Villino Stroganov. The view over Rome and the *genius loci*, as described by Vernon Lee (1856–1935), functioned as a sort of 'frame' for the Russian Count's collecting activities. 'To house his gigantic collection', recalled Buslaev, 'he built himself a house on the via Gregoriana in Rome, near Monte Pincio. There you will also find massive marble sarcophagi from the catacombs, and sepulchres, and heavy bas-relief marble slabs from recently dissolved Italian monasteries, and statues and statuettes, silver chalices, patens and cups, dishes, vases and covers, and diptychs of elephant ivory and metal, and all sorts of other vessels'.[42] Although the Count accumulated his collection of pictures under the guidance of Karl von Liphart (1808–91) (who lived in Florence from 1864 onwards), he was himself considered a prominent art expert; for example, he correctly identified Martini as the creator of the *Madonna from the Annunciation Scene*. According to contemporaries, many scholars and art enthusiasts frequented the Palazzo Stroganoff – Giovanni Cavalcaselle (1819–97), Giovanni Morelli (1816–91), Franz von Lenbach (1836–1904), Wilhelm von Bode (1845–1929), Bernard Berenson (1865–1959), Nikodim Kondakov (1844–1925) and others.

---

42 F. I. Buslaev, 'Moi vospominaniia', *Vestnik Evropy*, 5 (1891), 171. Today, the Bibliotheca Hertziana–Max Planck Institute for Art History in Rome is housed at the Palazzo and Villino Stroganov. On the history of this building, see E. Kieven, ed., *100 Jahre Bibliotheca Hertziana. Der Palazzo Zuccari und die Institutsgebäude 1590–2013* (Munich: Hirmer Verlag, 2013), pp. 276–91.

Throughout the eighteenth and the first half of the nineteenth century, Italian 'primitives' and Russian icons were evaluated primarily according to the norms of Classical art and Johann Joachim Winckelmann's (1717–68) aesthetics. However, the Romantic aesthetic which superseded it increasingly began to shape the curiosity of the first icon collectors in Russia, just as it began to shape interest in early Italian painting in Western Europe at the end of the eighteenth and beginning of the nineteenth centuries. The icon collections of Count Sergei Stroganov and Pogodin in Moscow appeared right on the wave of Romantic interest in national history and the religiosity of the folk. And Lord Lindsay's impassioned writings about the merits of the 'primitives' has clear connections with evaluations of the Russian icon by, for example, Russian litterateur and poet Nikolai Ivanchin-Pisarev (1790–1849), the archaeologist Ivan Sakharov (1807–63) and the famous connoisseur and collector Dmitrii Rovinskii (1824–95), who owned a huge collection of Russian folk religious prints (*lubki*). Moreover, in the mid-nineteenth century, this Romantic interest in medieval and folk life influenced the Russian imperial court, just as it influenced the British and Austrian courts, for example. Prince Albert's (1819–61) purchases of Italian 'primitives' (the works of Duccio, Bernardo Daddi (c. 1280–1348) and Fra Angelico), donated to London's National Gallery by Queen Victoria (1819–1901) after his death, belonged entirely to the spirit of the times. Early icons – long forgotten in the upper echelons of Russian culture, and preserved only in Old Believer collections and by a few admirers of Russian antiquities – became positively fashionable in Russia for the first time in many years, thanks to Nikolai Leskov's (1831–95) *The Sealed Angel* (1873), which was highly spoken of by the Emperor Alexander II (1818–81) himself.[43]

Artistic Form and the Idea of Pure Visibility

By the end of the nineteenth and the beginning of the twentieth century, there was every indication that tastes had changed. Suddenly, it was clear that Byzantine, early Italian and early Russian art not only represented a harmonious way of seeing the world, but also possessed aesthetic value.

---

43 See K. A. Lantz, ed., *The Sealed Angel and Other Stories by Nikolay Leskov* (Knoxville, TN: University of Tennessee Press, 1984).

The new fashion for Italian 'primitives', the proliferation of exhibitions, the development of great collections and their increasing presence in the antiquarian-art market inevitably had an impact on the emerging culture of 'new collecting' and the growing interest in early icons in Russia. That the young Russian critics Muratov, Shchekotov and Punin cited and drew on the works of Wölfflin, Berenson, Charles Diehl (1859–1944) and Gabriel Millet (1867–1953) in their publications testifies to the fact that Russian authors were well acquainted with both the latest research in the field of art theory, and with new publications in English and French Byzantine studies. 'Henceforth it became clear', noted Shchekotov in one of his articles, 'that the changes and transformations of artistic form in the art of Byzantium give us the right to consider its monuments with the help of those same methods that we use, for example, to study the art of the early Italian Renaissance'.[44] In other words, the *idea of pure visibility* and the basic theses of the Formalist School of German art studies arrived in Russia at the beginning of the twentieth century. English essays on art attracted no less interest, particularly the works of Walter Pater (1839–94), John Symonds (1840–93) and Vernon Lee. Together with Ruskin and William Morris (1834–96), Pater was recognized in Russia as a proponent of Victorian aesthetics and as responsible for laying the foundations for the theory of 'aesthetic criticism', the aim of which was to prepare the viewer for education in taste and to be able to perceive beauty.[45] It is therefore no coincidence that it was precisely *art critics*, not academics, who became the main new interpreters of medieval Russian icons. Their evaluations were based exclusively on visual criteria, and their observations and conclusions on early Russian painting were

---

44 N. M. Shchekotov, 'Ikonopis' kak iskusstvo. Po povodu sobraniia ikon I. S. Ostroukhov i S. P. Riabushinskogo', *Russkaia ikona*, 2 (1914), 115–42.

45 See W. Pater, *Renessans. Ocherki iskusstva i poezii*, trans. S. G. Zaimovskii (Moscow: Problemy estetiki, 1912); W. Pater, *Voobrazhaemye portrety. Rebenok v dome*, trans. P. P. Muratov (Moscow: V. M. Sablin, 1908); V. Lee, *Italiia. Volume 1: Genius loci. Vol. 2: Teatr i muzyka*, ed. P. P. Muratov, trans. E. S. Urenius (Moscow: n.p., 1914–15). Symonds' travel writings were published under the title *Obrazy Italii* (J. A. Symonds, *Sketches and Studies in Italy and Greece*, 3 vols. (London: J. Murray, 1907–14)). In the foreword to Vernon Lee's sketch, Muratov noted: 'The historic enthusiasm of the English for Italy is a wonderful phenomenon, not to be found in any other nation. All English literature went under the motto of Italy…' And, furthermore: 'No nation has done as much for knowledge of the Italian genius in all his manifestations from Giotto to Tiepolo and from Dante to Carlo Gozzi, as the English did in the period from the 1860s to 1880s' (*Italiia: Genius loci*, pp. 7–8).

shaped by the Western European academic works that popularized the Italian 'primitives' and the works of French Impressionists. Essentially, the texts discussing the early Russian icon address the same problems of artistic form as studies of Trecento artists or emerging trends in Russian and Western European art. This is particularly evident in the numerous comparisons drawn in Russian books and journals between Italian 'primitives', medieval Russian icons and the works of French and Russian Impressionism and Modernism.

The Formalist School of German art studies acquired particular significance for the re-evaluation of early Russian painting. This School raised the question of the content of artistic form inherent in the fine arts. The Formalist School endeavoured to prove that universal and objective laws of development are manifested in art: a timely advancement in the history of the discipline. New discoveries in the sphere of psycho-physiological vision provided ammunition in the formation of these theses; the works of Hermann von Helmholtz (1821–94) and Ernst Mach's (1838–1916) optical theory, which helped determine the very nature of the object perceived by sight, became exceptionally popular. According to the new aesthetical theories, the nature of the artistic form of a work of art derived not from the ideological backdrop of the era, but was determined by a special *visual intelligence*, the contents of which were declared unique and had nothing in common with other forms of cultural activity, be they religious, philosophical or literary. This *correct vision* was presumed to have one vital characteristic – it was able to reveal ideal forms, which reflect harmony and stability, in other words the permanent universal values of human activity by which the monuments of Classical art declare themselves.

These ideas first emerged in the intellectual community that coalesced in Florence in the 1880s, which included the philosopher Konrad Fiedler (1841–1895), the artist Hans von Marées (1837–87) and the sculptor Adolf von Hildebrand (1847–1921). The infatuation with Italy and Classical art resulted in the articulation of new aims: to apprehend the secrets of Classical form and define the very mechanisms of spiritual activity. It was Fiedler's idea of *Reine Sichtbarkeit* [pure visibility] that Hildebrand developed in his famous book *Das Problem der Form in der Bildenden Kunst* [*The Problem of Form in the Fine Arts*] (1893), translated from German and published in Russia in 1914. This notion influenced the way the issue of *artistic vision* was addressed in the works of Russian researchers in the first two decades of the twentieth century.[46] Moreover this *artistic vision*, which would be mentioned so often in the works of Muratov, Shchekotov and Igor Grabar (1871–1960), was understood not as a mechanical reflection of reality but as a product of intensive spiritual activity. More than that, according to Fiedler and Hildebrand, visual perception led to autonomous cognition, which should be distinguished from cognition conveyed in language. Thus, the content particular to the fine arts automatically corresponded with the physiology of visual perception. The Head of the Viennese School of Art History, Alois Riegl (1858–1905), for example, drew the essence of fine arts out of the laws of vision. His concept of *Kunstwollen* [artistic volition] is nothing other than objective visual conformity with regularity, which allows the history of art to be understood as a process of the changing of artistic forms and their objective development. Riegl set out his theory in *Grundlegungen zu einer Geschichte der Ornamentik* [*Problems of Style: Foundations for a History of Ornament*] (1893) and in his renowned monograph *Spätrömische Kunstindustrie* [*The Late Roman Art Industry*] (1901). It was precisely in ornamentation, Riegl suggested, that humankind's genuine artistic abilities were most clearly manifested, and this was true even at the dawn of human history. In ornament, too, those 'inner' artistic forms that began to be considered as the outward projection of the artist's subjective style were also laid bare. It is no coincidence that the development of this concept by Wilhelm Worringer (1881–1965) in his work *Abstraktion und Einfühlung* [*Abstraction and Empathy*] (1908) significantly shaped the art of the European avant-garde. Worringer traced the transformation from early eastern (abstract) art to the art of the ancient world (the 'art of empathy') by focusing on ornament, and became one of those first critics of Eurocentrism who defended the idea of multiple viewpoints on the world.

This new conception of visual arts led to more concentrated attention on medieval European art, and to a new consideration of Renaissance and Baroque art. The work of Wölfflin and Berenson, which so influenced the new research on the history of medieval Russian painting, is key here. Wölfflin was the first scholar to develop the

---

46 A. Hildebrand, *Problema formy v iobrazitel'nom iskusstve*, trans. N. B. Rozenfel'd and V. A. Favorskii (Moscow: Musaget, 1914).

conception of *a priori* forms, which was grounded in the visual analysis of artworks. A huge number of scholars – in Russia as elsewhere – began to consider artworks as optical phenomena following the publication of his eminent books *Renaissance und Barock* [*Renaissance and Baroque*] (1888), *Die Klassische Kunst* [*Classic Art*] (1899) and *Kunstgeschichtliche Grundbegriffe* [*The Principles of Art History*] (1915). Henceforth, even renowned Russian icon specialists like academicians Kondakov and Likhachev had to begin their analysis with visual impressions. That *The Principles of Art History* can be seen as a precursor to Structuralism is supported by the fact that it transformed into a dogma of artistic forms. The preface to the book shows that the author was striving to provide a sort of 'auxiliary framework', allowing the specificities of any artistic style to be more easily configured. Wölfflin never abandoned the idea of *pure visibility* discussed in Fiedler and Hildebrand's circle, to which Wölfflin was always connected via mutual interests.[47] Wilhelm Dilthey's (1833–1911) psychology was also immensely important for Wölfflin. He had attended Dilthey's lectures at the University of Berlin, and we can gain some idea of what Wölfflin studied in Berlin by reading Dilthey's seminal work *Einleitung in die Geisteswissenschaften* [*An Introduction to the Human Sciences*] (1883).

Echoes of those formal-psychological aesthetics – which many of those then writing about early Russian painting, particularly Muratov, had grasped precisely via the works of Wölfflin and Berenson – may be clearly traced in the workings out of the German Formalist School. According to the theories developed by Dilthey and Theodor Lipps (1833–1911), beauty is not an objective property of an artefact, but generated by the perceiving subject's feelings being inserted into the artwork. In his theory of *Einfühlung* [empathy], Lipps intended, amongst other things, to demonstrate that penetration of a painting is a special, spiritual practice which allows the viewer to be aware of themselves as a complete person. Lipps considered the artistic value and beauty of a work to be linked less with the content of an artwork than with subjective, intimate experience, the viewer's capacity and skill in revealing the hidden beauty of the contemplated object through special emotional effort. These ideas appeared especially clearly in the

---

47   See Wölfflin, *Principles of Art History*, trans. Levy and Weddigen.

works of Muratov and Shchekotov, for example, which will be discussed further below. But they were picked up earlier by the famous American art historian, dealer and collector Berenson, who – following Wölfflin and Hildebrand – began to develop the idea that painting possesses its own *intrinsic quality* which remains unchanged in essence while being modified across the centuries.[48] It was Berenson's work which most seriously influenced Muratov, as it did other young researchers of medieval Russian icons.

Berenson was born within the territory of the Russian Empire, in a small Lithuanian town not far from Vilnius. His family emigrated to the United States when he was ten, and, between 1884 and 1887, Berenson studied at Boston University and Harvard University. His acquaintance with Isabella Stewart Gardner (1840–1924), who inherited an enormous fortune and married one of the richest men in America, played a significant role in his career. Berenson was a key advisor in the formation of her famous Museum of Western European Art over many years, alongside artists James Whistler (1834–1903) and John Singer Sargent (1856–1925), and French writer Paul Bourget (1852–1935). The collection included genuine masterpieces by early Italian artists such as Giotto, Martini, Lippo Memmi (c. 1291–1356), and Fra Angelico. The private Isabella Stewart Gardner Museum was opened to the public in 1903, and included a special hall – the Early Italian Room – with works by Italian 'primitives'. The fifteenth-century Russian icon the *Ascension of Christ* remains in the museum to this day, creating that refined aura of high art so characteristic of private house-museums of the *Belle Époque*. The icon reflected the era's particular taste for mysticism, simplicity and the decorative qualities of medieval art. The connoisseur's celebrated conceptual approach as an advisor to collectors developed first in the ground of Berenson's collaboration with the extravagant Isabella, to whom he wrote in January 1895, 'If you will permit me to advise you in art matters as you have for a year past it will not be many years before you possess a collection almost unrivaled of masterpieces and masterpieces only...'.[49]

---

48 B. Berenson, *The Italian Painters of the Renaissance* (London: Phaidon, 1959), pp. 84–85.

49 As cited in E. Samuels, *Bernard Berenson: The Making of a Connoisseur* (Cambridge, MA: Harvard University Press, 1979), p. 240.

At the end of the 1880s, Berenson was already captivated by Italian painting. As he discovered for himself the creations of Giotto, Duccio and Fra Angelico, he ultimately emerged as one of the leading specialists in this field. Berenson's collecting, and his interrogation of style and artistic quality, was effectively combined with diligent research in his academic work, as is already clearly demonstrated in his first major work focused on Lorenzo Lotto (c. 1480–1556/57).[50]

It is important to register that finding a new way of attributing authorship to the vast number of dirty and repainted fourteenth- and fifteenth-century Italian paintings became art history's most important goal in this last quarter of the nineteenth century. Indeed, if a 'genuine' icon 'painted by Andrei Rublev' might be found in practically every wealthy Old Believer collector's oratory in nineteenth-century Russia (while today only one genuine Rublev icon – the *Trinity* (1411, or 1425–27, Tretyakov Gallery, Moscow) – is known), practically every large collection in Western Europe had acquired a 'genuine' Sandro Botticelli (c. 1445–1510) or Giorgione Barbarelli da Castelfranco (1477/78–1510). The exhibition of fifteenth- to seventeenth-century Venetian painting held in London in 1895, assembled from private collections, is a telling example of this. Berenson ruled out thirty-two of the thirty-three paintings attributed to Titian (c. 1488/90–1576) in the catalogue, while all eighteen of the paintings attributed to Giorgione turned out to be the work of other artists.[51] 'It became fashionable for wealthy lovers of art, with no critical standard of authenticity, to collect so-called works of Giorgione, and a multitude of imitations came into circulation', Pater observed, 'Yet enough remains to explain why the legend grew up, above the name, why the name attached itself, in many instances, to the bravest work of other men'.[52] It was indeed precisely in this period that a huge number of fakes circulated, mostly under the names of Botticelli, Giorgione, Raphael (1483–1520) and Leonardo da Vinci (1452–1519). Private collections in Western Europe and Russia were absolutely flooded with works from various periods and by various masters that

---

50 See B. Berenson, *Lorenzo Lotto* (Milan: Electa, 1955).
51 N. A. Belousova, 'Bernard Bernson i ego kniga', in B. Berenson, *Zhivopistsy ital'ianskogo Vozrozhdeniia* (Moscow: Iskusstvo, 1965), p. 19.
52 W. Pater, *The Renaissance: Studies of Art and Poetry* (n.p.: The Floating Press, 2010 [1873]), p. 137.

had been ascribed to Botticelli or Giorgione on the basis of random features, although there were a few exceptions in the form of famous, genuine paintings.

As a special sphere of art studies, connoisseurship was in an entirely fluid state for the duration of the eighteenth and nineteenth centuries. The expert of the eighteenth century was an art lover without the ability to judge a work of literature or painting. Evaluation of a painting was based on taste and the outward similarity of the artist's style. Jonathan Richardson (1667–1745) endeavoured to make sense of all the complexities of such expertise as early as 1719, in the section *Whether 'tis an Original, or a Copy* of his book on connoisseurship.[53] The connoisseur of the late nineteenth and early twentieth century also based their evaluation on a visual reading of the painting. But this judgement was now primarily built on the experience of psychological aesthetics (aesthetic empathy), and also on formal analysis grounded in the comparative anatomy method of Morelli.[54] The importance of Berenson's work in attribution lies wholly in his success at bridging the

---

53 See J. Richardson, *Two Discourses. I. an Essay on the Whole Art of Criticism as it Relates to Painting... II. An Argument in Behalf of the Science of Connoisseur* (London: W. Churchill, 1719),
https://archive.org/details/twodiscoursesia00conggoog

54 The concept of a connoisseur (*conoscitore*) first emerged in Italy and was used in contrast to *professore*, that is, to someone who engages with art as a professional and/or as a teacher. In other words, connoisseurs are enthusiasts and collectors first, scholars and researchers second. The essence of connoisseurship was most clearly expressed in this period by Max Friedländer (1867–1958), who counterposed historians and connoisseurs in his book *Der Kunstkenner* [*The Art Connoisseur*] (Berlin: Cassirer, 1919): connoisseurs favour collecting and the pure enjoyment of art, and they see in this the goal of artistic creativity. Historians pay greater attention to context: 'A work of art', Friedländer explained, 'should be viewed without a conscious, cognitive aim, and if at some moment or other inspiration suddenly strikes and some of our knowledge is confirmed or even enriched, then fine; one must never approach a work of art with a firm intention to resolve some question or other. We must allow [the work of art] to speak for itself, we must converse with rather than interrogate it'. See M. Friedländer, *Ob iskusstve i znatochestve*, trans. M. I. Korenev, 2nd ed. (Moscow: Andrey Naslednikov, 2013), p. 135. The theoretical grounds and criticism of connoisseurship are considered in detail in the section 'Art Forgery as the Connoisseur's Nightmare', in F. Lenain, *Art Forgery. A History of a Modern Obsession* (London: Reaktion, 2012), pp. 234–310. Researchers have also considered the special significance of the works of Pater and Hildebrand for Berenson: see P. Barolskii, 'Walter Pater and Bernard Berenson', *New Criterion*, 2 (1984), 47–57; M. A. Calo, *Bernard Berenson and the Twentieth Century* (Philadelphia, PA: Temple University Press, 1994), p. 8.

divide between German Formalism and Italian connoisseurship at the end of the nineteenth century; furthermore his concept of *tactile values* without doubt rested on enormous erudition, visual memory and, it would seem, clear ability to intuitively penetrate a painting. It is hard now to imagine just how authoritative Berenson was in the global art and antiquities market in the first three decades of the twentieth century. In the formation of the largest American collections, including the painting collections of Isabella Stewart Gardner, John G. Johnson (1841–1917) and Henry Clay Frick (1849–1919), who opened their private collections to the public, Berenson's word was final. Contemporaries recalled how, as well as captivating specialists, the mania for attribution based on Berenson's method of *tactile values* gripped even American tourists, who anticipated 'tactile imagination' in their fingertips as they stood before the masterpieces of Italian painting in the Florentine Academy of Arts.[55]

Between 1894 and 1907 Berenson published four volumes of his history of Italian Renaissance painting, and finally formulated the principles of scholarly connoisseurship, foregrounding visual perception, the artistic quality of a painting and innate taste. 'We must look and look and look till we live the painting and for a fleeting moment become identified with it', Berenson wrote in the spirit of the aesthetic ideas fashionable at the time.[56] It is also necessary to note that the American researcher constructed his concrete descriptions on the analysis of concepts like movement, space and colouring, as well as the notion of *tactile values*. For him, this concept of *tactile values* was not simply the tactile modelling of artistic form (as, for example, in the work of Giotto) but also 'the essence' of the image, which delights us and is apprehended swiftly and clearly. But how, and when, does a sensation and understanding of an artwork's essence manifest in the beholder? Berenson explained that it comes 'when we unconsciously translate our retinal impressions into ideated sensations of touch, pressure and

---

55   H. Hannay, *Roger Fry and Other Essays* (London: George Allen and Unwin, 1937), pp. 54, 71–72. 'It follows that the essential in the art of painting […] is somehow to stimulate our consciousness of tactile values, so that the picture shall have at least as much power as the object represented, to appeal to our tactile imagination' (Berenson, *Italian Painters of the Renaissance*, p. 40).
56   Berenson, *Italian Painters of the Renaissance*, p. xiii.

grasp'. This was the meaning of his concept of 'tactile values'.[57] In other words, in revealing the concept of the artistic form, Berenson had two aims: on the one hand, to penetrate the essence of the influence of the work of art on the psycho-physical nature of a person, and, on the other hand, to bring out 'the intrinsic quality' of a painting, which, soon after, young art critics in Russia began to seek in the early Russian icon. In Berenson's terminology, 'the Decorative' was opposed to 'Illustration' reflecting the ideological context of the epoch: 'Illustration is everything which in a work of art appeals to us, not for any intrinsic quality, as for colour or form or composition, contained in the work of art itself, but for the value the thing represented has elsewhere, whether in the world outside, or in the mind within'.[58] Scrutinizing the works of the Florentine and Sienese 'primitives' (Giotto, Duccio, Martini and others), Berenson therefore detected that they possessed 'decorative' worth as well as 'illustrative qualities' – in other words, these artists handled the construction of space beautifully, and created visually pleasing effects of masses and lines. On the basis of this methodology, Berenson determined both the stylistic characteristics of the Italian Renaissance's Schools of painting (Venetian, Florentine, Central Italian and North Italian) and the individual hand of many Italian artists.

In the long-term, Berenson's subjective-psychological ideas would be criticized by proponents of the avant-garde; he refused to accept their critiques through the course of his lifetime. At the beginning of the twentieth century, however, his ideas directly influenced the challenges identified and posed to a new generation of Russian researchers of early Russian icons. These challenges were brilliantly resolved, above

---

57 B. Berenson, *The Italian Painters in the Renaissance* (Oxford: Oxford University Press, 1952), p. 94. 'We remember that to realize form we must give tactile values to retinal sensations. Ordinarily we have considerable difficult in skimming off these tactile values, and by the time they have reached our consciousness, they have lost much of their strength. Obviously, the artist who gives us these values more rapidly than the object itself gives them, gives us the pleasures consequent upon a more vivid realization of the object, and the further pleasures that come from the sense of greater psychical capacity' (Berenson, *Italian Painters of the Renaissance*, p. 43).

58 Berenson, *Italian Painters of the Renaissance*, pp. 84–85. That said, Berenson's understanding of the 'intrinsic quality' of an artwork evoked fundamental doubts amongst his contemporaries. Bertrand Russell also pointed out the error of these views to Berenson. See Calo, *Bernard Berenson*, p. 13; and M. Schapiro, 'Mr. Berenson's Values', *Encounter*, 16 (1961), 57–65.

all, by an archetypal representative of Silver Age Russian culture, the famous art historian and critic Muratov. It was precisely in his works on the history of early Russian painting that the issue of the origin of the medieval Russian icon was first addressed in the context of artistic culture worldwide, distinguishing between different Schools and their respective stylistic characteristics.

2. From Images of Italy to Early Russian Art

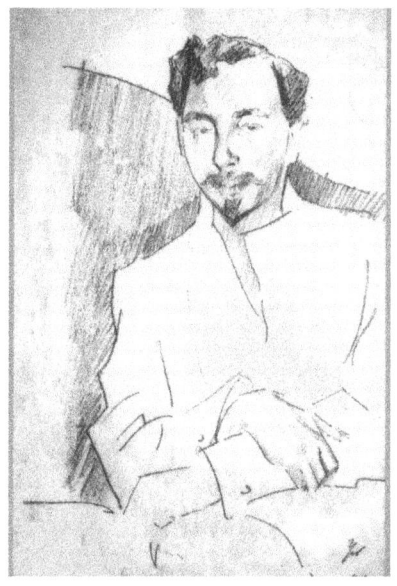

Fig. 2.1 Nikolai Pavlovich Ulyanov (1877–1949), *Portrait of Pavel Muratov* (1911), graphite pencil on paper, 24 x 18 cm. Private collection. Reprinted by permission of the owner. All rights reserved.

Pavel Muratov (1881–1950) came from the hereditary nobility and was educated as an engineer, but his love of art took him to Italy (see Fig. 2.1). His principal work, *Obrazy Italii* [*Images of Italy*], written in the genre of intellectual travel writing, was dedicated to the art and culture of Italy. It was this book that made Muratov famous and secured his place in history.[59] His multifaceted activity in the period from 1905 to 1914,

---

59 The fact that reprints of *Images of Italy* were made during the 1910s testifies to its popularity. See P. P. Muratov, *Obrazy Italii*, 2 vols. (Moscow: Izdanie Nauchnogo

however, cannot but evoke admiration. He visits Italy and travels widely in Western Europe, writing about Italian, French and Russian art; his is the foreword to Vernon Lee's (1856–1935) famous book *Italy*, which was published in Russian by the Sabashnikovs in two volumes in 1914–15.[60] He also prepared a translation of Italian Renaissance-era novels, with detailed commentaries.[61] Finally, it is in these years that Muratov laid the foundations of new scholarship in early Russian painting, publishing two highly significant works: the essay *Russkaia zhivopis' do serediny XVII veka* [*Russian Painting to the Mid-Seventeenth Century*] and *Drevnerusskaia zhivopis' v sobranii I. S. Ostroukhova* [*Medieval Russian Icon-Painting in the Collection of I. S. Ostroukhov*]. The former was published in the sixth volume of artist and historian Igor Grabar's (1871–1960) luxurious 1914 edition, and is, in essence, the first history of early Russian painting to draw on the restored and genuine masterpieces of Russian icon-painting from the fourteenth to the first half of the seventeenth century.[62] The latter book focuses on the practice of new collecting. Here, early Russian icons are subject to brilliant formal analysis as masterpieces; in other words, as artefacts exclusively of high artistic quality, which is what distinguishes Ilya Ostroukhov's (1858–1929) collection from others. The new type of collector is also discussed in this work.[63] Muratov finally leaves Russia in 1922, and lives in Berlin, Rome, Paris and London.[64] It is in the 1920s and 1930s that he does a great deal to popularize early Russian icons in the West. His book *Medieval Russian Painting* was published in Italian, as we have already noted, in 1925, and may be rightfully considered the first western publication on the aesthetic significance of early Russian icons.[65]

Slova, 1911–12). See also P. P. Muratov, *Immagini dell'Italia*, ed. R. Giuliani, trans. A. Romano, 2 vols. (Milan: Adelphi, 2019–21).

60 V. Lee, *Italiia. Volume 1: Genius loci. Vol. 2: Teatr i muzyka*, ed. P. P. Muratov, trans. E. S. Urenius (Moscow: n.p., 1914–15).

61 P. P. Muratov, ed. and trans., *Novelly ital'ianskogo Vozrozhdeniia*, 2 vols. (Moscow: n.p., 1913).

62 P. P. Muratov, 'Russkaia zhivopis' do serediny XVII veka', in *Istoriia Russkogo iskusstva*, ed. I. Grabar, 6 vols. (Moscow: Knebel, 1914–16), IV, 18–21.

63 P. P. Muratov, *Drevnerusskaia zhivopis' v sobranii I. S. Ostroukhova* (Moscow: K. F. Nekrasov, 1914).

64 On this period in P. P. Muratov's life, see in particular: 'Pis'ma P. P. Muratova (1923–1926). Publikatsiia P. Deotto i E. Garetto' (n.a.), in *Archivio russo-italiano 9: Olga Resnevic Signorelli e l'emigrazione russa: corripondenze*, ed. E. Garetto, A. d'Amelia, K. Kumpan and D. Rizzi (Salerno: Europa Orientalis, 2012), pp. 81–108.

65 P. P. Muratov, *La pittura russa antica*, trans. E. Lo Gatto (Rome: A. Stock, 1925). Two major works in German and English on the history of Russian icon-painting were

Two years later Muratov published *Les icones russes* [*The Russian Icons*] (1927) in French, the frontmatter of which was decorated with a colour reproduction of Ostroukhov's icon *Descent from the Cross* (from the late fifteenth century). One of the copies of this book would be printed especially for Bernard Berenson (1865–1959) and his wife Mary Smith (1864–1954) (see Figs. 2.2a and 2.2b).[66] At the same time, Muratov was also writing about Byzantine painting and Western European art. From 1928 to 1931, he was actively collaborating with Mario Broglio (1891–1948) and his publishers Valori plastici [Plastic Values] in Rome, where his monograph *La pittura bizantina* [*Byzantine Painting*] was published in Italian, as was a book on Fra Angelico (c. 1395–1455) (in Italian, French and English), and on Gothic sculpture (in French).[67] In this same period, Muratov played a key role in the foundation and work of the Icon Society in Paris, which aimed to promote the heritage of early Russian art.[68] Finally, Muratov summarized his observations and research in the field of Russian medieval painting in three essays: 'Otkrytiia drevnego russkogo iskusstva' ['Discoveries in Russian Medieval Art'], 'Puti russkoi ikony' ['Ways of the Russian Icon'] and 'Vokrug ikony' ['Around the Icon'], published in 1923, 1928 and 1933.[69] In 1933, Muratov read three lectures

---

       soon published in the West: O. Wulff and M. Alpatov, *Denkmaler der Ikonenmalerei* (Dresden: Avalun-Verlag, 1925); N. P. Kondakov, *The Russian Icon*, trans. E. Minns (Oxford: Clarendon Press, 1927). In contrast to these, Muratov's work is the first attempt to comment on the art of the Russian icon in terms of the development of style.

66 P. P. Muratov, *Les icones russes* (Paris: Schiffrin, 1927). The book was released by Pléiade, the publisher of the French translation of Berenson's seminal work, *The Italian Painters of the Renaissance*. I found this copy of the book at the *Berenson Library Archive*, Villa I Tatti, The Harvard University Center for Italian Renaissance Studies, Florence.

67 See P. P. Muratov, *La pittura bizantina* (Rome: Valori Plastici, 1928); P. P. Muratov, *Frate Angelico* (Rome: Valori Plastici, 1929); P. P. Muratov, *Fra Angelico. His Life and Work*, trans. E. Law-Gisiko (New York: F. Warne and Co., 1930); P. P. Muratov, *La sculpture gothique* (Rome: Valori Plastici, 1931).

68 The Icon Society was founded in Paris by V. P. Riabushinskii with the aim of studying early Russian painting. The society's founders were Riabushinskii (chairman), S. K. Makovskii, Prince S. A. Shcherbatov, B. K. Zaitsev, P. P. Muratov, the artists I. I. Bilibin and D. S. Stelletskii. Some of the major western specialists on Byzantine art, such as C. Diehl, G. Millet, O. M. Dalton and J. Strzygowski, were nominated as honorary members.

69 P. P. Muratov, 'Otkrytiia drevnego russkogo iskusstva', *Sovremennye zapiski*, 14 (1923), 197–218; P. P. Muratov, 'Puti russkoi ikony', *Perezvony*, 43 (1928), 1360–67; P. P. Muratov, 'Vokrug ikony', *Vozrozhdenie* (January 1933), 2787, 2799, 2803, 2809. These resources are included in P. P. Muratov, *Russkaia zhivopis' do serediny XVII*

on the 'Origin and Development of Russian Medieval Painting' at the Courtauld Institute of Art in London and also one lecture (2 November 1933) at the University of Cambridge, effectively summarizing the studies on early Russian art so dear to his heart.

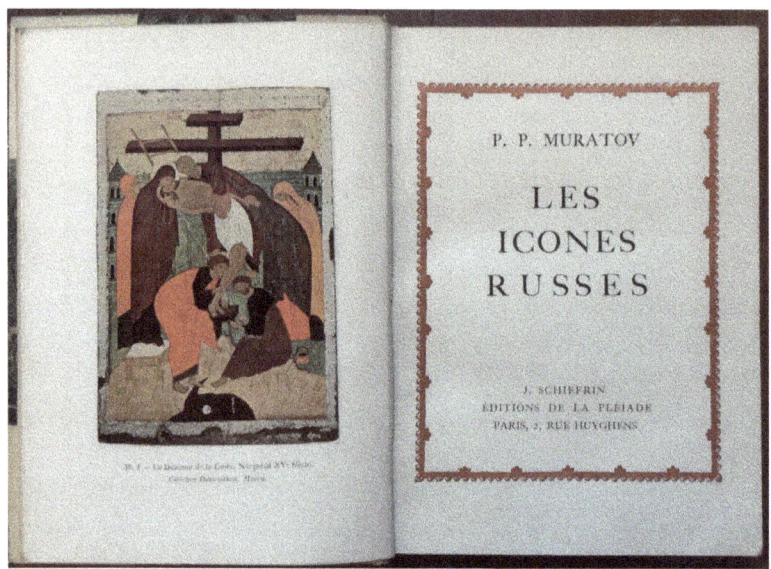

Figs. 2.2a–2.2b. Title page and dedication of a special copy of Pavel Muratov's book *Les icones russes*, printed for Bernard Berenson and Mary Smith (Paris: J. Schiffrin éditions de la Plèide, 1927). Villa I Tatti – The Harvard University Center for Italian Renaissance Studies, Florence. Photograph by the author (2018), Public domain.

The Art Critic as a Connoisseur

It would be a mistake to think that Muratov was the first or the only person writing about the artistic characteristics of early Russian icons in this period. He was, however, the first to apply the latest aesthetic theories to this subject, and managed to draw attention to the topic brilliant literary language. It was the spontaneous nature of Muratov's

veka. Istoriia otkrytiia i issledovaniia, ed. A. M. Khitrov (St Petersburg: Bibliopolis, 2008). Hereafter, I refer to this edition unless otherwise specified.

historiography of medieval Russian painting that revealed him as both a supreme stylist and consummate expert in the new methods of formal analysis. He was not only well versed in Berenson's works on the history of Italian Renaissance art but in the latest research by the Western European Byzantinists Charles Diehl (1859–1944), Ormonde Maddock Dalton (1866–1945) and Gabriel Millet (1867–1953).[70] His methodology draws on the work of founders of the Viennese School of Formalist analysis, such as Alois Riegl (1858–1905), Heinrich Wölfflin (1864–1945) and Adolf von Hildebrand (1847–1921). And, naturally, he demonstrates a brilliant grasp of the tradition of English literary and art historical essay writing, setting out his material in an elegant and artistic fashion reminiscent of the prose of Walter Pater (1839–94) and Vernon Lee. Moreover, he is interested in the very latest trends in Russian and Western European painting as well as in Italian Trecento and Quattrocento artists. He pens articles on the Sienese Madonna painted by Matteo di Giovanni (1430–95) (*Madonna and Child with Saints* (1490s, Museum of Fine Arts, Moscow)) and an unknown tondo from the School of Sandro Botticelli (c. 1445–1510), as well as essays on Paul Cézanne (1839–1906), Mikhail Nesterov (1862–1942) and Valentin Serov (1865–1919), which are published in the journals *Starye gody* [*Bygone Years*], *Vesy* [*The Scales*] and *Sofiia* [*Sophia*]. He also insightfully surveys Sergei Shchukin's (1854–1936) Moscow collection of French Impressionist and Modernist masterpieces, correctly anticipating the influence of this collection on the Russian avant-garde.[71]

---

70 In *Images of Italy*, alone, Muratov mentions Berenson forty times, Wölfflin twelve times. According to archival documents, Muratov was personally acquainted with Berenson (*Berenson Library Archive*, Villa I Tatti, The Harvard University Center for Italian Renaissance Studies, Florence: letters from P. Muratov to B. Berenson, 4 January 1927 and 23 January 1928). See also *Bernard Berenson and Byzantine Art. Correspondence, 1920–1957*, ed. G. Bernardi, with a contribution by S. Koulouris and preface by M. Bernabó (Turnhout: Brepols, 2023), pp. 363–65. Gabriel Millet's work, in particular, appealed to Muratov, as seen in his letter to I. S. Ostroukhov: 'Believe me, Ilya Semenovich, this book is what they call *indispensable* [in English in the original] for Old Russian painting. You will be convinced of this from your very first glance at it. Here is its proper title: Gabriel Millet, *Monuments byzantins de Mistra* Paris, 1910'. Letter from P. P. Muratov to I. S. Ostroukhov, 15 June 1912, in *Otdel rukopisei Gosudarstvennoi Tretiakovskoi Gellerei* [*State Tretiakov Gallery, Manuscript Division, Moscow*] (henceforth OR GTG), f. 10, ed. khr. 4391, https://bibliotheque-numerique.inha.fr/collection/item/16247-monuments-byzantins-de-mistra

71 P. P. Muratov, 'Pol' Sezann', *Vesy*, 12 (1906), 32–42; P. P. Muratov, 'Tvorchestvo M. V. Nesterova', *Russkaia mysl'*, 4 (1907), 151–58; P. P. Muratov, 'Shchukinskaia

The young critic was commissioned to contribute to the multivolume *Istoriia russkogo iskusstva* [*History of Russian Art*], edited by Grabar, under interesting circumstances. Muratov had not focused on early Russian painting until then, but he was well acquainted with the painting of the early Italian masters from Giotto (c. 1267–1337) and Duccio (c. 1255/60–c. 1318/19) onwards, as his 'Siena' chapter in *Images of Italy* testifies, as does his Sienese Madonna article in *Starye gody*, in which he substantiated a new authorship for the Rumiantsev Museum's altarpiece *Madonna and Child*.[72] 'If you want a beautiful and scholarly pre-Petrine era [volume], don't ask the "learned men", ask Pavel Muratov', wrote Baron Nikolai Vrangel (1880–1915) insisted in a letter to Grabar in August 1911. 'He has a thorough knowledge of the Italian primitives, as you are well aware, and would easily master, comprehend and even investigate their "cousins" – our iconographers. I discussed this topic with him this year, since I wanted to dedicate an issue of "Apollon" to the early icons, to an aesthetic rather than a scholarly evaluation of them, and Muratov was very interested and expressed his accord'.[73] Indeed, in Russia little was known about the early Italian masters prior to Muratov and his *Images of Italy*.[74] His journey from the Italian Trecento to early Russian art was entirely in keeping with the latest trends in European and Russian art criticism.

Commissioned by Grabar in January 1912 to write an essay on early Russian painting for the *History of Russian Art*, Muratov visited a

---

galereiia. Ocherki iz istorii noveishei zhivopisi', *Russkaia mysl'*, 8 (1908), 116–38; P. P. Muratov, 'Novoe tondo shkoly Bottichelli', *Starye gody* (May 1911), 29–34; see also Muratov's article on Serov (*Sofiia*, 3 (1914), 93–95).

72   Muratov worked for the curator of the Fine Arts and Classical Antiquities Department of the Moscow Public Museum and Rumiantsev Museum from 1910 to 1913. The Sienese Madonna was acquired by the Rumiantsev Museum from Dmitrii Khomiakov's (1841–1919) collection and was considered the work of Sano di Pietro (1405–81). Muratov attributes it to Matteo di Giovanni in his article, when publishing his essay on other works of Italian artists of the fifteenth to early sixteenth centuries in the museum's collection (Guidoccio Cozzarelli's (1450–1517) *The Baptism of Christ* (after 1486) and Matteo Balducci's (1509–54) tondo *Madonna and Child with St Joseph and Angels* (c. 1517)). See P. P. Muratov, 'Ocherki ital'ianskoi zhivopisi v Moskovskom Rumiantsevskom muzee. I: Sienskaia Madonna', *Starye gody* (November 1910), 605–11 and 'Ocherki ital'ianskoi zhivopisi v Moskovskom Rumiantsevskom muzee. II: Kvatrochento', *Starye gody* (October 1910), 3–11.
73   I. E. Grabar, *Pis'ma 1891–1917* (Moscow: Nauka, 1974), p. 426, fn 27.
74   Piecemeal information on the 'primitives' could be found, in particular, in slim illustrated publications (see *Dzhotto I dzhotisty* (n.a.) (Moscow: n.p., 1881); V. T. Khvoshchinskii, *Toskanskie khudozhniki. I. Primitivy* (St Petersburg: n.p., 1912).

series of medieval Russian towns and monasteries (Novgorod, Pskov, Yaroslavl, Vologda, Kirillo-Belozerskii Monastery, Ferapontovo and several others). He also investigated Moscow's most interesting and oldest churches, including the renowned Old Believer churches housing valuable collections of Antique icons, and the similarly famous private collections of early Russian painting owned by the artist Ostroukhov and the banker Stepan Riabushinskii (1874–1942). However, these were not the only sources Muratov relied on. He also incorporated into his analysis early Russian frescos from Novgorod's churches and from Moscow's cathedrals, as well as miniatures and embroidery. In this regard, the edition's selection of illustrations – luxurious, colour reproductions published on grey-toned, expensive paper – is remarkable. It comprised icons from the fourteenth to the sixteenth centuries from the collections of Ostroukhov, Riabushinskii, Aleksei Morozov (1867–1934), Alexander Anisimov (1877–1937) and others – icons that were, at that time, seen as most vividly embodying the national characteristics of early Russian painting. These were supplemented by photographs of Byzantine mosaics and Italo-Greek icons, and also works by the renowned Greek master Theophanes the Greek (c. 1340–c. 1410) and the lauded medieval Russian iconographers Andrei Rublev (1360–1428) and Dionisii (1444–1502). The description of these key works testified not only to the broad historical and cultural context within which the history of early Russian iconography was scrutinized, but also to the author's endeavour to change the way in which the medieval image was perceived: Muratov presented an anonymous artisan's creation like an authored work of art. As a result, the semiotic nature of the early icon changed in the reader's consciousness: since it was being examined aesthetically, rather than from the point of view of religious history, it began to be perceived as a unique work of *pure art*.

The Icon Painter as an Artist

This theoretical perspective generated a whole series of new questions – on the early Russian icon's origin, the specifics of its artistic language, the Hellenistic foundation of Byzantine and early Russian art, the formation of Schools, the relationship between iconographic forms and national psychology and various other issues, including how the language of the icon differed from that of Western European pictures.

Also discussed was the necessity of discerning, in the icon's artistic form, those original elements of painting and pure artistic values that were objective and universal (according to proponents of the Formalist School), in order to view the medieval Russian icon in the context of world culture. Outwardly the Old Russian master was contained by the framework of the canon, but – and it was vital to demonstrate this – he possessed a free, inner creativity. The source of this creative activity was 'divine inspiration', 'innate artistry' and 'a sense of style'. And if, for the famous Russian philosopher and theologian Pavel Florenskii (1882–1937), the artistic form of the icon constantly speaks in accord with the metaphysical dimension (about which we shall say more below), then, for Muratov, the early icon reflects *pure artistry*: it opens the eyes by a combination of elements ordered entirely according to the laws of *pure art*. The icon, then, serves as a pathway to the visual realm, where one could encounter those 'ideal types' of beauty, the starting point of which Muratov – following Wölfflin and Berenson – always considered to be the canons of *Classical* art. Moreover, rendering stylistic analysis absolute compelled him to consider the discovery of a new order of artistic form (whether it be an icon, picture or sculpture) as an event of equal – if not greater – magnitude to spiritual attainment. This prompted the endeavour to construct the history of early Russian painting exclusively on the basis of *masterpieces*, amongst the ranks of which Rublev's *Trinity* (1411, or 1425–27, Tretyakov Gallery) occupied a special place. 'Whatever school "Trinity" may belong to', Muratov explained in this regard, 'it [...] conveys the distinct impression of a first-class masterpiece'.[75] In other words, according to Muratov, the contribution a particular nation had made to global artistic culture could only be discussed through masterpieces. In particular, only masterpieces allowed the early Russian icon to be fairly juxtaposed with Italo-Byzantine artworks, and Trecento and Quattrocento painting – the works of Duccio, Simone Martini (c. 1284–1344), Ambrogio Lorenzetti (c. 1285/90–1348), Pietro Lorenzetti (c. 1280–1348), Fra Angelico and other renowned early Italian artists.[76]

---

75 Muratov, *Russkaia zhivopis' do serediny XVII veka*, p. 105.
76 P. P. Muratov, 'Vizantiiskoe mifotvorichesto', *Sofiia*, 2 (1914), 3–4. That sort of comparison may be found especially in the work of N. Sychev, who observed in Rublev's famous *Trinity* a combination of Martini's 'Sienese grace' and Duccio's inspired faces. See N. Sychev, 'Ikona sv. Troitsy v Troitse-Sergievoi lavre', *Zapiski*

This theoretical position is clearly in evidence in a brief note entitled 'Pereotsenki' ['Reappraisal'], that Muratov published in 1914 in the journal *Sofiia*, of which he served as editor-in-chief. In this note, he asserted that the criteria for evaluating the quality of an artwork are no less solidly established than the 'laws of light and gravity'. As an example, he used the paintings of Botticelli: 'I am free to assert that I don't like Botticelli', Muratov explained, 'but I am not obliged to first prove that Botticelli is bad'.[77] The reappraisal of a masterpiece, then, must exclude the sphere of individual preferences and remain within the framework of established norms. Muratov's position – like Berenson's – would later be challenged by supporters of the avant-garde, who demonstrated that the subjectivity of an interpretation of an artwork on the grounds of visual impressions is the main barrier to revealing the 'intrinsic quality' of artistic forms. However, when the study of medieval Russian painting was in its infancy, this position decidedly influenced the development of new analytical methods and the interpretation of the early Russian icon's stylistic characteristics.

Byzantine Tradition and Folk Culture

As with Italian Renaissance painting, Muratov presented the entire history of early Russian art in chronological order, divided into separate Schools according to both the nearest major administrative centre and the main named artists who central to entire eras and directions in the history of early Russian painting – Theophanes the Greek, Rublev and Dionisii. Since each School was distinguished by style, Muratov focused on formal indications of the painterly language of early Russian art, such as colour, line and silhouette.[78] He was one

---

  otdeleniia russkoi i slavianskoi arkhitektury Russkogo arkheologicheskogo obshchestva, 10 (1913), 1. The Russian artist Grishchenko compares the artistic characteristics of Fra Angelico's and Rublev's work in terms of 'the elements of painting' in his book *Russkaia ikona kak iskusstvo zhivopisi* (Moscow: Izdanie Avtora, 1917).

77 P. P. Muratov, 'Pereotsenki', *Sofiia*, 2 (1914), 3–4.
78 It is important to note that the search for the specifics of this pictorial language depended to a great extent also on Walter Pater's aesthetics. Pater had observed 'that true pictorial quality which lies between (unique pledge of the possession of the pictorial gift) the inventive or creative handling of pure line and colour, which [...] is quite independent of anything definitely poetical in the subject it

of the very first who endeavoured to provide stylistic characteristics for the Schools of medieval Russian iconography, and he grouped his data within the political and geographical framework represented by the specific state formations of Kievan Rus', the republic of Novgorod and the Muscovite principality. According to his model, three main 'Schools' of iconography may be distinguished in the history of Russian medieval painting – the Novgorod, Moscow and Stroganov Schools. That said, the Novgorod School of the fifteenth century was accorded special weight, comparable in significance with Florentine art of the same period. In Muratov's work, the Romantic aggrandizing of Trecento- and Quattrocento-era Siena and Florence clearly transferred to the art of medieval Pskov and Novgorod. A special creative impulse was detected in the Novgorodian icon, both a stylistic individuality and that very 'spirit' of national tradition that would be later noted in the example of a large icon made for church use – a hagiographical (or *vita*) icon of *St Theodore Stratelates* (late fifteenth century, Novgorod) – 'one of the finest creations in Russia's art of the icon' (see Fig. 2.3).[79] Elaborating this thought in his 1928 essay 'Ways of the Russian Icon', Muratov pondered in particular how:

> The Italian and Flemish primitives surmounted the Byzantine-Hellenistic graphic system and created their own graphic system, which also became the graphic system of European painting. Something entirely different happened in Russia [...] The Russian primitive was not in any way primitive in the western sense of the word. His foray into history's arena tells us that, over several centuries of effort, he brought the figurative, monumental, pictorial, aristocratic painting of Byzantium to the peasant art of the people, to the level of folkloric and decorative art. The history of Russian icon-painting reveals the interconnectedness of these two sources – Byzantine tradition on the one hand, and the influence of the village art of the people on the other.[80]

---

accompanies'. See W. Pater, *The Renaissance. Studies in Art and Poetry* (New York: Macmillan, 1888), p. 137, https://archive.org/details/renaissancestu00pate

79   P. P. Muratov, 'V Novgorodskikh tserkvakh', in P. P. Muratov and A. I. Anisimov, *Novgorodskaia ikona Sv. Feodora Stratilata* (Moscow: K. F. Nekrasov, 1916), pp. 3–8.

80   P. P. Muratov, 'Puti russkoi ikony', in Muratov, *Russkaia zhivopis' do serediny XVII veka*, p. 352.

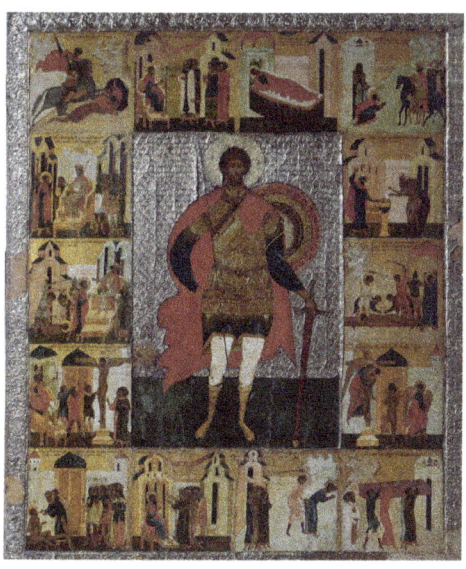

Fig. 2.3 Novgorod School, *St Theodore Stratelates* (late fifteenth century), tempera on wood, 136.5 x 109 cm. Novgorod State Museum-Reserve. Wikimedia, public domain, https://commons.wikimedia.org/wiki/File:Theodore_Stratelates_-_hagiography_icon.jpg

But how, and by which paths, were the Russian icon's features formed? What was novel about Muratov's contribution was that he scrutinized the crystallization of national artistic language of medieval Russian painting in the context of its historical origin and the evolution of form. It was precisely this aspect of Muratov's work which had the greatest value at the time. Muratov was one of the first to apply the so-called theory of the Palaiologan Renaissance (the Hellenistic foundations of Byzantine art) in his interpretation of medieval Russian painting of the fourteenth and fifteenth centuries, and he saw the Russian icon's originality in its ability to combine elements from both Byzantine and local folk traditions. Today, it seems obvious that high culture always draws additional resources from folk art (in other words, from uncanonical works which surpass or transgress established norms) to take innovative steps. The conceptual frame of the masterpiece could not accommodate the development of this idea in the eighteenth and nineteenth centuries. However, it was at the beginning of the twentieth century that the distinguishing features of the Russian icon, which Muratov later expanded upon in his emigration, were first discovered precisely through this approach. Early Russian art found its defining characteristics in the *poetry of folk art*: the early Russian (and especially the Novgorodian) icon introduced 'a natural folk taste for pattern' into the inherited tradition of Byzantine painting.[81]

Italy or Byzantium?

An interesting academic debate unfolds at the beginning of the twentieth century around the question of the early Russian icon's origins, which incorporates both the Italian 'primitives' and the Italo-Greek icon. A few scholars, working independently, saw these as the main sources of influence on Byzantine and medieval Russian art of the fourteenth and fifteenth centuries. Here, Italy – the land of art and standards of beauty – continued to provide the models by which the art of other countries and peoples was interpreted. The question of the relationship between Byzantine, early Italian and early Russian painting of the fourteenth and fifteenth centuries was broached in the theory of the abovementioned Russian archaeologists, Nikodim Kondakov (1844–1925) and Nikolai Likhachev (1862–1936), and in the concept of the Palaiologan Renaissance developed by French Byzantinists Millet and Diehl, and also by the University of Oxford professor Dalton. Seminal monographs by the Russian scholars came out in 1911: Kondakov published *Ikonografiia Bogomateri. Sviazi grecheskoi I russkoi ikonopisi s ital'ianskoi zhivopis'iu rannego Vozrozhdeniia* [*Iconography of the Mother of God. Greek and Russian Icons and Their Connections with Early Italian Renaissance Painting*], and Likhachev published *Istoricheskoe znachenie italo-grecheskoi ikonopisi. Izobrazhenie Bogomateri v proizvedeniiakh italo-grecheskikh ikonopistsev I ikh vliianie na kompozitsii nekotorykh proslavlennykh russkikh ikon* [*The Historical Significance of Italo-Greek Icon-Painting. Images of the Mother of God in the Works of Italo-Greek Iconographers and Their Influence on the Composition of Some Renowned Russian Icons*].[82]

---

81 It is notable that V. N. Lazarev also developed the very same idea towards the end of his creative career. See K. M. Muratova, 'Ital'ianskoe iskusstvo XIII I XIV vekov v russkoe kritike: sviazi, vzaimovliianiia, sud'by', in *In Christo. Vo Khriste. Obmen khudozhestvennymi i dukhovnymi shedevrami mezhdu Rossiei i Italiei*, ed. A. Melloni (Rome: Treccani, 2011), 521–68 (p. 556).

82 N. P. Kondakov, *Ikonografiia Bogomateri. Sviazi grecheskoi i russkoi ikonopisi s ital'ianskoi zhivopis'iu rannego Vozrozhdeniia* (St Petersburg: Tipografiia imperatorskoi akademii nauk, 1911); N. P. Likhachev, *Istoricheskoe znachenie italo-grecheskoi ikonopisi. Izobrazhenie Bogomateri v proizvedeniiakh italo-grecheskikh*

In the thinking of Kondakov and Likhachev, Italian models furnished those iconographic types of the Mother of God which conveyed maternal feeling and love – particularly images of the *Mother of God of Tenderness* (*Umilenie*), the *Virgo Lactans* or *Mother of God Nursing* (*Mlekopitatel'nitsa*), the *Konevskaia Mother of God* and the *Mother of God of the Passion* (*Strastnaia*) and several others. These ideal types are contrasted with compositions developed on Byzantine soil, for example the *Hodegetria*, the *Mother of God of the Sign* (*Znamenie*), and the *Pecherskaia Mother of God*. According to Kondakov and Likhachev, although the 'Tenderness' type appeared in Byzantium, it nevertheless ended up in early Russian painting via Italy (see Fig. 2.4).

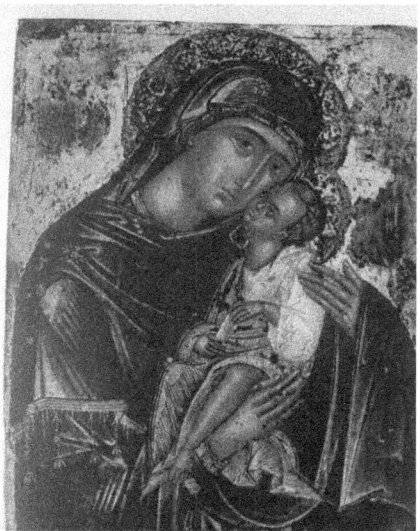

Fig. 2.4 Italo-Greek School, *Mother of God of Tenderness* (fifteenth century). Plate from Nikolai Likhachev, *Materialy dlia istorii russkogo ikonopisaniia: Atlas* (St Petersburg: Ekspedisiia zagotovleniia gosudarstvennykh bumag, 1906). Photograph by the author (2016), public domain.

---

ikonopistsev i ikh vliianie na kompozitsii nekotorykh proslavlennykh russkikh ikon (St Petersburg: Izdanie Russkago arkheologicheskogo obva, 1911). On the discovery and study of Byzantine and early Russian art in nineteenth-century scholarship, see G. I. Vzdornov, *The History of the Discovery and Study of Russian Medieval Painting*, ed. M. Sollins, trans. V. G. Dereviagin (Leiden: Brill, 2017); G. I. Vzdornov, 'Nikodim Kondakov v zerkale sovremennoi vizantinistiki', in *Nauka i restavratsiia. Ocherki po istorii i izucheniia drevnerusskoi zhivopisi* (Moscow: Indrik, 2006); I. Foletti, *From Byzantium to Holy Russia. Nikodim Kondakov (1844–1925) and the Invention of the Icon*, trans. S. Melker (Rome: Viella, 2011).

Kondakov also associated individual distinctive features of the early Russian icon's artistic form – in particular, the bicoloured highlights (*bliki*) on the clothing of saints, and the elongated proportions of the figures – with Italian sources. In sum, Kondakov and Likhachev erroneously made the formation of the national characteristics of early Russian painting contingent upon the development of the so-called Italo-Cretan School which, in their opinion, was itself the result of the influence of Italian thirteenth- and fourteenth-century 'primitives' on the art of Byzantium.

Meanwhile, in the works of Millet, Diehl and Dalton, a 'living creativity' distinguished the art of Byzantium: it had its own evolution just as all other art did.[83] In this regard, the Palaiologan Renaissance of the fourteenth century had no need for Italian models. The relative illusionism in Byzantine icons and frescos of the Palaiologan era was based on a return to the models of Antiquity. The wall paintings of Mistra, the mosaics of Kahrie Djami and the churches of Old Serbia (in which scenes and figures brimming with observations from life were detected) testified to a self-contained manifestation of art, independent of early Italian painting of the thirteenth and fourteenth centuries. Moreover, in the opinion of the western specialists, a more plausible case could be made for Byzantium's influence on Italy in the Trecento era. Duccio's painting, and that of the artists in his circle, had already proved convincing in this regard (see Fig. 2.5). Given the strength of the Byzantine resonances in Duccio's Sienese Madonnas, Berenson even suggested that Duccio might have studied in Constantinople.[84] Indeed, the Byzantine tradition was firmly established in Siena not only in the fourteenth century, but right up until the very end of the fifteenth

---

83   G. Millet, *Monuments byzantins de Mistra* (Paris: E. Leroux, 1910), https://bibliotheque-numerique.inha.fr/collection/item/16247-monuments-byzantins-de-mistra; C. Diehl, *Manuel d'art Byzantin* (Paris: A. Picard, 1910); O. M. Dalton, *Byzantine Art and Archaeology* (Oxford: Clarendon Press, 1911).

84   B. Berenson, *Central Italian Painters of the Renaissance* (New York and London: Putnam, 1897), p. 41. In commenting on Berenson's supposition, and once again comparing Duccio's work with the icons of Novgorod, Muratov suggested that 'one should seek the roots of Duccio's art, just like the roots of Novgorodian icon-painting, in the Palaiologan Renaissance'. See Muratov, *Obrazy Italii*, I, 258. See also B. Berenson, 'Two Twelfth-Century Paintings from Constantinople', in B. Berenson, *Studies in Medieval Painting* (New Haven, CT: Yale University Press, 1930), pp. 1–16.

century. Throughout this period, Sienese artists continued to reproduce the very same type of Madonna, passed down to them by Duccio and Martini. It is fair to say, moreover, that this 'Byzantine' type of Madonna appeared in fifteenth-century Russian painting too, as demonstrated by an icon from the former collection of Riabushinskii.[85]

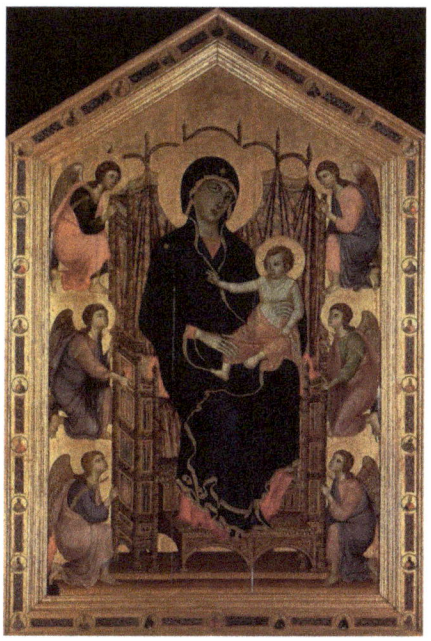

Fig. 2.5 Duccio (c. 1255/60–c. 1318/19), *Madonna Rucellai* (1285), tempera and gold on wood, 450 x 290 cm. Uffizi Gallery, Florence. Wikimedia, public domain, https://commons.wikimedia.org/wiki/File:Duccio_di_Buoninsegna_-_Rucellai_Madonna_-_WGA6822.jpg

Using this wealth of western and Russian scholarship on Byzantine and early Italian art, Muratov's own inclination was to draw out the entire history of Old Russian painting from Byzantine art of the Palaiologan era. He would later reject this approach, in part because of discoveries made by Grabar's Central Restoration Workshop between 1918 and 1929. The frescos of Vladimir's Cathedral of St Demetrius, the earliest Byzantine

---

85 See M. Alpatov's article on the influence of Sienese Madonna iconography from the School of Duccio on the composition of the fifteenth-century Novgorodian icon 'The Mother of God Enthroned', from Riabushinskii's collection. See M. Alpatov, 'K voprosu o zapadnom vliianii na drevnerusskoe iskusstvo', *Slavia*, 3 (1924), 94–113 (p. 94).

icons and early Russian icons of the twelfth and thirteenth centuries all convincingly demonstrated that the sources of medieval Russian painting should be sought in Byzantine culture at least as early as the Komnenian era (the eleventh and twelfth centuries) – in other words, considerably earlier than had seemed probable at the start of the 1910s. Nonetheless, the working hypothesis of the Palaiologan Renaissance was important in terms of broad historical-cultural understanding of the characteristics of the early Russian icon's artistic form, which Muratov set out so clearly. The researcher's taste for Antiquity and Classical art brought him, via the Palaiologan Renaissance, to a highly important thesis demanding thorough elaboration: the Byzantine and early Russian icon could not be understood in isolation, without attention to their Hellenistic origins.

In this regard, Muratov once again raised the question of the interconnections between Italian 'primitives' of the thirteenth to fifteenth centuries, the Italo-Cretan School and early Russian icons. Engaging in a detailed analysis of the development of the Italo-Cretan School in light of new discoveries in Byzantine painting of the Palaiologan era, Muratov convincingly demonstrated that 'in the fifteenth and sixteenth centuries it was Novgorod and Moscow that became metropolises of Byzantine-based art – not Crete or the southern Italian cities, nor even Athos'. Russian icons of the Mother of God drew on Byzantine monuments, rather than (as Kondakov and Likhachev had suggested) being dependent on Italian models. Most probably, Italian Trecento Madonnas revealed a dependence on Byzantine models.[86]

Italian influence can indeed be found in Greek iconography, but considerably later – from the second half of the fifteenth century to the sixteenth century. Icon workshops, producing works for the Orthodox East, were established in Italy in precisely this period. Greek workshops were also in operation in the territory of Greece itself (particularly in Crete, Cyprus and Corfu), which often incorporated Italian models to cater to the tastes of their Catholic clientele. This influence is felt, above all, in the scenery and draped figures of fifteenth- and sixteenth-century Italo-Greek icons. In sum, then, Muratov viewed Italo-Cretan icons

---

86 P. P. Muratov, 'Russkaia zhivopis'' do serediny XVII veka', in Muratov, *Russkaia zhivopis' do serediny XVII veka*, ed. Grabar, IV, 55. G. G. Pavlutskii, in particular, developed this line of thought. See G. G. Pavlutskii, 'K voprosu o vzaimnom vliianii vizantiiskogo i ital'ianskogo iskusstva', *Iskusstvo*, 5–6 (1912), 208–20.

as provincial artisan reflections of the models of Italian high art. The activity of these workshops had little in common with Byzantine art of the Palaiologan era.[87]

'Hellenistic Impressionism'

Muratov's approach to the problem of Hellenistic traditions evident in medieval art proved to be particularly fruitful. When elaborating on the question of its genesis, Muratov was consistently inspired by the idea of the unity of the Hellenic-Christian world, of which early Rus' was a part. He continuously stressed that Christianity came to Russia in Hellenistic forms, and that 'the entire history of Russian icon-painting is a history of the dissolving of Hellenistic forms'. Russian researcher Dmitrii Ainalov (1862–1939) and Polish-Austrian art historian Jòzef Strzygowski (1862–1941) had already convincingly demonstrated that the Hellenistic aesthetic never disappeared from the artistic consciousness of Byzantine culture.[88] Muratov, however, was among the first to identify the echoes of Antiquity in the artistic form of early Russian icons itself. Russia was introduced to Hellenist civilization through the Byzantine icon: the world of Hellenized Christianity became, for Russians, their 'national' world. This is why no Russian features may be discerned in Christ and the Mother of God on Russian icons, and the figures of Christian saints resemble the personages in Fayum portraits, dressed in Hellenistic himatia and chitons. In turn, winged angels, their heads decorated with ribbons, reiterate the genii from some ancient altars of victory.

The coloured highlights on the garments and cloths of the saints were also inherited from the ancient world. Comparing the architectural

---

87 Muratov, 'Russkaia zhivopis'' do serediny XVII veka', in Muratov, *Russkaia zhivopis' do serediny XVII veka*, ed. Grabar, IV, 70. In the context of this polemic, it is notable that Italo-Greek icons were reproduced on the first pages of the first issue of the *Russian Icon* collection (which included Muratov's flagship article), for comparison with early Russian examples. See *Russkaia ikona*, 1 (1914), illustrations on pp. 7, 10, 11, 13.

88 D. V. Ainalov, *Ellinisticheskie osnovy vizantiiskogo iskusstva* (St Petersburg: n.p., 1900); J. Strzygowski, *Orient oder Rom: Beitrag zur Geschichte der spätantiken und frühchristlichen Kunst* (Leipzig: Hinrichs, 1901). For a long time, in fact, Ainalov's research was unknown in Western academia. His book was translated into English only in 1961. See D. V. Ainalov, *The Hellenistic Origins of Byzantine Art*, ed. C. Mango, trans. E. Sobolevitch and S. Sobolevitch (New Brunswick, NJ: Rutgers University Press, 1961).

forms on Russian icons with the architecture depicted in the frescos of Pompei and Roman plaster reliefs also delivered surprising results. Muratov observed similar columns and porticos in both cases, and also the shape of a four-cornered atrium, covered by a tent-shaped awning, in addition to the *velum* motif – a cloth draped between the roof of the house and a tree or column standing alone. The rocky scenery of Antiquity also appears in Russian icons, as well as in Byzantine mosaics and Italian Trecento painting. A Russian-American historian of Antiquity, Mikhail Rostovtsev (1870–1952), and art historian Wolfgang Kallab (1875–1906), writing at this time about Hellenistic landscapes, located the origins of these rocky landscapes in the ancient world and pointed out the influence of such scenery on fourteenth-century Italian art.[89] According to Muratov, this scenery was retained in an original purity in the Russian icon: 'One cannot conceive of the Russian icon of the fourteenth to the sixteenth century', the researcher stressed, 'without Hellenist mountains, without fantastic and picturesque "Alexandrian" architecture'.[90]

Finally, this deep connection between the art of Antiquity and the Russian icon may be discerned in iconography which depicts Hellenistic personifications of the sea, rivers, land and deserts. The god of the river Jordan features in scenes of the Baptism of the Lord, and figures personifying the Earth and the Desert may be seen in compositions of the Synaxis of the Mother of God. Russian icons thus made it possible to experience a shared visual impression that, for Muratov, evoked the lost easel paintings of Ancient Greece. Muratov communicated this unexpected discovery to Moscow collector Ostroukhov in a letter: 'One may see something like the visual impression conveyed by Greek easel painting of the fifth and sixth centuries B.C. only in the Russian icon of the fourteenth and fifteenth centuries […] I am positively certain that you will discover traces of the style traditional in the Hellenistic world as you discover ancient Novgorod'.[91]

---

89 M. Rostovtsev, *Ellinisticheski-rimskii arkhitekturnyi peizazh* (St Petersburg: n.p., 1908); W. Kallab, *Die toskanische Landschaftsmalerei in XIV und XV Jahrhundert* (Vienna: Vienna Holzhausen, 1900).

90 Muratov, 'Russkaia zhivopis' do serediny XVII veka', in *Istoriia Russkogo iskusstva*, ed. Grabar, IV, 101.

91 OR GTG, f. 10, ed. khr. 4394, ll. 1–4 (Letter from P. P. Muratov to I. S. Ostroukhov, 10 September 1912). Influenced by Muratov, Ostroukhov himself later wrote about

Muratov employed the concept of 'Hellenistic Impressionism', which conveyed real life observations and impressions, in discussing Byzantine and early Russian art's foundations in Antiquity. Viewed through this lens, the bicoloured highlights on saints' clothing might echo real, coloured overtones in Greek textiles, and the icon's red and pink hills might reflect the reality of mountainous terrain lit by the setting sun. Muratov also discerned these features in Daphni's eleventh-century mosaics and in the fifteenth-century mosaics of Kahrie Djami, as well as in Byzantine icons of the same period. They were revealed, too, in the frescos of Vladimir's churches, and in early Russian icons of the fifteenth and sixteenth centuries.

Aided by this understanding of 'Hellenistic Impressionism', Muratov also developed a series of identifiable contrasts between the stylistic traits of Western European and Eastern Christian art, and also of differences between the Italian 'primitives' and early Russian icons. And if the illusionism of Byzantium was preserved in Russia's fourteenth-century art, then early Russian painting of the fifteenth century (especially that of the Novgorodian School) found its own formula for iconography. Fifteenth-century Novgorodian icons, therefore, may be easily distinguished from both Byzantine and Balkan artworks by the way their symbolic language constantly draws on the rhythms of liturgy and prayer. In this regard, an early Russian icon's composition is always distinguished by a particular *musical rhythm* (see Fig. 2.6).[92] In contrast, western masters in the age of Charlemagne (747–814) and in the era of Romanesque art in Italy and Flanders intensified the traits of realism in their pictorial systems, and, as a result, the Italian and Flemish 'primitives' went beyond the Byzantine-Hellenistic canon

---

the 'Greco-Roman roots' of the early Russian icon. See *Rossiiskii gosudarstvennyi arkhiv literatury i iskusstva* [*Russian State Archive of Literature and Art*] (henceforth RGALI), f. 822, ed. khr. 128.

92 Muratov, 'Russkaia zhivopis' do serediny XVII veka', in Muratov, *Russkaia zhivopis' do serediny XVII veka*, ed. Grabar, IV, 313. Grabar also observed that 'This rhythmic nature and stamp of melody basically distinguishes the way all Russian icons are painted' (I. E. Grabar, 'Vvedenie v istoriiu russkogo iskusstva', in *Istoriia russkogo iskusstva*, I, ed. Grabar, p. 48). Later, Nikolai Tarabukin's (1889–1956) paper 'Ritm i kompozitsiia v drevnerusskoi zhivopisi', delivered on 22 December 1923 at the Institute of Art History in Petrograd, would focus in on the special rhythm of early Russian icons. See N. M. Tarabukin, *Smysl ikony* (Moscow: Pravoslavnogo bratstva Sviatitelia Filareta, 1999), pp. 204–06.

and thereby established the groundwork for the pictorial system upon which European Renaissance painting was built.

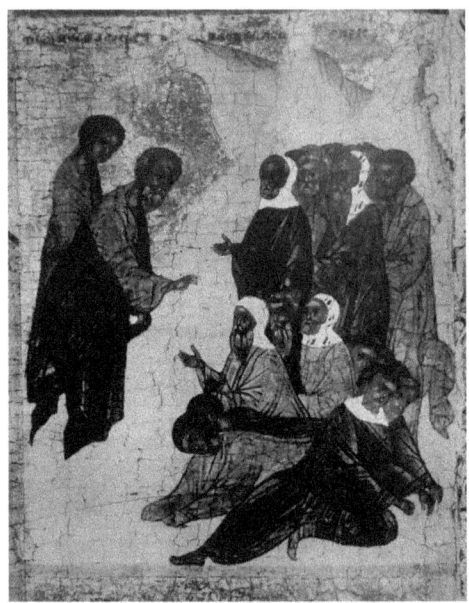

Fig. 2.6 *St John Theologian with Scenes from His Life* (c. 1500). Icon detail, reproduced in Pavel Muratov, *La pittura russa antica* (Rome: A. Stock, 1925), as a characteristic example of the musical and rhythmic composition of medieval Russian icon. Photograph by the author (2020), public domain.

Muratov's broad historical-cultural approach to understanding the early Russian icon found an interesting interpretation in the programme of the journal *Sofiia*, founded in 1914 by Muratov in collaboration with the publisher Konstantin Nekrasov (1873–1940). Since the new journal strove to set the early Russian icon in the context of the development of art globally, articles on early Russian painting appear in parallel with materials on the history of Hellenistic portraits, Italian Trecento painting, the art of ancient China and also notes and essays by famous researchers and philosophers on the aesthetics and theories of contemporary avant-garde movements. The medieval Russian icon was therefore presented as heir to the traditions of Byzantium and Antiquity. It was also compared to the schematic nature of Buddhist art and even of Pablo Picasso's (1881–1973) Cubist painting, the arrival of which promoted an aesthetic re-evaluation of 'the primitive'. In order to facilitate the comparison of the characteristics of Russian icons with the characteristics of ancient paintings, Baron Vladimir von Gruneizen's (1868–1932) extensive research article 'Illiuzionisticheskii portret' ['The Illusionistic Portrait'] was published in the fourth number of *Sofiia*: the public juxtaposition of illustrations of ancient images with reproductions of early Russian icons graphically convinced the reader that Byzantine and medieval Russian painting was grounded specifically in the Hellenistic portrait.[93] Publications on the theory of art, and, in particular, certain articles by Berenson and Waldemar Deonna (1880–1959), also had particular significance for Muratov.[94] Muratov's identification of the Schools of medieval Russian painting was undoubtedly grounded in the famous – and Berenson was, at that time, one of the most important specialists on Italian 'primitives' – American researcher's argument for the significance of formal elements in discerning an artist's individual style.[95] The intention behind employing methods of stylistic analysis and contemporary theories in interpreting early Russian artworks was to demonstrate that the icon occupied a worthy place in the history of European art and could be readily compared with the finest examples of early Italian and Flemish painting. This explains the multiple comparisons of early Russian icons with the paintings and altarpieces of the Trecento and Quattrocento. Comparisons were necessary, in some cases, to reveal the 'shared artistic spirit' in the beauty of Novgorodian icons and Sienese Madonnas. In other cases, comparisons brought unique elements in the construction of the icon to light, clarifying their connection with the Palaiologan Renaissance of the fourteenth

---

93 W. de Gruneizen, 'Illiuzionisticheskii portret', *Sofiia*, 4 (1914), 5–59. Russian researcher Baron Vladimir Gruneizen (Wladimir de Grüneisen) was also the author of a work dedicated to the Roman Church of Santa Maria Antiqua. See W. de Grüneisen, *Sainte Marie Antique* (Rome: Bretschneider, 1911).

94 B. Berenson, 'Osnovy khudozhestvennogo raspoznavaniia', *Sofiia*, 1 (1914), 40–69; W. Deonna, 'Iskusstvo i deistvitel'nost'. Voprosy arkheologicheskogo metoda', *Sofiia*, 5 (1914), 22–48.

95 It seems that especial interest was garnered by the section on 'Artistic Morphology', in which the Berenson developed Giovanni Morelli's (1816–91) formal-anatomical method. Berenson divided all the formal elements of a picture into three classes according to their suitability for identifying the artist's style. According to his theory, the most suitable elements are the hands, folds in clothing and scenery; hair, eyes and mouth are less useful; and, finally, the most difficult to apply are the skull and chin, the structure and movement of a figure. See Berenson, 'Osnovy khudozhestvennogo raspoznavaniia', 66–68; see also B. Berenson, 'The Rudiments of Connoisseurship (A Fragment)', in B. Berenson, *The Study and Criticism of Italian Art* (London: G. Bell and Sons, 1902), pp. 111–48.

century. And if (in accordance with these approaches) the Trecento era proved to be a turning point in the history of Italian painting in terms of the gradual overriding of Byzantine tradition, then, in the history of Russian icon-painting, this period was viewed as generating creative reinterpretations of Byzantine models and as crystallizing national traits in the language of art.

Muratov's wide circle of interests as an art critic and a gifted art historian, as a connoisseur and a fine judge of Italian culture, thus directly influenced his aesthetic evaluation of the early Russian icon. The methodology of new European studies of art helped him not only to set out the historical evolution of medieval Russian icon-painting in relation to the periodization of Byzantine painting, but also to insightfully outline the Russian icon's original stylistic features, to clarify that decorative and musical-rhythmic principle of its composition that has always distinguished it from Greek and Eastern Slavic works of art.

3. The New Museum of Medieval Icons

> Primitives stepped into the shoes of the High Renaissance artists.
>
> —Aleksei Grishchenko (1883–1977)[96]

In his 1831 short story *Le Chef-d'œuvre inconnu* [*The Unknown Masterpiece*], Honoré de Balzac (1799–1850) attempted to convince the reader of the impossibility of creating an absolute masterpiece. A masterpiece is an unattainable ideal, sought by the mind of the artist. At the beginning of the twentieth century, however, the concept of the masterpiece changed. Suddenly, far more works were deemed masterpieces, and an entirely new link between the collected object and the personal, aesthetic experience of the individual art lover became of primary importance. The new collector 'discovers' a masterpiece, and simultaneously aims to attract attention to it both as a researcher and as a representative of the art market. Moreover, with the rampant rise of capitalism and the swift concentration of capital within the narrow sector of the new bourgeoisie, the market began to extend its reach into the process of sacralizing the masterpiece. It greatly influenced the 'discovery' of new artists and the production of counterfeits; it put ownership of masterpieces beyond the reach of the ordinary person, while better quality colour illustrations, advertisements and exhibitions imprinted these masterpieces on the public eye. In other words, significant developments were taking place concerning the masterpiece, its interpretation and its increasing prominence in the art and antiquities market. New art critics were not alone in their concern for the expression and quality of artistic form,

---

96   A. Grishchenko, *Russkaia ikona kak iskusstvo zhivopisi* (Moscow: Izdanie Avtora, 1917), p. 243.

and for the early Russian icon's national style and individuality – the new collectors were also worried. The conception of early Russian icons (and Italian 'primitives') as masterpieces of painting became a sensitive subject amongst the new collectors precisely in the era of the *Belle Époque* (c. 1871–1914).

The Artist's Gaze: A New Masterpiece of Painting

Ilya Ostroukhov (1858–1929) occupied a special place in this dynamic, as an artist and collector, academician of art and trustee of the Tretyakov Gallery, and as the founder of the best private collection of medieval Russian art in Russia (see Fig. 3.1). Ostroukhov may also be considered the founder of the new private museum, in which Russian medieval icons were displayed as masterpieces of painting in special halls.[97] Initially, the icons were arranged in Ostroukhov's private residence amongst works by Russian and Western European painters such as Ilya Repin (1844–1930), Valentin Serov (1865–1919), Edgar Degas (1834–1917) and Édouard Manet (1832–83). However, we know that in 1910, or thereabouts, Ostroukhov planned a special exhibition space for the icons; this may be discerned from sketches preserved in his archive that show a carefully worked out display of the items he had collected. It is clear that the stylized forms of Russian wooden architecture provided the starting point for this space, as did the characteristic elements of the icon walls in Old Believer prayer houses (free of the strict system that governs the iconostasis). This display is the genesis of the icon's emancipation from the context of religious and ecclesiastical practice. It follows a fundamentally different theory and is intended for Kantian, 'disinterested' contemplation. Revealing the universal nature of creativity, the frame of the exhibition essentially articulates the possibility of positioning the icon alongside any work of art and permits the eye to focus on each icon as an individual art object. This reception of the icon as *pure art* at the same time introduced the secular aura of a national museum, which was characteristic of that era.

---

97   P. P. Muratov, *Drevnerusskaia zhivopis' v sobranii I. S. Ostroukhova* (Moscow: K. F. Nekrasov, 1914), p. 4.

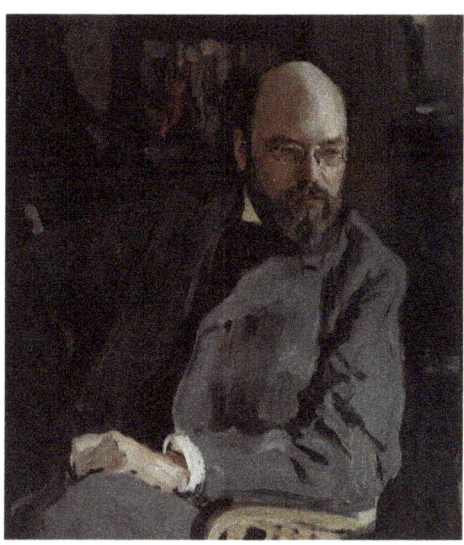

Fig. 3.1 Valentin Serov (1865–1919), *Portrait of the Artist Ilya Ostroukhov* (1902), oil on canvas, 87.5 x 78.2 cm. Tretyakov Gallery, Moscow. Wikimedia, public domain, https://commons.wikimedia.org/wiki/File:Portrait_of_the_Artist_Ilya_Ostroukhov.jpg

The museum was open to specialists and art lovers around 1911, but its masterpieces were soon accessible to all. By 1917, it housed 125 icons and over 600 items of ecclesiastical plate; 237 pictures by Russian artists and around 40 works by Western European masters, including Jean-Baptiste-Camille Corot (1796–1875), Degas, Auguste Rodin (1840–1970) and Manet; 20 sculptures and around 100 examples of art from Ancient Egypt, Greece, Rome, China and Japan. The museum also had an extremely rich library, with around 15,000 Russian and foreign publications on art, in addition to art magazines and a multitude of books on history, aesthetics and philosophy.[98] The museum was nationalized after the 1917 October Revolution, and, in 1920, was named 'The I. S. Ostroukhov Museum of Icons and Paintings'. By an irony of fate, its former owner was appointed the director. After the collector's death, the museum was dissolved (1929), its contents dispersed around various collections, and its interiors vanished into the glittering mists of Russia's cultural past. Such is the brief history of this unique place,

---

98   I. S. Ostroukhov, *Alfavitnyi ukazatel' biblioteki I. S. Ostroukhova* (Moscow: n.p., 1914).

which offers a glimpse of the fascinating historical and cultural realities of the very start of the *new collecting* of Russian medieval painting.

Born into a merchant family and highly educated, Ostroukhov first gained prominence as a talented artist. He was drawn to art by a close relationship with Savva Mamontov's (1841–1918) family in Abramtsevo, where he took painting lessons with the landscape artist Aleksandr Kiselev (1838–1911). Thanks to his unique abilities he soon garnered extraordinary success. His *Siverko* painting (1890, Tretyakov Gallery, Moscow) was purchased by Pavel Tretiakov (1832–98), and lauded by all (most notably by Isaac Levitan (1860–1900), Repin and Serov) as a masterpiece of Russian landscape painting. In 1891, Ostroukhov joined the Society of Wandering Art Exhibitions; in 1903, he entered the Union of Russian Artists; and, in 1906, he became a full member of the Imperial Academy of Arts. He was not, however, attracted by a career as a landscape artist. After his 1889 marriage to N. P. Botkina (the daughter of Piotr Botkin (1831–1907), a prominent tea-merchant), Ostroukhov devoted more time to collecting Russian and foreign art. The contents of his diverse collection were shaped by his natural talent and taste. It included a fairly large number of Russian and foreign artists of secondary importance, a substantial collection of studies, sketches and watercolours, and a limited number of the large, finished paintings that wealthy collectors always sought to secure. It should be noted, however, that all works were of markedly high artistic quality, which testifies to the good taste of this strict aesthete. According to Baron Nikolai Vrangel (1880–1915), the prominent art critic, Ostroukhov's museum presented such striking examples of work by second-rank artists that they looked like 'entirely new and unknown masters'.[99]

Ostroukhov opposed the collection of icons long after his associates had taken up the practice with enthusiasm. Significant early enthusiasts included the scholar-archaeologists Nikodim Kondakov (1844–1925) and Nikolai Likhachev (1862–1936), the entrepreneur Pavel Kharitonenko (1852–1914), as well as those Old Believer collectors from prominent merchant families – the Riabushinskiis, the Morozovs, the Saldatenkovs and others. One of the founders of European Byzantine

---

99 N. N. Vrangel, 'Sobranie I. S. Ostroukhov v Moskve', *Apollon*, 10 (1911), 5–14 (p. 9).

studies, Kondakov, although not a 'professional' collector like Wilhelm von Bode (1845–1929), for example, owned a collection of icons – small but nonetheless interesting in its own way. Kondakov acquired icons – mainly of Italo-Greek style – from time to time on his many travels around the Mediterranean and Near East. Apparently, they aided in the scholar's understanding of the evolution of Byzantine and post-Byzantine painting, and they inspired him when writing *Ikonografiia Bogomateri. Sviazi grecheskoi I russkoi ikonopisi s ital'ianskoi zhivopis'iu rannego Vozrozhdeniia* [*Iconography of the Mother of God. Greek and Russian Icons and Their Connections with Early Italian Renaissance Painting*] (1911). He also collected Russian icons and, in particular, works from those renowned centres of Russian folk icon-painting, Palekh, Mstera and Kholui. A letter of thanks dated 6 December 1909, from Grand Prince Georgii Mikhailovich (1863–1919) to Kondakov, records how, in 1909, the scholar – already then eminent – gave his collection to the Russian Museum of His Imperial Majesty Alexander III (now the State Russian Museum) in St Petersburg: 'A colleague of mine at Emperor Alexander III's Russian Museum, which I direct', the Prince wrote, 'has brought to my attention the fact that you have donated a systematically assembled collection of early Russian icons and examples of peasant handicrafts made in the Vladimir region villages of Mstera, Kholui and Palekh to the Russian Museum. I consider it a pleasant task to convey to Your Excellency my sincere and deep gratitude for such a valuable and rare academic offering to the treasury of native icon-painting. With sincere respect, Georgii'.[100]

Academician Likhachev, who amassed one of the biggest collections in Europe of medieval Russian, Byzantine and fifteenth- to seventeenth-century Italo-Greek icons, undoubtedly stands out here. Likhachev's icon collection (totalling around 1,500 examples) was exhibited in several halls of his own St Petersburg mansion, built especially to

---

100 On N. P. Kondakov's icon collection, see *Mir Kondakova. Publikatsii. Stat'i. Katalog vystavki*, ed. I. L. Kyzlasova (Moscow: Russkii put', 2004). Wilhelm von Bode also donated his collection of Renaissance majolica to the Museum of Applied Arts, the Kunstgewerbemuseum, in Berlin. Before this, it was published in his book *Die Anfänge der Majolikakunst in Toskana* (Berlin: Julius Bard, 1911). See A. F. Moskowitz, *Stefano Bardini 'Principe degli Antiquari'. Prolegomenon to a Biography* (Florence: Centro Di, 2015), pp. 75–76.

house his huge collection. This scholar's interests encompassed not only medieval works of art, but also examples of material culture which served as sources for his numerous academic works in the most diverse spheres of knowledge – art history, archaeology and sphragistics. His collection therefore included Eastern and Western European manuscripts, eleventh- to sixteenth-century Byzantine and Russian seals, Antique coins and a great deal more besides the Byzantine, medieval Russian and Italo-Greek icons. Embarking on research in palaeography in 1894, Likhachev first became interested in the inscriptions on icons as historical sources; by 1895, however, he had already decided to engage in original research on Russian iconography. His primary focus was the mutual connections between the Russian icon and Byzantine painting, Italian 'primitives' and Italo-Greek icons. His travels in Western Europe, Greece, Constantinople and Athos were accompanied by active collecting. In sum, Likhachev was one of the first who strove to demonstrate how icon-painting developed in the Eastern Mediterranean, and he was practically the first to reveal the historical, cultural and artistic value of post-Byzantine art. We know that Italy, and, above all, Venice – which by the second half of the nineteenth century was already becoming the chief centre for trade in medieval icons – played a special role in Likhachev's collecting. He made major purchases from Rome's antiquarians too, and in Florence, Naples, Milan and Bari. Italian academic colleagues also helped him. Thanks to the director of the Museo Trivigiano (the Treviso town museum), Luigi Bailo (1835–1932), his collection was enriched with several outstanding examples of Italian 'primitives', in particular the Master of Imola Triptych of the *Madonna and Child with Saints*, from the 1430s, and also Italo-Greek icons of the Mother of God. This active collecting and research bore fruit in the two-volume atlas *Materialy dlia istorii russkago ikonopisaniia* [*Materials for a History of Russian Icon-Painting*] (one volume of which presented Byzantine and post-Byzantine icons), published in 1906, and *Istoricheskoe znachenie italo-grecheskoi ikonopisi. Izobrazhenie Bogomateri v proizvedeniiakh italo-grecheskikh ikonopistsev I ikh vliianie na kompozitsii nekotorykh proslavlennykh russkikh ikon* [*The Historical Significance of Italo-Greek Icon-Painting. Images of the Mother of God in the Works of Italo-Greek Iconographers and Their Influence on the Composition of Some Renowned Russian Icons*], published in 1911. Emperor Nicholas II (1868–1918) acquired the entire collection in 1913, and thus laid the foundations for the Russian Medieval Painting section of the Russian Museum in St Petersburg.[101]

Finally, Stepan Riabushinskii (1874–1942), who continued the Old Believer tradition of collecting, was one of the first to perceive the icon as a work of high art as well as a holy object.[102] Small, medieval icons for personal devotions predominated in eighteenth- and nineteenth-century Old Believer oratories. Riabushinskii began to collect large-format icons, which reminded his contemporaries of early Italian artists' altarpieces painted on boards, and he was also the first to realize the need to uncover the original paint layer of early works. Old icons decorated the oratory and several rooms of his mansion on Malaya Nikitskaya Street in Moscow, built in 1900–03 by Fyodor Schechtel (1859–1926), one of the most famous architects of Russian Art Nouveau. Today, with the help of the surviving oratory wall paintings and a drawing of the iconostasis, we may only imagine the originality and bravery of combining bright, Art Nouveau-style ornamentation with the exquisite silhouettes of medieval icons. The elegant iconostasis was set in an alcove, along the edges of which ran a stylized ornamental grapevine; large icons of Christ and the Mother of God were supplemented by smaller, personal devotional images, and the Holy Doors of the iconostasis incorporated a netlike ornamentation

---

101 See N. P. Likhachev, *Materialy dlia istorii russkogo ikonopisaniia: Atlas* (St Petersburg: Ekspeditsiia zagotovleniia gosudarstvennykh bumag, 1906), chs. 1–2. For further detail on Likhachev's icon collection see: V. T. Georgievskii, 'Kollektsiia drevnikh ikon N. P. Likhachev', *Novoe vremiia* (29 July 1913), n.p.; P. Neradovskii, 'Boris i Gleb iz sobraniia N. P. Likhacheva', *Russkaia ikona*, 1 (1914), 63–77; N. Punin, 'Zametki ob ikonakh iz sobraniia N. P. Likhacheva', *Russkaia ikona*, 1 (1914), 21–45; *Iz kollektsii akademika N. P. Likhacheva. Katalog vystavki v Gosudarstvennom Russkom muzee* (n.a.) (St Petersburg: Seda-S, 1993).

102 Riabushinskii was born into an Old Believer dynasty and to one of the richest merchant families in Russia. Once Old Believer churches were opened, after the 1905 imperial edict of toleration, Riabushinskii built new Old Believer churches in Moscow, filling them with old icons. By 1914, he had amassed one of the best private collections of medieval icons in Moscow. After the revolution of 1917, he emigrated to Western Europe and died in Milan in 1942. In 1918, Riabushinskii's vast collection was nationalized and distributed mainly between the Tretyakov Gallery and the Historical Museum in Moscow. After 1928, many icons from Riabushinskii's former collection were sold abroad by the Soviet government.

which clearly came from Scottish Art Nouveau – the work of Charles Rennie Mackintosh (1868–1928) was popular at that time. A distinctive pageantry arose, therefore, at the junction of various epochs and arts. Gazing upon the decorated walls and ornamental icon settings, the religious experience of encountering old icons was overshadowed by the aesthetic experience. The medieval icons found themselves in a religious and philosophical-symbolic context typical of Art Nouveau, reflecting the personality of one of the first connoisseurs of medieval Russian painting's authentic beauty.

Meanwhile, in 1909, Ostroukhov – by then already prominent as an artist, philanthropist and collector – bought the fifteenth-century Novgorodian icon *Elijah the Prophet* (in Russian, *Ilya Prorok*, Ostroukhov's namesake) (Tretyakov Gallery, Moscow) on his name day (see Fig. 3.2). This was the start of his famous collection of early Russian painting.[103] From this point, he practically abandoned collecting canvases and entirely dedicated himself to medieval icons, spending huge amounts by the standards of the day to acquire them for his collection. Ostroukhov's genuine passion to discover this still mysterious sector of European art was observed by many of his contemporaries: 'It became his overriding passion', Prince Sergei Shcherbatov (1874–1962) wrote about Ostroukhov's fascination with icons:

> He didn't buy anything else, only at times the odd, rare publication or book which was added to his fine library. Paintings no longer interested him, although earlier he had collected them, and indeed almost nothing else existed for him – everything had been swallowed up by a burning passion that was adolescent-like, almost manic. Of course he valued [...] external aspects, too: he loved to dominate in Moscow as the authoritative, refined expert, the foremost patron in a field which was then still new and therefore had excited public interest not only amongst Russians but also among foreigners, who visited the Ostroukhov museum like a sort of landmark.[104]

---

103 According to Igor Grabar's (1871–1960) memoirs, Ostroukhov bought his first icon *Elijah the Prophet* precisely on his name day in 1909: 'And the entire collection followed from there' (I. E. Grabar, *Moia zhizn'. Avtomonografiia. Etiudy o khudozhnikakh* (Moscow: Respublika, 2001), p. 250). Image available at *Belygorod*, http://www.belygorod.ru/img2/Ikona/Used/293Ikona3.jpg

104 S. Shcherbatov, *Khudozhnik v ushedshei Rossii* (New York: Izdate'stvo imeni Chekhova, 1955), pp. 207–09.

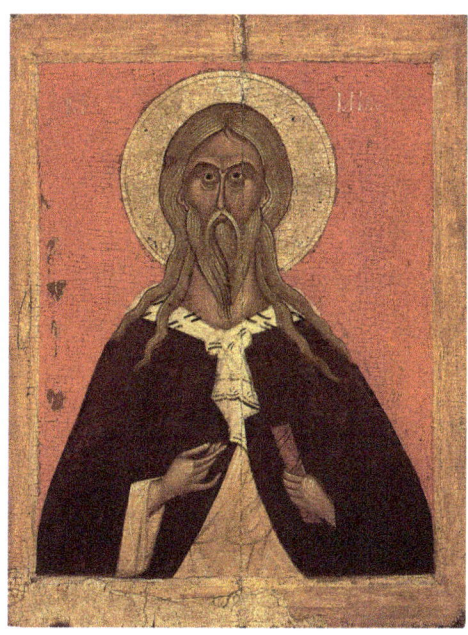

Fig. 3.2 Novgorod School, *Elijah the Prophet* (fifteenth century), tempera on wood, 75 x 57 cm. From the collection of Ilya Ostroukhov in Moscow. Tretyakov Gallery, Moscow. Reproduced as a color illustration in Nikolai Punin's article 'Ellinizm i Vostok v ikonopisi' ['Hellenism and the East in icon painting'], *Russkaia ikona* (1914), 3. Photograph by the author (2023), public domain.

It seems possible that the 1908 preparations for a *Starye gody* [*Bygone Years*] exhibition in St Petersburg had some influence on Ostroukhov's turn to icon-collecting. A fifteenth-century Netherlandish *Mater Dolorosa* from his collection was loaned to the exhibition. Within a few years, Ostroukhov had not only begun collecting icons himself, but had also inspired a wider group of art enthusiasts in Moscow to join in the pursuit of collecting these works. An article on the exhibition, published in the journal *Starye gody*, stressed that the work of European 'primitives' clearly represents aesthetic value, since it manifests 'the transition from the Gothic, constrained by spiritual bonds, to consciously free creativity'. Moreover, the meaning of the term 'primitive' was also explained to a wide circle of readers: 'The conventionality of this term, which entered the international jargon of art scholarship via French enthusiasts', the author noted, 'impedes thorough investigation of the essential aspect of Northern Renaissance painting, which was by no means distinguished by simplicity but, on the contrary, was distinguished rather by the complexity of ideas somehow intrinsic to all transitionary eras in the history of art'.[105]

The Antiquities Market: Some Parallels

That Ostroukhov unexpectedly began to collect icons in 1909, exactly when we see the greatest demand for Italian 'primitives' in the European art market, is significant in this regard. Specialists have observed that the periods 1908–09 and 1920–21 saw the biggest price rises for Italian 'primitives' in Europe. As may be recalled, from the second half of the nineteenth century, this market was actively shaped by writers, collectors and enthusiasts of Italy. Major collectors, such as John Leader (1810–1903), Frederick Stibbert (1838–1906) and Herbert Horne (1864–1916), entered the market, turning their homes in Florence into private museums of art history and the daily life of the Italian Renaissance. The formation of major American collections also contributed to market demand for 'primitives' during the *Belle Époque*, which was, in turn, greatly facilitated by Bernard Berenson's (1865–1959) new methods of attribution, discussed in Chapter Two.[106] It was further significant that the fact that the fullest collection of Italian 'primitives' in Russia (seventy works) was donated to Emperor Alexander III's Museum of Fine Arts in Moscow precisely in 1909. This superb collection, gifted to the museum while it was still under construction, was amassed by the Russian Consul General in Trieste, Mikhail Sergeevich Shchekin (1871–1920), mentioned in Chapter One. The museum's opening was intended to be an important event in Moscow's cultural life. The newspaper *Russkoe slovo* [*Russian Word*] wrote about the extremely rare, genuine

---

105 D. A. Shmidt, 'O primitivakh. Vozrozhdenie na Severe', *Starye gody* (November–December 1908), 661, 663–64; see also F. Gevaert, 'Vystavka "Zolotogo Runa" v Briugge', *Starye gody* (December 1907), 616–17.

106 It is also noteworthy that tax on the importation of artworks was abolished in the USA precisely in 1909. See Moskowitz, *Stefano Bardini. 'Principe degli Antiquari'*, p. 112; R. Cohen, *Bernard Berenson: da Boston a Firenze*, trans. M. Gini (Milan: Adelphi, 2017), pp. 119–96. It is no coincidence that interest in Byzantine and post-Byzantine icons also gradually grew in this same period. According to Hans Belting (1935–2023), the German art historian Oskar Wulff (1864–1946) (author of the first article on reverse perspective, published in 1907) began to acquire Russian icons for the Berlin museum even before the First World War. See H. Belting, *Obraz i kul't. Istoriia obraza do epokhi iskusstva*, trans. K. A. Piganovich (Moscow: Progress-Traditsiia, 2002), p. 35.

works in this collection. Among the exhibits, the work of Jacobello del Fiore (c. 1370–1439) clearly stood out. The *Crucifixion with the Virgin, Saint John the Evangelist and Carmelite monks* (c. 1405) was presented on a red background which resembled the red background of Novgorod icons of the fifteenth century.[107] In that same year of 1909, the journal *Starye gody* published an extensive article by Vrangel and Aleksandr Trubnikov (1882–1966) on the Roman collection of Count Grigorii Stroganov (1823–1910), mentioned in Chapter One, which contained reproductions of early Italian painting such as Duccio's (c. 1255/60–c. 1318/19) *Madonna and Child* (c. 1300, Metropolitan Museum, New York), Simone Martini's (c. 1284–1344) *Madonna from the Annunciation Scene* (1333, State Hermitage, St Petersburg), and the *Stroganov Tabernacle* (c. 1425–30, State Hermitage, St Petersburg) painted by Fra Angelico (c. 1395–1455) – in other words, works by those artists who would, a little later, be compared with the medieval Russian masters of the fourteenth and fifteenth centuries by Pavel Muratov (1881–1950).[108] One cannot with certainty assert that all this directly prompted the new direction in collecting by an individual already then famous for collecting Russian and foreign art, but, unquestionably, Ostroukhov knew the European art market well, was familiar with the new wave of collecting Italian and Flemish 'primitives', and travelled Western Europe exploring museums and galleries of antiquities often and for extended periods.[109] Ideas about

---

107 V. E. Markova, 'Ital'ianskie "primitivy" v traditsii russkogo sobiratel'stva', in *Chastnoe kollektsionirovanie v Rossii. Materialy nauchnoi konferentsii 'Vipperovaskie chteniia-1994'*, ed. I. E. Danilova (Moscow: Gosudarstvennyĭ muzeĭ izobrazitel, nykh iskusstv im. A.S. Pushkina, 1995), pp. 186–99 (p. 197). The journal *Starye gody* informed its readers that 'M. S. Shchekin has donated his valuable collection of Italian "primitives" to the Fine Arts Museum of Alexander III in Moscow'. See *Starye gody* (December 1909), 695.

108 N. N. Vrangel and A. Trubnikov, 'Kartiny sobraniia grafa G.S. Stroganova v Rime', *Starye gody* (March 1909), 115–36. Judging by archival documents, Ostroukhov was acquainted with the Count and even had some business dealings with him. Their correspondence from 1909, which discusses three framed portraits that Ostroukhov purchased from Stroganov, is evidence of this: *Otdel rukopisei Gosudarstvennoi Tretiakovskoi Gellerei* [*State Tretiakov Gallery, Manuscript Division, Moscow*] (henceforth OR GTG), f. 10, ed. khr. 562 (Letter from I. S. Ostroukhov to G. S. Stroganov, 30 April 1909); f. 10, ed. khr. 6055 (Letter from G. S. Stroganov to I. S. Ostroukhov, 4 April 1909); f. 10, ed. khr. 6056 (Telegram from G. S. Stroganov to I. S. Ostroukhov, 1 May 1909).

109 'Ostroukhov was a Westernizer', Grabar recalled, 'he couldn't live without an annual trip to Paris or Biarritz, exalting all that was foreign and forever busy with

the genuine rediscovery of the early Italian masters' artistic value, which the new generation of Western European scholars, headed by Berenson, so effectively portrayed as world class, were clearly circulating in the wider intellectual milieu.

The history of the Moscow collectors' 'unexpected insight' into the artistic value of medieval Russian painting was revived by the new discovery and re-evaluation of the 'primitives' in the European culture of the *Belle Époque*. It reinforced Ostroukhov's view of medieval Russian icons as typologically equal to the Italian masters of the Trecento and Quattrocento, and more than that, his recognition of their great beauty and value. It is no coincidence that in one of the letters he sent to the Trustee of the Russian Museum, Grand Prince Georgii Mikhailovich, he pointedly observed that 'our medieval Russian icon-painting is beginning to qualify as the greatest world art [...], more significant [...] than the great primitives of Italy'.[110]

The major European exhibitions of Italian, Flemish, Catalonian and French 'primitives', which acquainted the wider public with this new type of art for the first time, were of great importance here.[111] Museums and private collectors from Russia took part in several of them; in particular, the State Hermitage's *Madonna and Child* (1434–36) painted by Jan van Eyck (1390–1441) was shown at the *Exposition des Primitifs flamands et d'Art ancient* [*Flemish Primitives and Early Art*] exhibition in Bruges (1902). That same year, an exhibition of Catalonian 'primitives' was organized in Barcelona, and, within two years, there had been a whole series of exhibitions dedicated to medieval and pre-Renaissance art. An exhibition of *German Medieval Painting* was held in Dusseldorf in 1904. In turn, a grassroots audience learned that painting 'on gold backgrounds' existed in France, thanks to an exhibition of 'French primitives': the 'suspicion' of these works, that had taken hold in the

---

one of the visiting "distinguished foreigners", especially the museum workers, art historians, artists, collectors'. See Grabar, *Moia zhizn'*, p. 237.

110 See *Rossiiskii gosudarstvennyi arkhiv literatury i iskusstva* [*Russian State Archive of Literature and Art*] (henceforth RGALI), f. 822, op.1, ed. khr. 1173, l. 17 (Letter from I. S. Ostroukhov to Grand Prince Georgii Mikhailovich).

111 F. Haskell, 'Les expositions des Maritres anciens et la seconde "redecouverte des primitifs"', in *Hommage à Michel Laclotte. Etudes sur la peinture du Moyen Age et de la Renaissance*, ed. F. Bologna and M. Laclotte (Milan: Electa, 1994), pp. 552–6 4; F. Haskell, *History and Its Images. Art and Interpretation of the Past* (New Haven, CT: Yale University Press, 1995), pp. 461–68.

era of Classicism, began to disperse. Until then, a fair number of old boards bearing the faces of saints 'served as shelves in farms', in the words of Germain Bazin (1901–90).[112] Finally, the most remarkable of these exhibitions was the one of *Early Sienese Painting*, held in Siena from April to August 1904, at which a number of early Italian masterpieces from Stroganov's Roman collection – including the abovementioned *Madonna and Child* by Duccio – were presented.[113] The catalogue that accompanied this exhibition was luxurious by the standards of the day, including reproductions by the Alinari firm and conveying a sense of the grand scale of this breath-taking exhibition.[114] The exhibition was arrayed over forty rooms in Siena's Palazzo Pubblico, and included paintings and works of decorative and applied arts from museum and private collections, and also from functioning churches in Siena and its environs. Paintings were displayed in special venues, with drawings exhibited in glass cases. Large-scale works were exhibited separately, and works by 'the old masters of Siena' were displayed alongside icons in the *maniera bizantina* [Byzantine style], in room number thirty-six. Works by the fifteenth-century artist Stefano di Giovanni (c. 1392–1450), also known as Sassetta, and the Sienese Madonnas by Duccio, Lippo Memmi (c. 1291–1356) and Matteo di Giovanni (1430–95), evoked such genuine rapture in an international public that within several months the exhibition had been shown in London at the Burlington Fine Arts Club, and the English edition of the catalogue was furnished with coloured illustrations and a foreword by the famous British art critic, Robert Langton Douglas (1864–1951).[115] An exhibition of Italo-Greek art held in 1905–06 in the Greek monastery of Grottaferrata near Rome is also worthy of note. This was the first exhibition in Italy dedicated

---

112 G. Bazen, *Istoriia istorii iskusstva. Ot Vazari do nashikh dnei*, trans. K. A. Chekalov (Moscow: Progress, 1995), p. 100.
113 F. Mason Perkins characterized the 'Stroganov Madonna' as Duccio's 'most valuable work', which was noted in the catalogue of Count Stroganov's collection. It was displayed as N 1960 in the exhibition. See A. Muñoz and L. Pollak, *Pièces de choix de la collection du Comte Gregoire Stroganoff à Rome*, 2 vols. (Rom e: Impr. de "Unione editrice, 1912), II, 9.
114 The exhibition in Siena had 4000 visitors, and 2714 exhibits. See R. Corrado, ed., *La mostra dell'antica arte senese. Aprile–Agosto 1904. Catalogo generale illustrato* (Siena: L. Lazzeri, 1904). On this exhibition, see F. M. Perkins, 'La pittura alla Mostra d'arte antica a Siena', *Rassegna d'Arte*, 4.10 (1904), 145–53.
115 R. L. Douglas, ed., *Exhibition of Pictures of the School of Siena, and Examples of the Minor Arts of that City* (London: Burlington Fine Arts Club, 1904).

exclusively to medieval art. In particular, items from the Roman collection of Giulio Sterbini (d. 1911) and also from the collections of Count Grigorii Stroganov, the Russian Ambassador in Rome Aleksander Nelidov (1835–1910) and the Chair of the Moscow Archaeological Society Countess Praskovia Uvarova (1840–1924), were displayed to a wide audience.[116]

The first international exhibitions at which medieval Russian icons were shown, held at the beginning of the twentieth century, should also be mentioned here. Even before icons made an appearance amongst works by Serov, Degas, and Manet in Ostroukhov's Moscow mansion, they were exhibited in Paris by the famous theatre and art impresario Sergei Diaghilev (1872–1929), together with paintings by the Russian artists Mikhail Vrubel (1856–1910), Repin, Filipp Malyavin (1869–1940) and Natalia Goncharova (1881–1962). Alive to all things new, Diaghilev included icons from Likhachev's collection in his first exhibition project, *Deux Siècles de peinture et de sculpture russes* [*Two Centuries of Russian Painting and Sculpture*], under the auspices of the Salon d'Automne in Paris (1906). 'The exhibition was not restricted to a display of the creativity of artists from the "World of Art"', Alexandre Benois (1870–1960) later recalled, but 'with a fullness unusual for the time, medieval Russian icons were presented'.[117] Artist Leon Bakst (1866–1924), who designed the display for the *Le Primitive Russe* [*Russian Primitives*] exhibit, presented the 'Russian primitives' on gold brocade, perhaps thereby drawing parallels between the medieval Russian icons and early Italian painting 'on golden backgrounds'.[118] According to the press, the Russian section of the exhibition was a huge success, and its icon display was shaped by the 1902 and 1904 exhibitions of 'primitives'. It should be stressed that this was the first exhibition in which medieval Russian icons were shown together with the works of modern Russian artists. The following year, Princess Maria Tenisheva (1858–1928) organized an exhibition of works from her own collection in the Museum of Decorative Arts in Paris, entitled *Objets d'Art Russes Anciens* [*Artworks of Medieval Russia*], in which

---

116 For further detail on this exhibition, see G. Gasbarri, *Riscoprire Bisanzio. Lo studio dell'arte bizantina a Roma e in Italia tra Ottocento e Novecento* (Rome: Viella, 2015), pp. 164–65.
117 A. Benois, *Moi vospominaniia*, 2 vols. (Moscow: Nauka, 1993), II, 453.
118 S. Diaghilev and A. Benois, *Salon d'automne. Exposition de l'art Russe* (Pari s: Moreau frères, 1906), pp. 167–201.

'medieval Russian primitives' featured prominently. Icons such as the sixteenth-century *Mother of God of Smolensk*, the fifteenth-century *Saviour not Made by Hands* and the sixteenth-century *Protecting Veil* were amongst those exhibited. The now famous *Madonna and Child Enthroned, with Scenes from the Life of Mary* (1275–80, Museum of Fine Arts, Moscow) by a Tuscan master was also included in the display.[119]

The 'primitives' were finally established in the art and antiquities markets of Western Europe and the United States of America in this same period. Here, yet again, we recall Berenson – not simply as a scholar and expert, but as a collector and intermediary involved in significant antiquarian deals, who elevated the collecting of early Italian painting to a truly global scale. Moreover, he not only helped shape the celebrated American collections of Isabella Stewart Gardner (1840–1924), John G. Johnson (1841–1917), Henry Clay Frick (1849–1919) and many others, but also amassed a wonderful collection of Italian 'primitives' at his own Villa I Tatti in Settignano, including works by Sassetta, Matteo di Giovanni, Taddeo Gaddi (c. 1290–1366) and other Trecento and Quattrocento masters.[120] And while Berenson did not pursue Byzantine art, to this day, several fifteenth- and sixteenth-century Italo-Greek icons are found within his collection; evidently the eminent scholar felt that

---

119 I. Barchtchévski and D. Laroche, *Objets d'art Russes anciens faisant partie des collections de la Princesse Marie Tenichev, exposes au musée des arts décoratifs du 10 Mai au 10 Octobre, 1907* (Paris: Gauterin, 1907). The thirteenth-century icon by the Tuscan master was acquired for Princess Tenishev in Krakow in 1898. See O. B. Strugova, 'M. K. Tenisheva – neokonchennyi portret', in *Kniaginia M. K. Tenisheva v zerkale Serebrianogo veka. Katalog vystavki v Gos. Istoricheskom muzee*, ed. Gosudarstvennyi istoricheskii muzei (Moscow: GIM, 2008), p. 169. Cf. V. Markova, *Italiia VIII–XVI vekov. Sobranie zhivopisi Gos. Muzeia izobrazitel'nykh iskusstv im. A. S. Pushkina. Katalog*, 2 vols. (Moscow: Galart, 2002), I, 51–53.

120 As a result of Berenson's active antiquities dealing and consultancy work, his collection at Villa I Tatti was already taking shape by 1910. The surviving bills and receipts reveal the enormous sums that Berenson paid for Florentine and Sienese antiquaries between 1899 and 1909. See C. B. Strehlke, 'Bernard and Mary Collect: Pictures Come to I Tatti', in *The Bernard and Mary Berenson Collection of European Paintings at I Tatti*, ed. C. B. Strehlke and M. B. Israels (Florence: Villa I Tatti, 2015), pp. 26–27; M. B. Israels, 'The Berensons "Connosh" and Collect Sienese Painting', in *Bernard and Mary Berenson Collection*, ed. Strehlke and Israels, p. 62; see also G. Mazzoni, 'La cultura del falso', in *Falsi d'autore. Icilio Federico Joni e la cultura del falso tra otto e novecento*, ed. G. Mazzoni (Siena: Protagon, 2004), p. 74; Moskowitz, *Stefano Bardini. 'Principe degli Antiquari'*; W. A. Weaver, *A Legacy of Excellence: The Story of Villa I Tatti* (New York: Harry N. Abrams, 1997); R. Cohen, *Bernhard Berenson: A Life in the Picture Trade* (New Haven, CT: Yale University Press, 2013).

the inclusion of such artworks in no way marred the overall aesthetic impression of the collection, and housing them within a single, indoor environment was entirely appropriate. Furthermore, a whole string of books on medieval Russian painting can be found in his library at I Tatti – testimony that the medieval Russian icon had gradually secured an international audience. These were the works of Muratov, Likhachev, Kondakov, Oskar Wulff (1864–1946) and Mikhail Alpatov (1902–86), as well as three issues of the 1914 publication *Russkaia ikona* [*The Russian Icon*] and several others. Berenson was acquainted with Muratov's book on Ostroukhov's collection (the library had a luxurious Art-Nouveau style copy), and also with Muratov's works published in the 1920s in Italian, French and English – *La pittura russa antica* [*Ancient Russian Painting*], *Les icones russes* [*Russian Icons*], *La pittura bizantina* [*Byzantine Painting*] and his monograph on Fra Angelico.[121]

Meanwhile, if Berenson played a key role in the rediscovery of Italian 'primitives' in Western Europe, the collector-artist Ostroukhov played a key role in Moscow's rediscovery of medieval Russian painting. This points to yet another shared characteristic of the relationships between collecting, scholarly research and the art market in evidence in Russian and Western Europe during the *Belle Époque*. In London, Florence and Moscow, people directly involved in the fine arts – artists and art critics, rather than academics – began to play an important role in the re-evaluation of medieval 'primitives'. In addition to collecting 'primitives' in London and Florence, Horne (an architect by education) engaged in the graphic arts and designed for the English *Burlington Magazine*, which he founded together with Berenson and the artist Roger Fry (1866–1934) in 1905.[122] A special issue of the Moscow journal *Sredi kollektsionerov* [*Among Collectors*], celebrating forty years of Ostroukhov's

---

121 See *Berenson Library Archive*, Villa I Tatti, The Harvard University Center for Italian Renaissance Studies, Florence. P. P. Muratov, *La pittura russa antica*, trans. E. Lo Gatto (Rome: A. Stock, 1925); P. P. Muratov, *La pittura bizantina* (Rome: Valori Plastici, 1928); P. P. Muratov, *La peinture byzantine*, trans. J. Chuzeville (Paris: Editions G. Crès, 1928); P. P. Muratov, *Frate Angelico* (Rome: Valori Plastici, 1929); P. P. Muratov, *Fra Angelico*, trans. J. Chuzeville (Paris: Editions G. Crès, 1929); P. P. Muratov, *Fra Angelico. His Life and Work*, trans. E. Law-Gisiko (New York: F. Warne and Co., 1930).

122 Horne authored a book on Sandro Botticelli (c. 1445–1510), which remains significant to this day in terms of both the quantity and value of the materials collected. See H. Horne, *Alessandro Filipepi Commonly Called Sandro Botticelli, Painter of Florence* (London: G. Bell and Sons, 1908).

collecting, also testifies to the part artists played in revealing the aesthetic importance of the 'primitives'. Ostroukhov's efforts as an art connoisseur were summarized with the aid of concepts such as 'intuition' and 'artistic vision' in articles by Muratov, Igor Grabar (1871–1960), Nikolai Shchekotov (1884–1945) and Abram Efros (1888–1954). His collection taught one to look with precision. In an article entitled 'Novoe sobiratel'stvo' ['The New Collecting'], Muratov discussed Ostroukhov as a 'participant' in the creativity of the medieval artist, via his intuitive penetration of the early icon's artistic form.[123] Grabar also wrote about Ostroukhov's 'inner vision' in his article 'Glaz' ['The Eye'], according to which many contemporaries were able to perceive the medieval Russian icon as a work of *pure art* solely due to the Moscow collector's keen ability to discern value and beauty.[124] Finally, Efros noted, in his article 'Peterburgskoe i moskovskoe sobiratel'stvo' ['Petersburg and Moscow Collecting'] that Ostroukhov's collection continued a tradition of Moscow collecting in which the masterpiece was often 'discovered' by the collector himself and only then confirmed by art criticism.[125] In other words, Ostroukhov rediscovered and collected masterpieces of medieval Russian painting during a period of fundamental change in tastes of and knowledge about art.

But how, and by which paths, did this *new collecting* develop? Ostroukhov's position in Moscow's art and antiquities circles largely facilitated the successful development of his museum's icon collection. By 1909, he was already a renowned collector and, moreover, served as a trustee of the Tretyakov Gallery, actively contributing to the expansion of the holdings of this major museum. Constantly surrounded by a stack of catalogues, Ostroukhov knew practically all the major Moscow antique dealers, whose galleries were then concentrated in the Sukharev tower region, in the Hotel 'Slavianskii bazaar', Lavrushinskii Lane and the Arbat. These were relatively large spaces, owned by Mikhail Savostin (1860–1924), Sergei Bol'shakov (1842–1906), Ivan Silin (d. 1899) and several others. Ostroukhov had a particularly close relationship with Savostin, who owned antique shops in both St Petersburg and Moscow.

---

123 P. P. Muratov, 'Novoe sobiratel'stvo', *Sredi kollektsionerov*, 4 (1921), 1–3 (p. 3).
124 I. E. Grabar, 'Glaz', *Sredi kollektsionerov*, 4 (1921), 3–5 (p. 4).
125 A. A. Efros, 'Peterburgskoe i moskovskoe sobiratel'stvo (Paralleli)', *Sredi kollektsionerov*, 4 (1921), 13–20 (pp. 14, 17–19).

A few Greek icons in Ostroukhov's collection came from Savostin, who travelled to Constantinople in 1914 and brought back a large selection of Byzantine and Italo-Greek icons. One of these, notably, was the famous Byzantine icon of *Christ Pantocrator* (Constantinople, first half of the fifteenth century, State Museum of Fine Arts, Moscow) which specialists today sometimes associate with the Cretan master Angelos Akotantos (1390–1457) (see Fig. 3.3).[126] That same year, near Hadrianopolis (now Edirne), Ostroukhov himself obtained a Greek icon of *Saint Panteleimon* from the second half of the fifteenth century.[127] The juxtaposition of Greek and Russian icons in Ostroukhov's collection was intended to clearly show the unbroken development of the Byzantine tradition in Rus'.

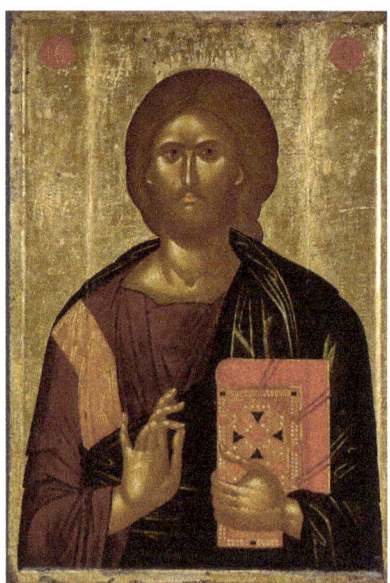

Fig. 3.3 Constantinople School, *Christ Pantocrator* (first half of the fifteenth century), tempera on wood. From the collection of Ilya Ostroukhov in Moscow. The Pushkin State Museum of Fine Arts. Wikimedia, public domain, https://commons.wikimedia.org/wiki/File:Pantokrator_by_byzantine_anonim,_poss._by_Angelus_(15th_c.,_Pushkin_museum).jpg

---

126 Y. D. Varalis, 'The Painter Angelos in Constantinople? Answers from the Pantokrator Icon at the State Pushkin Museum, Moscow', *The Annual Journal of the Benaki Museum*, 13–14 (2013–14), 79–88.

127 See I. E. Danilova, ed., *Gosudarstvennyi muzei izobrazitel'nykh iskusstv im. A.S. Pushkina. Katalog zhivopisi* (Moscow: n.p., 1995), p. 72. Ostroukhov also bought Russian and Western European paintings in M. M. Savostin's shop. See OR GTG, f. 10, ed. khr. 523 (Draft of a Letter from I. S. Ostroukhov to M. M. Savostin); f. 10, ed. khr. 527 (Letter from I. S. Ostroukhov to M. M. Savostin, 1912).

Since the issue of the original painted surface is key in the discovery of a masterpiece of Russian medieval painting, Ostroukhov established a workshop in his mansion for his personal icon painter and restorer Evgenii Briagin (1888–1949). In contrast to the majority of Italian 'primitives', medieval Russian icons were overpainted many times. The whole impact of the discovery of an early icon lay in the master restorer's success in layer-by-layer cleaning, which removed each repeated repainting of the original work. This was the case for the restoration of medieval icons in Riabushinskii's collection, which Aleksei Tiulin (d. 1918) and Aleksandr Tiulin (1883–1920) worked on. The Tiulins were icon painters and restorers, migrants from the village of Mstera, and had long been involved in the trading and restoration of old icons.[128] Riabushinskii, notably, had used the new method of cleaning earlier. This is confirmed by the *Ascension of Christ* icon from the beginning of the fifteenth century – according to Aleksei Tiulin, one of the first and most important in Riabushinskii's famous collection (see Fig. 3.4). Riabushinskii was also one of the first to witness the original paint layer of fourteenth- and fifteenth-century Novgorodian icons being revealed, when he actively participated in the construction of new Old Believer churches after Emperor Nicholas II's (1868–1918) 17 April 1905 edict of religious toleration. He was the first, too, to set up a restoration workshop at his personal mansion on Bolshaya Nikitskaya Street in Moscow. There, he came to fundamentally revise the Old Believer tradition of restoration work, and his observations are laid out in his article 'O restavratsii I sokhranenii drevnikh sviatykh ikon' ['On the Restoration and Preservation of Early Holy Icons']. This article concluded, for the first time, the necessity of preserving the authentic painted foundations.[129] In Old Believer circles, the restoration of early icons, in essence, meant updating the painted surface. Old icons were cleaned and then repainted.[130] Now, in the era of *Belle Époque*

---

128 O. Tarasov, *Icon and Devotion. Sacred Spaces in Imperial Russia*, trans. R. Milner-Gulland (London: Reaktion, 2002), pp. 52–57.

129 S. Riabushinskii, 'O restavratsii i sokhranenii drevnikh sviatykh ikon', *Tserkov*, 50 (1908), 1701–05.

130 It should, however, be noted that this was essentially a so-called 'antiquarian' restoration, which aimed to imitate the paint layer and craquelure in damaged places on old icons. Similar restoration methods were a feature of the European antiquities market in Italian 'primitives'. See Moscowitz, *Stefano Bardini. 'Principe degli Antiquari'*, p. 44, figs. 20, 21.

aestheticism, the new cleaning techniques were almost equated with devotion. The original medieval painting acquired especial worth. The icon's aura as a devotional image seamlessly merged with experiencing it as an authentic aesthetic object. It is therefore entirely appropriate to call the new restoration process an *aesthetic* one.

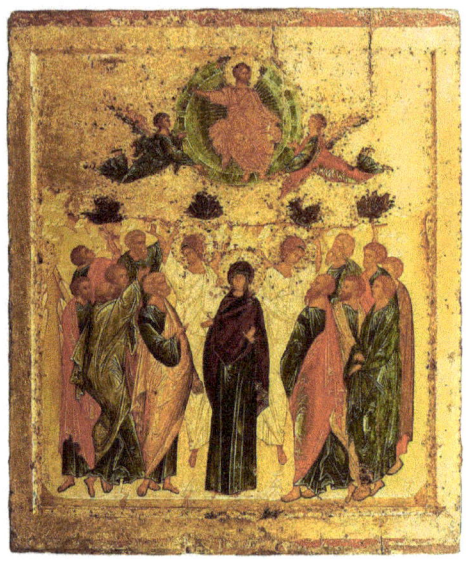

Fig. 3.4 Andrei Rublev (1360–1428) School, *The Ascension of Christ* (1410–20s), tempera on wood, 71 x 59 cm. From the collection of Stepan Riabushinskii in Moscow. Tretyakov Gallery, Moscow. Wikimedia, public domain, https://commons.wikimedia.org/wiki/File:Ascension_(1410-20s,_GTG).jpg

In other words, old icons were being swiftly transformed from objects of ecclesiastical antiquity into priceless masterpieces of medieval painting. The *Belle Époque* was clearly a golden age of icon collecting, according to the memoirs of many contemporaries. The fashion for medieval icons reached the Russian aristocracy and members of the imperial family. Literally within a few years, interest in Russian icons had gripped a new circle of wealthy individuals; ladies of the highest society, including the extravagant Princess Maria Tenisheva and Varvara Khanenko (1852–1922), as well as scholars, architects, poets and artists, were captivated by icons. Among their ranks was one of the brightest lights of the Russian avant-garde, Natalia Goncharova, whose 'primitivist' works were so clearly influenced by the language of the icons and *lubki* [traditional woodcut prints] she collected. 'A more serious and loving relationship with the elements of painting', wrote the artist Grishchenko in this period, 'naturally engendered in us an artistic interest in, and attraction to, the medieval icon. It was an *echo of the French artists' striving to primitivism* in both the sphere of painting generally, and in sculpture. Primitives stepped into the shoes of the artists of the High Renaissance'.[131] In other words, there was an altogether new fascination with Primitivism: in this period, the canvases of Henri Matisse (1869–1954) and Paul Gaugin (1848–1903) displayed characteristics in common with the aesthetic value of medieval icons and works of Western European painting 'on golden backgrounds'. The famous Moscow collector of Impressionists and Modernists, Sergei Shchukin (1854–1936), ordered Matisse's paintings *Dance* (1910, State Hermitage) and *Music* (1910, State Hermitage) for his Moscow mansion, and persuaded Ostroukhov of the value of these works. He did so, precisely, by citing the opinion of the main specialist on Italian 'primitives', Berenson: 'I would like to convince you', he wrote to Ostroukhov in 1909, 'that my fascination for Matisse is shared by people who are genuinely devoted to art. In Paris I managed to speak with Berenson, one of the best experts on early art. He called Matisse "the artist of the era"'.[132] Incidentally, Berenson is known to have met Matisse in 1908 (through Maurice Denis (1873–1945) and the Steins (Leo and Gertrude)) and even acquired a landscape from him which, within two years, was shown in London in the *Manet and Postimpressionism* exhibition (1910) organized by British artist and critic Fry.[133] There is a photograph of the first version of *Dance*, which Matisse was working on from March 1909 and which Berenson, in time,

---

131 Grishchenko, *Russkaia ikona*, p. 243 (my emphasis). In this same period, the medieval 'primitives' become models for new Catholic art. In 1919, under the auspices of the Paris Catholic Institute, the Symbolist artist Maurice Denis founds a 'religious art workshop' in which the medieval image is rethought. Later (to a great extent thanks to the Dominicans and, above all, to the artist monk Marie-Alain Couturier) we see the creation of renowned complexes like the Notre Dame de Toute-Grâce Church in Assy, in the French Alps (Fernand Léger, Henri Matisse, Pierre Bonnard, Georges Rouault, Georges Braque, Marc Chagall, and others), the Rosary Chapel in Vence (Henri Matisse), the Notre-Dame du Haut Chapel in Ronchamp (Le Corbusier). See A. Leroy, *Histoire de la peinture religieuse des origine origins à nos jours* (Paris: Amiot-Dumont, 1954); W. S. Rubin, *Modern Sacred Art and the Church of Assy* (New York: Columbia University Press, 1961).
132 OR GTG, f. 10, ed. khr. 7276 (Letter from S. I. Shchukin to I. S. Ostroukhov, 10 November 1909).
133 E. Samuels, *Bernard Berenson. The Making of a Legend* (Cambridge, MA: Harvard University Press, 1979), p. 66.

reviewed very favourably, preserved in Berenson's archive at the Villa I Tatti.[134] We may also recall here Matisse's own rapturous response to the medieval Russian icons in Ostroukhov's museum, which he saw when visiting Moscow in October 1911 on the invitation of Shchukin: 'I am familiar with the ecclesiastical creativity of various countries', Matisse said to the correspondent of the Moscow newspaper *Utro Rossii* [*Russia's Morning*] 'and nowhere else have I seen such feeling laid bare, mystical mood, on occasion religious awe [...] I've already managed to see Mr Ostroukhov's collection of early icons, to visit the Dormition and Annunciation cathedrals, the Patriarch's sacristy in Moscow. And everywhere that same brightness and manifestation of great strength of feeling'.[135] During this visit, Matisse supervised the hanging of his *Dance* and *Music* paintings in the hall of the grand staircase in Shchukin's mansion on Znamenskii Lane. In the archive of the Tretyakov Gallery we find an interesting letter from Ostroukhov to Shchukin concerning Matisse's Moscow visit, which reveals how the two Moscow collectors spent time with the famous French artist: 'Dear Sergei Ivanovich', Ostroukhov wrote,

> kindly let Matisse know the following programme [of activities] (with me). There's no concert tomorrow, and I'm not coming over. 29th [October] Saturday. At 11am I'm calling for you both, and we will go to Novodevichy monastery, and from there perhaps breakfast at Kharitonenko's (he wants to sketch a view of the Kremlin, and they have *several interesting icons*). 30th [October] Sunday. I'm coming to you by car at around 1–1:30, so we can go to the Rogozhskoe cemetery and the Edinoverie monastery [famous centres of Old Belief with collections of old icons]. 1st [November] Tuesday. I'm calling by at 3 o'clock so we can go to a synodal choir concert put on especially for you [...] That's [what is planned] for the next few days [...] I'm sending a parcel with Kondakov's book; please give it to him from me as a *souvenir of the icons*. Your I. Ostroukhov. P.S. If tomorrow, Friday, Matisse is free in the evening, then I'd be delighted if you would both drop in on us.[136]

---

134 See C. Pizzorusso, 'A Failure: Rene Piot and the Berensons', in *Bernard and Mary Berenson Collection*, ed. Strehlke and Israels, p. 677, fig. VI.3.

135 See the article 'Matiss v Moskve: V Tret'iakovskoi galeree. V krugu estetov' (n.a.), *Utro Rossii*, 248 (27 October 1911), 4. See also A. G. Kostenevich and N. Y. Semenova, eds., *Matiss v Rossii* (Moscow: Avangard, 1993).

136 OR GTG, f. 10, ed. khr. 680 (Letter from I. S. Ostroukhov to S. I. Shchukin, 27 October 1911) (my emphasis).

There are grounds, therefore, for suggesting that Ostroukhov discovered the artistic significance of the medieval Russian icon while the renowned collectors Shchukin and Ivan Morozov (1871–1921) were still acquiring Impressionist and Modernist works.[137] Indeed, the collections of Modernist works played a crucial role in shaping a new frame of reference in Moscow, in which intuition about the potential of a work, as well as a keen eye, provided the courage needed to make a judgement. Ostroukhov's merits and success should be seen, then, in the fact that he clearly was one of the first to discern the significance of the medieval Russian icon in the context of the collecting of Italian 'primitives', being able to bring together the expertise of Old Believer collectors and icon-painting antiquarians with his personal aesthetic experience as an artist and collector.

I have already written about the customs and language of the pedlars of antiquities and wandering traders in medieval icons. The Russian North and Volga region were interlaced with trade routes used for the sale of antiquities in the eighteenth and nineteenth centuries.[138] It was this efficient trading system that facilitated the huge flow of medieval icons into the Moscow market after the opening of Old Believer churches in 1905, and which allowed Riabushinskii, Ostroukhov, Aleksei Morozov (1867–1934) and others to establish their extraordinary collections of medieval Russian painting in such a short space of time. (The main

---

137 On Shchukin's and Morozov's Impressionist and Modernist collections, see A. Baldassari, *Icones de l'art moderne. La collection Chtchoukine* (*Livres d'art*) (Paris: Fondation Louis Vuitton, 2016); N. Semenova and A-M. Delocque-Fourcaud, *The Collector: The Story of Sergei Shchukin and His Lost Masterpieces* (Haven, CT: Yale University Press, 2018); N. Semenova, *Morozov: The Story of a Family and a Lost Collection*, trans. A. Tait (New Haven, CT: Yale University Press, 2020), https://doi.org/10.2307/j.ctv17z848g

138 In Russia, trade in medieval icons was shaped by Russia's distinct religious history. Since Russian Old Believers only venerated and valued icons that pre-dated the mid-seventeenth-century schism, a unique (in comparison with Balkan countries) market for medieval icons developed in Russia, centred in Mstera. Itinerant pedlars from Vladimir gubernia, with distinct customs, rules of behaviour, and even their own argot, pursued this trade from at least from the eighteenth century onwards. This secret language allowed traders of medieval icons to communicate between themselves when striking deals. A unique corpus of folk expertise relating to particular Schools of Old Russian painting (Moscow, Novgorod, Stroganov etc.) also developed in Old Believer circles. For further detail, see O. Tarasov, *Ikona i blagochestie: Ocherki ikonnogo dela v imperatorskoi Rossii* (Moscow: Progress-Kul'tura, 1995), pp. 200–36; Tarasov, *Icon and Devotion*, trans. Milner-Gulland, pp. 55–57.

icon collection in Ostroukhov's museum, for example, was assembled between 1909 and 1914.) Moreover, if the earlier trade in old icons was confined to a narrow circle of Old Believers, it now reached the wider circle of aesthetes and art lovers. It led to the appearance of a *new* type of antiquarian and icon painter-restorer. A good example is Grigorii Chirikov (1891–1936), from a family of icon painters in the village of Mstera. The Chirikov brothers' workshop in Moscow had been set up back in the 1880s. However, on the wave of this *new collecting* of medieval icons their workshop gained prominence and began to play a role somewhat similar to that of Italy's antiquarian restoration establishments, such as Stefano Bardini's (1836–1922) and Elia Volpi's (1858–1938) in Florence. Chirikov uniquely navigated the new and evolving relationships between collectors, researchers and antiquarians. He acquired and supplied things for the most eminent collectors; many holy objects and masterpieces of Old Russian painting, including the *Mother of God of Vladimir* (first quarter of the twelfth century, Tretyakov Gallery, Moscow), the *Donskoi Mother of God* (1382–95, Tretyakov Gallery, Moscow), and Rublev's *Trinity* (1411 or 1425–27, Tretyakov Gallery, Moscow), were restored by him; he served on numerous committees and academic commissions; he published about restoration work; and he played an active part in important exhibitions of *Vystavka drevne-russkogo iskusstva* [*Old Russian Art*] held in St Petersburg in 1911, and in Moscow in 1913. In doing so, he (together with other commissioners) forged fresh ties with the spheres of advertising and the art and antiquities market. It was through his workshop that, in 1907, Likhachev obtained the pearl of his collection – the fourteenth-century *Saints Boris and Gleb* icon, which subsequently graced the walls of the Russian Museum (see Fig. 3.5). Thanks to Chirikov, a whole series of masterpieces enriched Ostroukhov's collection, above all the *Descent from the Cross* and *Deposition in the Tomb* icons from the end of the fifteenth century, which evoked genuine rapture amongst art critics of the time, and to this day are considered among the Tretyakov Gallery's finest exhibits.[139]

---

139 The receipt from Chirikov's 1912 icon sale to Ostroukhov survives: OR GTG, f. 10, ed. khr. 6950.

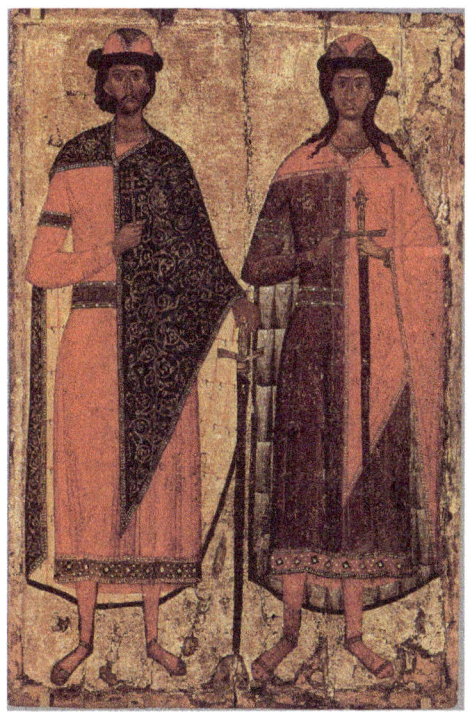

Fig. 3.5 Novgorod School, *St Boris and St Gleb* (mid-fourteenth century), tempera on wood, 142.5 x 95.4 cm. From the collection of Nikolai Likhachev. State Russian Museum, St Petersburg. Wikimedia, public domain, https://commons.wikimedia.org/wiki/File:%D0%A1%D0%B2%D1%8F%D1%82%D1%8B%D0%B5_%D0%91%D0%BE%D1%80%D0%B8%D1%81_%D0%B8_%D0%93%D0%BB%D0%B5%D0%B1.jpg

The Grigorii and Mikhail Chirikov brothers' workshop also painted copies and imitations. It is not impossible that some of these were intended to be substituted for medieval icons in certain old Novgorodian churches. The practice of substituting old icons with copies had existed amongst Old Believers since at least the eighteenth century. In the context of religious rivalry, stealing old icons from the official Russian church was framed as 'saving the faith' by Old Believers.[140] However, during the 'icon craze' of the 1910s, this practice lost its religious colouring and began to flourish in entirely different soil. Grabar – an active participant in the cultural life of those years – testifies to this:

---

[140] From the point of view of the official church, such forgery was sacrilege. For further details, see O. Tarasov, *Ikona i blagochestie*, pp. 213–19.

> Pedlars wandered the North, bartering new icons for old with priests and church wardens [...] The old icons were usually lying around in belltowers [...] thrown there as decrepit fifty years earlier. But sometimes it was necessary to steal them away from the iconostases of working churches, too, swapping copies for the originals, [a task] for which restorers from Mstera were called upon. In such instances the latter would make a close copy of the old icon, with all its cracks and other marks, under the pretence of restoration, and put it in the place of the valuable original – which would end up in one of the Moscow collections. During the revolution I came across more than a few of these counterfeit icons while on various expeditions to the North. This was how the provenance of many famous works of art was clarified.[141]

At the same time, firms accorded the name 'purveyors to the court' – that of the Chirikovs, of Mikhail Dikarev (d. after 1917), Nikolai Emel'ianov (1871–1958) and Vasilii Gur'ianov (1866–1920) – copied numerous old icons to decorate Old Believer prayer houses, as well as official churches and the churches of the Russian imperial court. Icons from Emil'ianov's workshop, for example, graced the Feodorovskii Icon Cathedral in Tsarskoe Selo (1909–12, architect Vladimir Pokrovskii (1871–1931)). Mastering the new techniques of restoration, pastiche and reconstruction, Moscow workshops repaired a whole raft of new specimens of 'old' icon-painting. The main aim of such aesthetic restoration was not only to create an effect of the original's well-preserved state, but to make it attractive, and often according to the tastes of *Belle Époque* culture. Riabushinskii's icon *Saints Boris and Gleb with Scenes from Their Lives* (fifteenth century, with later restoration, Tretyakov Gallery, Moscow) is a good example of this: its central panel is set in a seventeenth-century frame with hagiographical scenes, and most likely dates to the period when the Novgorodian painting from the fifteenth century underwent repainting – in other words, likely in the early 1900s. Interest in the bright colours and refined outlines of the modern era, and in the picturesque effect of the icon as a whole, prompted additions to the original layer, the erasure of unsuitable elements, changing the background, and so on. And what is interesting is that researchers observe the same practices in the restoration of Italian 'primitives'. The activities of the Moscow workshops and those of the antiques restoration establishments in Italy therefore have much in common.

---

141 Grabar, *Moia zhizn'*, p. 250.

As demand for fifteenth-century Novgorodian icons burgeoned in Moscow during the 1910s, in Florence and Siena the antiquities and restoration establishments of Bardini and Volpi likewise flourished, driven by the great interest in the Sienese Madonnas of the Trecento and Quattrocento.[142] It is notable that the first issue of the Italian magazine L'antiquario [The Antiquarian], founded in 1908 to promote the profession's interests, opened with a substantial article about Bardini, and also reproduced an anonymous Italian 'primitive', a *Madonna and Child* of the Italo-Byzantine School. This, apparently, was no coincidence, since in Bardini's house-museum in Florence, a separate installation was dedicated to small altarpieces of the Madonna, many of which – incontrovertibly – underwent the same aesthetic restoration that medieval Russian icons were subjected to in famous Moscow workshops. 'Bardini made himself an expert in a variety of restoration techniques', Anita Fiderer Moskowitz notes, 'and demonstrated enormous skill in transforming ruined works of art into marketable items'.[143] The private museum of antiquarian and former artist Volpi in the Palazzo Davanzati also attracted particular attention in Florence; it conveyed the 'very spirit' of the Florentine way of life in the fourteenth and fifteenth centuries, and often served as a venue for significant art deals. Its neo-Renaissance interiors were subsequently mirrored in the Florida and Cap Ferret villas of American and European millionaires. These were, of course, decorated with Sienese Madonnas.

---

142 It is fitting here to recall Berenson's thoughts about the European art market, and the rising prices for the works of fifteenth-century Sienese masters in these years: 'Although the arts of the Italian Quattrocento were never quite so forgotten or unknown as these, yet, with a few rare exceptions, they were little appreciated. Thus, in the Napoleonic years, although the interest in them was already reviving, a Guercino was valued at 30,000, a Baroccio at 45,000 and a Caracci at 100,000 francs, but a Botticelli at only 1500 francs. What a Sienese painter would have fetched we do not know, for the reason, apparently, that the question never came up. Little over a hundred years ago, the pre-historic frescos in the cave of Altamira were scarcely less present in the minds of people than the master-pieces of the Sienese fifteenth century'. See B. Berenson, *Essays in the Study of Sienese Painting* (New York: Frederic Fairchild Sherman, 1918), pp. 81–82. In the same period, the 1910s, the success of fifteenth-century Novgorod icons on the Moscow market led to a genuine 'iconomania': prices for them grew from year to year and reached fantastic figures before the revolution of 1917. This is testified to in documents from the personal archive of I. S. Ostroukhov (RGALI, f. 822, op. 1, ed. khr. 1041, ll. 1–9).

143 See Moskowitz, *Stefano Bardini. 'Principe degli Antiquari'*, pp. 35, 39.

The huge success of Italian 'primitives' on the international market generated numerous forgeries, which flowed from Florence and Siena to the galleries of London and New York. Researchers have observed that forgeries and imitations with older elements began to appear once British and American collectors began to actively seek out works by Duccio, Pietro Lorenzetti (c. 1280–1348), Sano di Pietro (1405–81), Matteo di Giovanni, Benvenuto di Giovanni (1436–c. 1518) and other Tuscan painters of the Trecento and Quattrocento. At the same time, sarcastic pieces about Giovanni Morelli's (1816–1891) attribution method began to be published increasingly often, and, in addition to Berenson, von Bode, Max Friedländer (1867–1958), Frederick Mason Perkins (1874–1955), Harold Parsons (1882–1967) and others joined the new circle of influential experts.[144] The Sienese Madonnas of Duccio, Benvenuto, Matteo, Lorenzetti and Sano were counterfeited most often. Famous experts in the restoration, copying and forgery of thirteenth- to fourteenth-century 'primitives' such as Icilio Federico Joni (1866–1946), Bruno Marzi (1908–81) and Umberto Giunti (1886–1970) were working in Italy during this period. At the same time, the master Alceo Dossena (1878–1937) was flooding the international market with counterfeit works by the famous thirteenth-century sculptor Nicola Pisano (c. 1220/25–c. 1284).[145] Joni, who worked in Giovacchino Corsi's (1866–1930) Sienese antiquities and restoration studio, later wrote an autobiography with the fairly ironic title *Le memorie di un pittore di quadri antichi* [*Memoirs of*

---

144 B. Santi, 'Falsificazione dell'arte o arte della falsificazione', in *Falsi d'autore*, ed. Mazzoni, pp. 11–12; see also G. Mazzoni, *Quadri antichi del Novocento* (Vicenza: Neri Pozza, 2001). The experience of connoisseurship in this period found its reflection, above all, in the works of Bernard Berenson, Max Friedländer, and Roberto Longhi, which set out the grounds for attributing Italian and Flemish 'primitives'. See, in particular, M. Friedländer, *Ob iskusstve i znatochestve*, trans. M. I. Korenev, 2nd ed. (Moscow: Andrey Naslednikov, 2013).

145 Many specialists have observed the influence of photography on imitations and forgeries. Adolfo Venturi's *Istorii ital'ianskoi zhivopisi* (1907) was often drawn on for details of clothes and landscapes, and for characteristics of the movement of figures and the faces of Florentine and Sienese Madonnas, as were reproductions by the photography firms of Alinari and Brogi, licenced to reproduce copies of the Uffizi Gallery's masterpieces. The topic of 'forgeries', then, is broader than the market in antiquities alone, but also engages questions of taste, and issues of the study and collection of works of art. For comprehensive treatment of this topic, see F. Zeri, *Cos'e un falso e altri conversazioni sul'arte*, ed. M. Castellotti (Milan: Longanesi, 2011); S. Radnoti, *The Fake: Forgery and Its Place in Art* (Lanham: Rowman and Littlefield, 1999); P. Craddock, *Scientific Investigation of Copies, Fakes and Forgeries* (Amsterdam: Elsevier, 2009).

an Artist of Old Paintings], which was published in Italian in 1932. Within four years it was translated into English and released by Faber and Faber.[146] Joni reveals many of the secrets of the copying and falsification of Italian 'primitives' in his memoirs. He describes in detail, for instance, how the Madonna's missing clothes were filled in on a painting by a fifteenth-century Florentine artist, how a copy of a Benvenuto triptych was made for a Sienese antique dealer and how frescos were removed from old church walls. Finally, he recounts in depth the methods of ageing paintings to look like Trecento and Quattrocento works.[147] Joni, well connected with antiquities dealers and Anglo-American collectors, including Berenson, also sold imitations and early paintings.[148] The unprecedented demand for masterpieces of early Italian painting led to new developments in restoration methods and to new discoveries of the techniques used by old masters. During the *Belle Époque*, concepts such as *original*, *imitation* and *forgery* become commonplace not only in the Moscow market, but in Florence, Venice and Siena. Italian specialists, like Russian experts restoring medieval icons, removed the soot from works from the thirteenth to fifteenth centuries, touched up the missing parts of the image, and (not infrequently) completely repainted poorly preserved images on boards and 'golden backgrounds', giving them a complete and finished look. They might also make an exact copy of the original on an old board. The Russian restorer, artist and copyist Nikolai Lokhov (1872–1948) stands out amongst such specialists in Florence.

---

146 A bilingual parallel text of the book was published in Siena in 2004. See I. F. Joni, *Le memorie di un pittore di quadri antichi. A fronte la versione in inglese "Affairs of a painter"*, ed. G. Mazzoni (Siena: Protagon Editori, 2004).

147 Ibid., pp. 154–56, 170, 296, 302.

148 There are several pieces which are Joni's work in Berenson's collection in Villa I Tatti (F. Russoli, ed., *The Berenson Collection* (Milan: Arti Grafiche Ricordi, 1964), pp. 15–16). And although Joni writes about how Berenson could buy his works 'as genuine' and declare original works to be fakes, we should treat such statements with the utmost caution (Joni, *Le memorie di un pittore di quadri antichi*, ed. Mazzoni, pp. 308–10, 312). As the most recent research reveals, Joni's fakes were obtained by Berenson via the Sienese antiquarian Lodovico Torini at the end of the 1890s, in other words, as he began collecting and dealing in art. Berenson even kept several of these works in his office; they evidently helped him recognize the tricks of imitation art. In this same period, Joni also furnished Berenson with genuine paintings, and prepared Italian Renaissance-style frames for him. See Strehlke, 'Bernard and Mary Collect', pp. 24–25; Israels, 'The Berensons "Connosh" and Collect', pp. 57–58; G. Mazzoni, 'The Berensons and the Sienese Forger Icilio Federico Joni', in *Bernard and Mary Berenson Collection*, ed. Strehlke and Israels, pp. 639–56.

Lokhov lived in Florence from 1907, copying Renaissance frescos and paintings by Tuscan artists for the Alexander III Museum of Fine Arts in Moscow.[149] Since knowledge of the characteristic stylistic elements of Old Italian masters reached new heights precisely at the beginning of the twentieth century, the production of imitations and forgeries was similarly elevated. These entered the Florentine and Sienese antiquities market in great quantities, through the hands of cunning dealers, just as better imitations and forgeries of the 'Old Novgorodian style' began to circulate in the markets of Moscow and St Petersburg. As an anonymous contributor to *Starye gody* acutely observed in 1909, 'The market in forged medieval icons is as yet almost entirely unstudied, but there can be no doubt that it exists – and rather successfully too'.[150]

The Popularization of a Masterpiece

The popularization of a new masterpiece, its promotion and entry into academic circulation, became a vitally important constituent of the new relationships between collectors, critics and antiquarians. The masterpiece acquired a new life, taking on a celebrity status, propelled by monographs, numerous advertisements and exhibitions. Muratov's *Drevnerusskaia zhivopis' v sobranii I. S. Ostroukhova* [*Medieval Russian Icon-Painting in the Collection of I. S. Ostroukhov*], is particularly interesting in this regard. This was, in essence, the first book about the collector and a new type of medieval Russian icon collection, which the author presented in the context of the history of icon collection in Russia.

---

149 We know that Lokhov was copying frescos for the Museum of Fine Arts in Moscow, but, with the events of the 1917 October Revolution in Russia, these were no longer sought after. On Berenson's recommendation, Helen Clay Frick (1888–1984) acquired them for her private museum in Pittsburgh. Mary Smith (1864–1945) dedicated a special article to Lokhov. See M. Logan (Berenson), 'A Reconstructor of Old Masterpieces', *The American Magazine of Art*, 21 (1930), 628–38; W. R. Hovey, *The Nicholas Lochoff Cloister of the Henry Clay Frick Fine Arts Building* (Pittsburgh, PA: University of Pittsburgh, 1967); T. V. Beresova and M. G. Talalai, *Chelovek Renessansa. Khudozhnik Nikolai Lokhov i ego okruzhenie* (Moscow: Staraya Basmannaya, 2017). See also R. C. Pisani, *The Angeli Workshop: Federigo and the Angeli Workshop. Palazzo Davanzati. Dream and Reality* (Florence: Sillabe, 2010). In the same period, the Italian magazine *L'Antiquario* published a series of pieces on copies and forgeries ('I falsi degli Uffizi' (n.a.), *L'Antiquario*, 5 (1908), 38–39; *L'Antiquario*, 12 (1909), 89–92).

150 'O poddel'nikh kartinakh' (n.a.), *Starye gody* (June 1909), 339–40; see also V. Ivolgin, 'Nravy ikonotorgovtsev', *Peterburgskii listok* (30 July 1913), n.p.

Written in striking prose and containing around eighty phototype pictures of the Ostroukhov collection's core masterpieces, it was read like a captivating novel in its day, especially compared to the rather dry articles included in the catalogues of other collections. According to the author, only a gifted individual could recognize a masterpiece. This encapsulates the essence of Ostroukhov's characterization as an educated European collector and artist. Able to grasp the 'unmediated nuance of creativity' in medieval Russian icons, Ostroukhov became the first to elevate them to the ranks of world art treasures – in other words, to create that 'astonishing collection of genuine masterpieces' in which both the tradition of Hellenistic painting and the tradition of the great Italian masters of the Early Renaissance was resurrected.[151] Muratov's book breathed new life into icon collecting and clearly accords with his essay for volume six of Grabar's *Istoriia russkogo iskusstva* [*History of Russian Art*] (1914), which included, as noted in Chapter Two, a huge number of pictures of Ostroukhov's icons. Ostroukhov's icons thus provided the basis for a new history of medieval Russian art, and were compared with the most famous monuments of medieval Russian culture at that time. Since Muratov's text was not 'specialist' and was aimed at a wide readership, the new wave of collectors could fully appreciate the description of one of the best icon collections and the book had significant impact.[152]

The book's wide circulation also facilitated a close and amicable connection between the art critic and the collector. Italy as 'an image of beauty and joy in life' occupied a special place in this relationship, as numerous documents, postcards and letters testify.[153] It may be that Ostroukhov's acquaintance with the catalogues of Italian collections

---

[151] Muratov was especially delighted by the 'Elijah the Prophet' icon. He saw its red background as harking back to 'Hellenistic traditions', and its colouring, as a whole, reminiscent of the colour palette of Duccio's works. 'We know of no icon painted more powerfully', he concluded (Muratov, *Drevnerusskaia zhivopis'*, pp. 6, 13).

[152] The possibility of publishing a second edition was evidently considered as early as 1917, given Ostroukhov's new acquisitions: 'Your news and the fate of our book make me very happy', Muratov wrote to the collector. 'It ought, of course, to be supplemented and republished'. OR GTG, f. 10, ed. khr. 4440 (Letter from P. P. Muratov to I. S. Ostroukhov, 21 October 1917, ll. 1–1 ob.).

[153] Nikolai Berdiaev (1874–1948) accurately identified Italy's significance for Russians at the time. See N. Berdiaev, 'Chuvstvo Italii', in N. Berdiaev, *Filosofiia tvorchestva, kul'tury i iskusstva*, 2 vols. (Moscow: Iskusstvo, 1994), I, 367.

and exhibitions crystallized the idea of creating, with Muratov's help, a catalogue of his own collection. Since Ostroukhov was planning to travel to Rome in the autumn of 1912, Muratov wrote to him from Italy about what was worth seeing in connection with their shared interest in icons and 'primitives'. The Roman collection of Pope Leo XIII's (1810–1903) financial advisor, Sterbini, which Muratov tracked down at Ostroukhov's request but did not manage to view, could have been of particular interest. At that point in time, Sterbini's collection was kept at the palazzo on via del Banco di Santo Spirito in Rome, and included 'Greek icons' and works by Tuscan masters of the Trecento. Many of these had been exhibited at the above mentioned 1905–06 exhibition of Italo-Greek art in Grottaferrata – notably the so-called *Sterbini Diptych* with images of the *Mother of God*, the *Crucifixion* and *Saint Louis of Toulouse* (after 1317, Palazzo Venezia, Rome).[154] Berenson also bought a number of works by Sienese masters from this collection. Since Sterbini's collection was famous for its works in the *maniera bizantina*, we may assume that Ostroukhov – who, at this point, had also developed an interest in Byzantine icons – set off to Rome in order to make a number of acquisitions.

Muratov's letter suggests that this was not easy. 'Dear Ilya Semenovich', Muratov wrote,

> I embarked upon a search for Sterbini on receiving your letter, and delayed answering you in the expectation of visiting Sterbini and viewing his collection. I still haven't managed to achieve that. My acquaintance, the well-known local professor Antonio Muñoz, passed on a letter to Sterbini but the latter has still not given me any reply. I have dropped by three times and not once managed to catch him in. I'm ready to give it up as a bad job or, more accurately, to pass all the information on to you in the hope that you will be luckier than me [this] autumn. So, Sterbini – the elder and the collector – died recently. He leaves behind three sons, one of whom – A. Niccolò Sterbini – is in charge of the collection. They all live in a magnificent old house (their own) – a little palazzo with a marble cherub on the façade and a beautiful courtyard, on the corner of Banchi Vecchi and Banco di Santo Spirito streets, near the Ponte St Angelo. Their name is 'd'un certaine consideration' in Rome, and Muñoz was vague when questioned about the possibility of purchases…

---

154 On this collection see A. Venturi, *La Galleria Sterbini a Roma. Saggio illustrativo* (Rome: Casa editrice de l'Arte, 1906), https://archive.org/details/lagalleriasterbi00vent; see S. Moretti, *Roma bizantina. Opere d'arte dall'impero di Costantinopoli nelle collezioni romane* (Rome: Campisano, 2014), pp. 123–30.

The same letter talks about Antonio Muñoz (1884–1960) preparing a catalogue of icons in the Vatican Library's Museum of Religious Art (Museo Sacro della Biblioteca Vaticana). At the same time, Muñoz authored the second volume of a catalogue of a hundred masterpieces from Count Grigorii Stroganov's collection. Muratov strongly recommended Ostroukhov to take a careful look at the Count's collection, which had made a great impression on him: 'It is a whole museum [...] You absolutely must see the Stroganov house on via Sistina [this] autumn'.[155] Ostroukhov stayed in the Hotel Hassler, near the Palazzo Stroganov, during his trip to Rome in October of that same year, and clearly had the opportunity to compare his own collection of medieval Russian icons with the Italian 'primitives' and Byzantine icons of the Stroganov collection, and – above all – with the aforementioned *Madonna and Child* by Duccio. It is most likely that the Moscow collector also knew about the exhibition held that same year (1912) in Siena, dedicated to Duccio and his School.[156] While in Rome, Ostroukhov received an open letter from his young friend. In it, Muratov recounted his trip to the Russian North and his visit to Ferapontov Monastery, where he had acquired a rare 'Stroganov style' icon of the *Trinity*.[157]

Surviving documents and Muratov's correspondence with Ostroukhov and Berenson reveal that collecting and participation in the art and antiquities market became an integral part of the creative biographies of the new generation of Russian critics and historians of art, just as they did for Berenson or Perkins in Italy.[158] Muratov's

---

155 OR GTG, f. 10, ed. khr. 4391 (Letter from P. P. Muratov to I. S. Ostroukhov, 15 June 1912); see also Muñoz and Pollak, *Pièces de choix*.

156 On this exhibition, see Museo dell'Opera del Duomo, *Mostra di opere di Duccio di Buoninsegna e della sua scuola. Catalogo. Siena, Museo dell'Opera del Duomo, Settembre, 1912* (Siena: L. Lazzeri, 1912); F. M. Perkins, 'Appunti sulla mostra ducciana a Siena', *Rassegna d'Arte*, 13 (1913), 5–9, 35–40. Interestingly, V. Khvoshchinskii's work also came out this same year. In his foreword, the author noted that it was guided entirely by the 'artistic significance' of the works being published (V. T. Khvoshchinskii, *Toskanskie khudozhniki. I. Primitivy* (St Petersburg: n.p., 1912)). In the letter from 15 June 1912, Muratov advised Ostroukhov to visit Khvoshchinskii's house in Rome 'for the sake of several lauded Russian paintings and one good primitive'. See OR GTG, f. 10, ed. khr. 4391 (Letter from P. P. Muratov to I. S. Ostroukhov, 15 June 1912), p. 4.

157 OR GTG, f. 10, ed. khr. 4395 (Open letter from P. P. Muratov to I. S. Ostroukhov, 25 October 1912).

158 On Berenson's collection, which is today kept at the Villa I Tatti near Florence, see *Bernard and Mary Berenson Collection*, ed. Strehlke and Israels. On Perkins' collection, see F. Zeri, *La collezione Federico Mason Perkins* (Turin: Allemandi, 1988).

collection (which was not large, and was amassed before he emigrated in 1922) included not only medieval icons, but also engravings by Giovanni Battista Piranesi (1720–78) (about whom he was preparing to write a book), Japanese woodblock prints and Antique cameos. As discussed, Muratov advised Ostroukhov on art in Italy, and also helped his Yaroslavl publisher Konstantin Nekrasov (1873–1940) to assemble a collection of medieval icons. This is evidenced by an open letter he sent Nekrasov from Venice, in October 1914: 'Dear Konstantin Feodorovich', Muratov wrote, 'I have made one further (final) purchase – I bought a large icon of the Mother of God with two medallions for 190 francs. In my opinion it's an interesting piece from the fourteenth century. If I'm not mistaken, the outstanding specimens of the fourteenth, fifteenth and sixteenth centuries will be connected specifically with Venice'.[159] We discover that Muratov took an expert interest in Byzantine artefacts and Italo-Greek icons in 1914 from one of his letters to Ostroukhov, in which he recounted his plans to go to Venice and hunt for Byzantine icons which Likhachev and Kondakov 'might pass', as he put it.[160] Among the new generation of Russian art critics and colleagues of Muratov and Ostroukhov, it is worth recalling Alexander Anisimov (1877–1937), who undoubtedly owned one of the most interesting collections of icons at that time. During the wave of new collecting, the young scholar and expert managed to discover and acquire valuable examples of twelfth- to sixteenth-century medieval Russian icon-painting. Amongst these were genuine masterpieces, which today grace the displays of key museums and exhibitions abroad. These include the two-sided icon the *Mother of God of the Sign and Saint Juliana* (twelfth to thirteenth century, Tretyakov Gallery, Moscow), the *Saviour Enthroned* (fourteenth century, Tretyakov Gallery, Moscow), the *Prophets Daniel, David and Solomon*

Today, part of Perkins' collection is held at the Museum complex of the Basilica of St Francis in Assisi. It is interesting to note that Perkins not only collected famous masters and Sienese Madonnas from the fourteenth and fifteenth centuries, but also the folk icons of the *madonneri*, which clearly indicates his increasing interest in the artistic 'primitive' at this time. The fullest collection of the works of *madonneri* in Italy is in Ravenna, in the museum that now occupies the monastery cloisters near the church of San Vitale. See G. Pavan, ed., *Icone dalle collezioni del Museo Nazionale di Ravenna* (Ravenna: Il Museo, 1979).

159 See I. V. Vaganova, 'Iz istorii sotrudnichestva P. P. Muratova s izdatel'stvom K. F. Nekrasova', *Litsa: Biograficheskii al'manakh*, 3 (1993), 155–265.

160 OR GTG, f. 10, ed. khr. 4400 (Letter from P. P. Muratov to I. S. Ostroukhov, 15 June 1914).

(fifteenth century, Tretyakov Gallery, Moscow), *Saint Paraskeva Piatnitsa* (sixteenth century, Tretyakov Gallery, Moscow). After graduating from Moscow University's history and philology faculty in 1904, Anisimov became interested in medieval Russian art while working in Novgorod region. Just as Perkins surveyed the churches of Tuscany and organized exhibitions in 1904 and 1912 in Siena while collecting 'primitives', in 1910 and 1911 Anisimov surveyed medieval Novgorodian churches and collected examples of medieval icon-painting which were shown at the exhibition of medieval art in Novgorod, organized as part of the Fifteenth Russia-wide Archaeological Congress in 1911.[161] In the same period, Anisimov also helped create the Museum of the Novgorod Diocese, to which he transferred part of his collection. Muratov recalled a visit to Novgorod in the winter of 1912, when he was preparing his essay on medieval Russian painting for the abovementioned *History of Russian Art*:

> I was hosted by A. I. Anisimov while he was still living in a teacher training college in Novgorod region. It was winter. The town itself, and all the surrounding area, crisscrossed by rivers, was covered by astonishingly deep, pure and even snow. For days on end Alexander Ivanovich and I travelled from church to church and from monastery to monastery on little sledges. There was an enormous wealth of art [...] with pounding hearts Anisimov and I stood before the most wonderful and ancient icons, sometimes huge in size, sometimes even not completely repainted but simply very blackened by the old, spoiled oil varnish that was so easy to remove.[162]

---

161 See A. I. Anisimov, 'Tserkovnaia starina na vystavke XV arkheologicheskogo s'ezda v Novgorode', *Starye gody* (October 1911), 40–47. Cf. Perkins, 'Appunti sulla mostra ducciana', 5–9, 35–40. For more information about the Anisimov collection, see O. Tarasov, *Ten Icons of the 15th–16th centuries from a Private Collection. From the History of Collecting and Studying Medieval Russian Painting in Soviet Russia* (Rome: Editoriali e Poligrafici, 2023), pp. 26–28, 109–120.

162 P. P. Muratov, *Vokrug ikony* (1933), in P. P. Muratov, *Russkaia zhivopis' do serediny XVII veka. Istoriia otkrytiia i issledovaniia*, ed. A. M. Khitrov (St Petersburg: Bibliopolis, 2008), pp. 56–58. After the 1917 October Revolution, Anisimov headed up, amongst other things, the Department of Medieval Russian Art in the Institute of Art Historical Research and Museum Studies (INKhUK), and also worked as an academic consultant in the Central State Restoration Workshops established under Grabar's supervision. His was the first research on early Russian icons of the twelfth and thirteenth centuries, and it retains scholarly significance to this day. Anisimov also took part in preparing the famous Exhibition of Old Russian Icons in Western Europe and the USA from 1929 to 1932. Anisimov's publication of his book *The Vladimir Icon of Mother of God* (Prague: Seminarium Kondakovianum,

Meanwhile, large-scale circulation publications were particularly significant in promoting Ostroukhov's Museum of Medieval Russian Painting in the 1910s. Information about the museum percolates through the newspapers and magazines *Utro Rossii, Tserkov'* [*Church*], *Apollon* [*Apollo*], *Starye gody, Khudozhestvennye sokrovishcha Rossii* [*Artistic Treasures of Russia*] and many others. And, of course, along with Muratov's *Sofiia* [*Sophia*], the periodical *Russkaia ikona* played a special role. This luxurious art publication was issued under the auspices of the Society for the Study of Medieval Russian Icon-Painting, with financial support from Riabushinskii, Ostroukhov, Bogdan Khanenko (1848–1917), Varvara Khanenko (1852–1922) and several others. In a review of this new publication, the journal *Sofiia* noted that it was conceived 'as a masterpiece in typographical art', and its aim was to introduce private collections of medieval Russian icons, one by one, to academic circles.[163] *Russkaia ikona* was connected with the antiquities market: the publication was targeted at the affluent collector, had a limited print-run, and its advertisement declared that '50 sets are printed on Dutch paper, and – reflecting the desires of our subscribers, are numbered'. The inclusion of Shchekotov's polemical article in the second issue is significant. In 'Ikonopis'' kak iskusstvo. Po povodu sobraniia ikon I. S. Ostroukhova i S. P. Riabushinskogo' ['Icon-Painting as Art. On I. S. Ostroukhov's and S. P. Riabukhinskii's Icon Collections'], Shchekotov called into question academic methods of studying the form of medieval Russian painting. Masterpieces owned by Moscow's two most renowned collectors were presented by the author as a new type of art that testified to the 'original artistic achievements' of pre-Petrine Rus'. Moreover, it was Ostroukhov's icons, specifically, that Shchekotov considered of revolutionary import for academia: 'Just as the frescos of Mistra's churches and the mosaics of Constantinople's Chora monastery provided the first reliable evidence

---

1928), amongst Russian émigré circles, served as one of the reasons for his arrest in the USSR in 1932. Like Pavel Florenskii, he died in Stalin's camps (in 1937). In these same years, his collection was confiscated and transferred to the Tretyakov Gallery. In Berenson's library we find one of Anisimov's books, *The Novgorod Icon of Theodore Stratelates*, which was co-authored with Muratov and printed by the aforementioned publisher Nekrasov. See A. I. Anisimov and P. P. Muratov, *Novgorodskaia ikona Feodora Stratilata* (Moscow: K. F. Nekrasov, 1916). On Anisimov, see also I. L. Kyzlasova, *Aleksandr Ivanovich Anisimov (1877–1937)* (Moscow: Izd. Moskovskogo Gosudarstvennogo Gornogo universiteta, 2000).

163 'Peterburgskaia "Russkaia ikona"' (n.a.), *Sofiia*, 96 (1914), n.p.

of the rich artistic life that nourished Byzantine art', Shchekotov wrote, 'the icons in I. S. Ostroukhov's collection call for a complete turnaround in the study of [Russia's] medieval painting'. As a talented artist himself, Ostroukhov was the first collector of icons to be 'governed primarily by artistic sense'.[164]

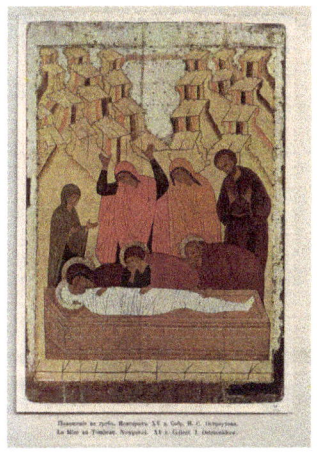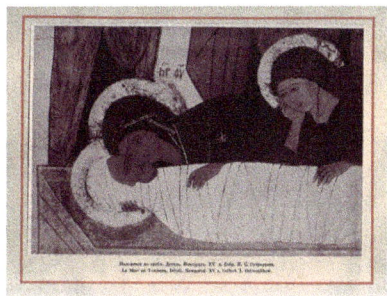

Figs. 3.6a–3.6b Novgorod School, *The Entombment of Christ* (late fifteenth century), tempera on wood, 90 x 63 cm. From the collection of Ilya Ostroukhov in Moscow. Tretyakov Gallery, Moscow. Reproduced as a color inset in Nikolai Shchekotov's article 'Ikonopis' kak iskusstvo' ['Icon Painting as Art'], *Russkaia ikona* (1914), 2. Photographs by the author (2019), public domain.

A new kind of reproduction, intended to penetrate the very essence of art, also accompanied the *Russkaia ikona* anthology. Reading the icon as a masterpiece of painting required analysis of form rather than commentary on content, and it therefore became more important to show rather than to tell. Especial skill and attention were given to framing the shot, and also to fragments of silhouettes and faces conveying nuances of emotion. The new illustration *educated the eye*, taught it to see nuances of form; the new illustration, then, conveyed that the 'inner' vision (which Berenson and Muratov had pondered) had nothing in common with an ordinary reflection of the surrounding world but was the result of strenuous spiritual labour (see Figs. 3.6a and 3.6b). Improved

---

164 N. Shchekotov, 'Ikonopis' kak iskusstvo. Po povodu sobraniia ikon I. S. Ostroukhova i S. P. Riabushinskogo', *Russkaia ikona*, 2 (1914), 115–42 (pp. 140–41).

colour reproduction, halftone etching and the fine detail of heliographic engraving (photographic illustration) shaped the conviction that a reproduction could adequately stand in for the original. As the reader turned to *Russkaia ikona*'s high-quality illustrations (the work of one of the finest firms of the day, the R. Golike and A. Vilborg company), they seemed to 'attain' the masterpieces. The emotional tone and literary worth of the individual articles made these masterpieces accessible and understandable to a wide readership. Special publications dedicated to the most important works also facilitated this access.

The journal *Starye gody* is also relevant here. This luxurious art publication 'for the lover of art and olden times', was published from 1907 until 1916. Right from the beginning, the journal introduced works of medieval Russian painting in the context of the art and antiquities market in Russia and Western Europe, and of world art collecting. Periodically, the journal included a column headed 'On Auctions and Sales', which published information about the most interesting acquisitions, including Italian, Flemish and German 'primitives'. Famous Russian and foreign researchers – Kondakov, Benois, Adolfo Venturi (1856–1941), Friedländer, von Bode and many others – collaborated with the journal. Essays on medieval Russian icons and frescos were often placed alongside articles on Western European art, and showed icons in the context of collections and exhibitions of early Italian and Flemish painting. In the reader's mind, then, research on Italian Madonnas illustrated by the works of Duccio and Martini was combined with Russian authors' reflections on the perspectives of new collectors such as Ostroukhov, Riabushinskii, Morozov and others.[165] Since the journal's aesthetic stance (like that of *Sofiia* and *Russkaia ikona*) was that art history should be studied via the very best examples, the *masterpiece* – whether that be a Persian miniature, an Italian 'primitive' or a medieval Russian icon – was consistently defined on its pages as

---

165 From 1909 onwards, Muratov is simultaneously writing about Italian and medieval Russian art in the pages of *Starye gody*. See P. P. Muratov, 'Ocherki ital'ianskoi zhivopisi v Moskovskom Rumiantsevskom muzee. I: Sienskaia Madonna', *Starye gody* (November 1910), 605–11 and 'Ocherki ital'ianskoi zhivopisi v Moskovskom Rumiantsevskom muzee. II: Kvatrochento', *Starye gody* (October 1910), 3–11; P. P. Muratov, 'Vystavka drevnerusskogo iskusstva v Moskve. I. Epokhi drevnerusskoi ikonopisi', *Starye gody* (April 1913), 31–38; P. P. Muratov, 'Ikonopis'' pri pervom tsare iz Doma Romanovykh', *Starye gody* (July–September 1913), 25–33.

a work of exceptional quality. Finally, it was the *Starye gody* journal that published two of the most important reviews of the celebrated *Old Russian Art* exhibition held in Moscow in May 1913, as part of the Romanov tercentenary festivities. These were Muratov's 'Vystavka drevnerusskogo iskusstva v Moskve' ['The Eras of Medieval Russian Icon-Painting'] and Shchekotov's 'Nekotorye cherty stiliia russkikh ikon XV veka' ['Some Stylistic Traits of Russia's Fifteenth-century Icons'], which clearly reflect the connection between the 'new collecting' and the new methods of reading the language of medieval Russian art.[166]

According to the memoirs and observations of contemporaries, large numbers of cleaned, medieval icons from private collections were first viewed by the general public at two major exhibitions. In St Petersburg, this was the 1911–12 exhibition in the Imperial Academy of Arts, and in Moscow the 1913 exhibition in Delovoi dvor ['Business precinct'], organized by the Nicholas II Moscow Archaeological Institute. Comparing these two exhibitions, moreover, allows us to appreciate the genuinely innovative way of displaying medieval Russian icons employed by Ostroukhov in his museum, and in the organization of the 1913 exhibition in Moscow. In the 1911–12 exhibition, the icons from the collections of the artist Viktor Vasnetsov (1848–1926), Likhachev, Kharitonenko and others were displayed together with crosses, ecclesiastical plate and embroidery. The inclusion of Italo-Greek icons from Likhachev's collection likely aimed to highlight the Italian influences on Russian icons through the 'Italo-Cretan School'. The catalogue's introductory article and a review of the exhibition, both by the art historian Vasilii Georgievskii (1861–1923), convincingly demonstrated that the exhibition was still operating with the traditional understanding of the icon as a work of ecclesiastical culture.[167] Moreover, the icons were exhibited in the halls of the Academy of Arts in St Petersburg, which attracted a special kind of audience, closely associated with academic and artistic circles.

---

166 Muratov, 'Vystavka drevnerusskogo iskusstva v Moskve'; N. M. Shchekotov, 'Nekotorye cherty stiliia russkikh ikon XV veka', *Starye gody* (April 1913), 38–42.
167 V. T. Georgievskii, 'Obzor vystavki drevnerusskoi ikonopisi i khudozhestvennoi stariny', *Trudy Vserossiiskogo s"ezda khudozhnikov*, 3 (1913), 163–74 (including the exhibition catalogue).

What was innovative about the 1913 Moscow exhibition was, firstly, that large-scale medieval Russian icons were hung in a separate display; in other words, they were exhibited in a way that – until then – had been reserved for the paintings of named Russian and foreign artists. Secondly, because the exhibition was part of the Romanov festivities, celebrating three hundred years of the Romanov dynasty, the icon was presented as *pure art* for the first time to the *general public*. The exhibition had such an unexpected and deep impact on this broad audience that many refused to believe the exhibited works were genuine. Stripped of their religious and ordinary church context, the general public was asked to view icons for the first time as vivid works of medieval Russian painting: 'the primary significance of the Moscow exhibition of medieval Russian art', Muratov wrote in his summary, 'is the extraordinary power of the artistic impression conveyed by the examples of Old Russian painting brought together in it. For many, almost for all, this impression is one of surprise. An enormous new field of art has opened up before us so suddenly [...] it is strange that no one in the West has yet seen these strong, gentle colours, these skilful lines and animated faces'.[168] Time and again, Muratov returned to Likhachev's and Kondakov's theory about Italian influence on the Russian icon, and to the innate Byzantine and Russian ability to bring Antiquity back to life, as if contesting the way the Academy of Art's 1911 exhibition was conceived. His brilliant prose and emotional engagement with the topic convinced the viewer, time and again, that what was before them were genuine masterpieces, each reflecting the individual style of a medieval Russian master-painter.

---

168 Muratov, 'Epokhi drevnerusskoi ikonopisi', 31. 'It tears down many firmly-held views on the art of Russia's medieval icon painters', Muratov wrote in the foreword to the exhibition catalogue; 'No one will call Russian icon-painting dark, monotonous and unskilled in comparison with contemporary western models'. See *Vystavka drevnerusskogo iskusstva, ustroennaia v 1913 godu v oznamenovanie 300-letiia Doma Romanovykh* (n.a.) (Moscow: Imperatorskii Moskovskii Arkheologicheskii Institut Imeni Imperatora Nikolaia II, 1913), p. 3.

3. *The New Museum of Medieval Icons* 107

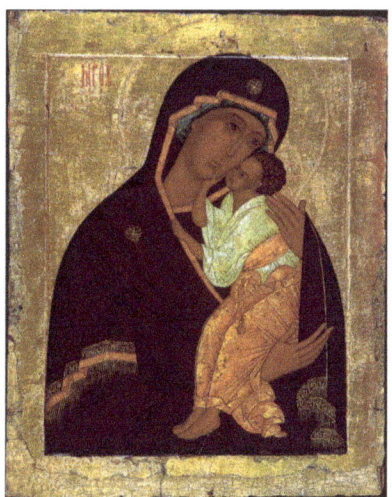

Fig. 3.7 Novgorod School, *Mother of God of Tenderness* (fifteenth century), tempera on wood, 54 x 42 cm. From the collection of Ilya Ostroukhov in Moscow. Tretyakov Gallery, Moscow. Wikimedia, public domain, https://commons.wikimedia.org/wiki/File:Mary_Mother_of_jesus1.jpg

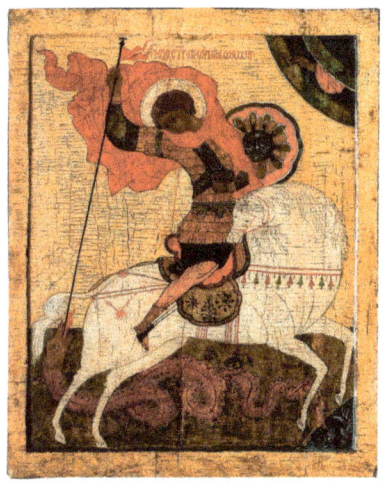

Fig. 3.8 Novgorod School, *St George and the Dragon* (end of the fifteenth century), tempera on wood, 82 x 63 cm. From the collection of Ilya Ostroukhov in Moscow. Tretyakov Gallery, Moscow. Wikimedia, public domain, https://commons.wikimedia.org/wiki/File:Georges_icon.jpg

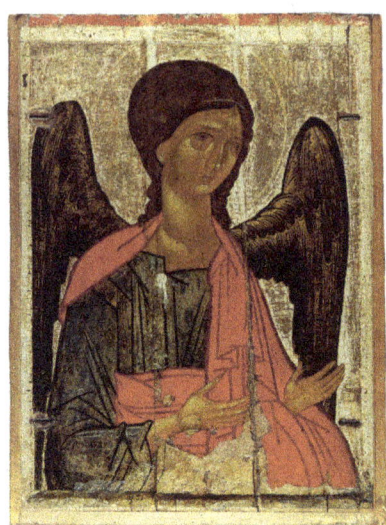

Fig. 3.9 Novgorod School, *Archangel Michael* (fourteenth century), tempera on wood, 86 x 63 cm. From the collection of Stepan Riabushinskii in Moscow. Tretyakov Gallery, Moscow. Wikimedia, public domain, https://commons. wikimedia.org/wiki/File:The_archangle_Michael_(Novgorod).jpg

For his part, Shchekotov drew out the common characteristics of those works included in the exhibition through formal analysis. Ornamentality, rhythmic repetitions and 'musicality' of composition were observed in the most vivid examples, and revealed Shchekotov's efforts to employ a fundamentally new, contemporary framework for understanding the artistic forms of these works.[169] Both authors especially admired the fifteenth-century Novgorodian icons that had such a prominent place in the exhibition. According to Muratov, icons such as the *Mother of God of Tenderness* (see Fig. 3.7), *Descent from the Cross* and *St George and the Dragon* (see Fig. 3.8) from Ostroukhov's collection, and the *Archangel*

---

[169] N. M. Shchekotov, 'Nekotorye cherty stilia russkikh ikon XV veka', *Starye gody* (April 1913), 38–42. Efforts to find musical and rhythmical analogies in the composition of medieval Russian icons were clearly grounded in the contemporary understanding of music as the highest of the arts, as was Walter Pater's (1839–94) conviction that 'all art constantly aspires towards the condition of music'. W. W. Pater, *The Renaissance. Studies in Art and Poetry* (New York: Macmillan, 1888), p. 140, https://archive.org/details/renaissancestu00pate). We find the forms of painting and the art of sound approximated not only in the work of Alexander Scriabin (1872–1915), Aleksey Remizov (1877–1957) and Shchekotov, but also in the artist and collector Ostroukhov's notes about icons: 'we may see the forms of medieval icon-painting as grounded in laws close to the laws of musical rhythm and acoustic harmony' (RGALI, f. 822, ed. khr. 76, l. 3).

Michael (see Fig. 3.9) and the *Ascension of Christ* from Riabushinskii's collection, could be compared with the greatest works of Early Renaissance painting. Muratov was especially captivated by the *Descent from the Cross* icon, which reminded him of Duccio's work and prompted discussion of the historical conundrum of the 'Russo-Byzantine Renaissance'. Given the painterly methods borrowed from monumental art in these specific works (and in the *Ascension* and *Archangel Michael* icons from Riabushinskii's collection), Muratov detected in them a close connection with Palaiologan art. He also observed a lightness and purity of style that distinguished the Russian icon not only from the icon-painting of other nations, but also from Italian Trecento painting: 'There is much in an icon as beautiful as the "Entry into Jerusalem" that calls to mind Duccio', wrote Muratov, 'but this of course is evidence only that Duccio was practically a Byzantine master, and that Berenson was not far wrong when he suggested that he had studied in Constantinople. In Italy and even in Siena Duccio is [...] an exception, and not long after him Simone Martini is already a master of Gothic. In contrast, Ostroukhov's "Entry into Jerusalem" sits naturally amongst other Russian icons of the fifteenth century...'.[170]

Almost all commentators on the Moscow exhibition observed the participation of collectors of the new wave – art lovers and collectors of the most diverse types of art. It is worth recalling that other famous individuals besides Ostroukhov owned major art collections before they began collecting icons; Aleksei Morozov, for example, was considered one of Russia's leading collectors of porcelain, while Kharitonenko and the Khanenkos possessed significant collections of Russian and Western European painting. That they all valued this new collectible as a *new type of art*, just like Western European collectors appreciated early Italian paintings on 'gold backgrounds', is without doubt. 'The native Russian art of the icon', recalled Shcherbatov, 'immediately joined the ranks of Ravenna's sublime, internationally significant artworks, the best frescos of Italian cathedrals, the best primitives, moreover a special Russian tenderness, combined with gravity and festive, joyous colours, distinguished them from all that was familiar to

---

170 Muratov, 'Epokhi drevnerusskoi ikonopisi', 35; see also P. P. Muratov, 'Drevniaia ikonopis', *Russkoe slovo*, 36 (13 February 1913), 2.

us in religious painting'.[171] In this regard, the close connection between the Moscow exhibition of 1913 and the new realities of collecting and investing in antiquities was mentioned more than once in the newspapers: 'It will not be long', wrote the *Utro Rossii* correspondent, 'before foreign collectors and connoisseurs turn their attention to this unexpected discovery [...] Russian icon-painting's turn to be the Parisian art market's object of desire will come...'.[172] Such sentiments were only reinforced by icons from Ostroukhov's and Riabushinskii's collections featuring on the pages of the Parisian journal *L'Art decoratif* [*Decorative Art*].[173]

Finally, the particular significance of the exhibition for the development of the very latest trends in Russian painting featured in many commentaries and reviews. Benois summed up his impressions in the newspaper *Rech'* [*Speech*], generalizing about the exhibition's impact in the context of the artistic reflection characteristic of the *Belle Époque*: 'Even ten years ago', he wrote,

> the 'Pompei of icons' would not have made any kind of impression on the art world [...] It wouldn't have entered anyone's head to 'learn' from the icon, to view it as a salvific lesson amid public disorientation. Now things are viewed entirely differently, and it seems as though one would have to be blind not to believe in the salvation offered by the icon's artistic impact, by its enormous power of agency in contemporary art and by its unexpected proximity to our times. Moreover, some fourteenth-century 'Nicholas the Wonderworker' or 'Nativity of the Mother of God' helps us understand Matisse, Picasso, Le Fauconnier or Goncharova. And, in turn, through Matisse, Picasso, Le Fauconnier and Goncharova we are able to better feel the enormous beauty of these 'Byzantine' paintings...[174]

---

171 It was Ostroukhov who attracted Prince Shcherbatov to collecting medieval Russian icons. See S. Shcherbatov, *Khudozhnik v ushedshei Rossii* (Moscow: Soglasie 2000), pp. 210–11.

172 See the summary of press commentary on the exhibition: 'Prazdnik drevnerusskogo iskusstva' (n.a.), *Tserkov'*, 8 (1913), 180; 'Vystavka drevnerusskogo iskusstva' (n.a.), *Svetil'nik*, 3 (1913), 33–35.

173 'Have you seen the issue of *L'Art decoratif* magazine that includes your and Riabushinskii's icons?' Muratov wrote to Ostroukhov from Paris on 15 June 1914. The same letter notes that Nikolai Riabushinskii (Stepan Riabushinskii's brother) was trying to instigate the sale of old icons in Paris (OR GTG, f. 10, ed. khr. 4400, ll. 1–2).

174 A. Benois, 'Ikony i novoe iskusstvo', *Rech'*, 93 (1913), 2; see also A. Benois, 'Russkie ikony i Zapad', *Rech'*, 37 (1913), 2.

3. The New Museum of Medieval Icons

In that same year of 1913, Russian avant-garde artists Mikhail Larionov (1881–1964) and Goncharova organized an exhibition of folk icons and *lubki* [traditional woodcut prints] in Moscow. The exhibition catalogue observed: 'Such a wonder of masterly painting and spirituality as the thirteenth-century icon of the "Mother of God of Smolensk", or the "Archangel Michael", has not lost what we might call patterns and a lubok-like quality'.[175] Kazimir Malevich (1879–1935), too, recalled his fascination with icons in these years: 'despite the naturalistic training of my feelings towards the natural world, icons created a deep impression on me. I sensed something familial and wonderful in them. The Russian people in its entirety, with all its emotional creativity, was revealed to me in them'.[176] It seems likely that Malevich's iconic *Black Square* (1915, Tretyakov Gallery, Moscow), as a new work of *pure art*, was influenced by both the 1913 exhibition and the perception of medieval icons as works of *pure painting*. Malevich first showed his Suprematist works at the *Poslednyaya futuristicheskaya vystavka kartin: 0,10* [*Last Futurist Exhibition of Painting 0,10*] in 1915, placing his *Black Square* in the corner of the exhibition hall where the icon corner was traditionally set up (see Fig. 3.10).[177] It is noteworthy that in the exhibition hall of Ostroukhov's private museum, one of his most spectacular icons was placed in the same corner. This was the Novgorodian icon of *Saint George and the Dragon* (end of the fifteenth century, Tretyakov Gallery, Moscow).

---

175 N. Goncharova, *Vystavka ikonopisnykh podlinnikov i lubkov, organizovannaia M. F. Larionovym* (Moscow: Khudozhestvennyi salon, 1913), p. 10. The display was organized as part of the March–April 1913 exhibition in Moscow of works by Target (*Mishen'*), an open group of avant-garde artists.

176 Cited in N. Khardzhiev, *K istorii russkogo avangarda* (Stockholm: Hylea Prints, 1976), pp. 117–18.

177 See O. Tarasov, 'Spirituality and the Semiotics of Russian Culture: From the icon to Avant-Garde Art', in *Modernism and the Spiritual in Russian Art: New Perspectives*, ed. L. Hardiman and N. Kozicharow (Cambridge: Open Book Publishers, 2017), pp. 115–28 (pp. 124–28, figs. 5.2, 5.3 and 5.4), https://doi.org/10.11647/OBP.0115.05. For a wider discussion of the significance of this place of the 'Black Square' in the exhibition hall see O. Tarasov, *Framing Russian Art: From Early Icons to Malevich*, trans. R. Milner-Gulland and A. Wood (London: Reaktion, 2011), pp. 344–53.

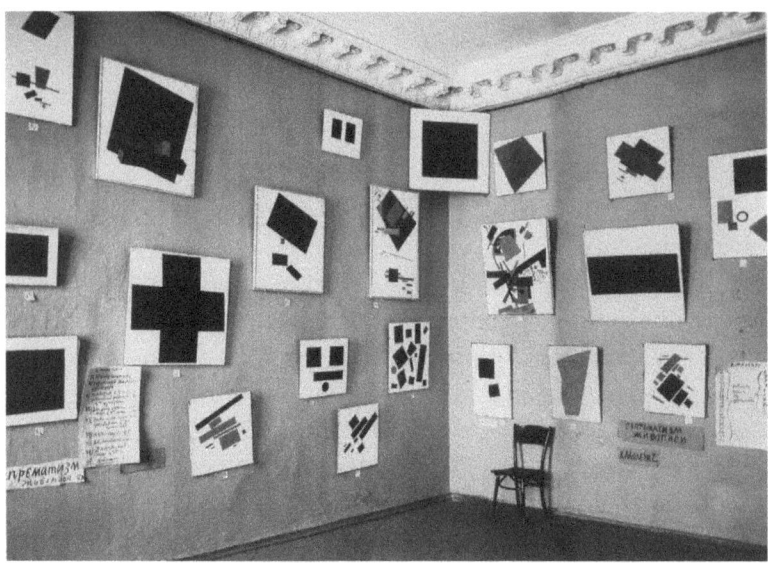

Fig. 3.10 Photograph of *Poslednyaya futuristicheskaya vystavka kartin: 0,10* [*Last Futurist Exhibition of Painting 0,10*] (1915). Wikimedia, public domain, https://commons.wikimedia.org/wiki/File:0.10_Exhibition.jpg

Two books by the abovementioned artist Grishchenko, *O sviaziakh russkoi zhivopisi s Vizantiei i Zapadom* [*On the Links of Russian Painting with Byzantium and the West*] (1913) and *Russkaia ikona kak iskusstvo zhivopisi* [*The Russian Icon as the Art of Painting*] (1917), provided the most accurate characterization of the *Old Russian Art* exhibition (and also of the Russian avant-garde's interest in the icon more generally). According to the author, the Russian avant-garde came into being largely due to Shchukin's Moscow collection of new French painting, and Ostroukhov's collection of medieval Russian icons. The first book, therefore, was dedicated to Shchukin and a special copy of the second book was printed for Ostroukhov. 'The exhibition of Old Russian art', Grishchenko mused, 'convinces me even more of the deep significance of early icon-painting. What unusual pageantry this rare exhibition presents in our pitiful, grey, humdrum life! The S. P. Riabushinskii collection's "Archangel Michael", a Novgorod-style icon from the end of the fourteenth century – the best thing in the exhibition – is striking in its stern beauty and surprising masterfulness. The same may be said about other icons from I. S. Ostroukhov's priceless collection'.[178] 'When the exhibition of medieval Russian art opened exactly three years ago', Grishchenko recalled, 'artists responded to the icon most vitally and enthusiastically, engaged as they were at that time in similar endeavours. For them, the medieval icon painters spoke an understandable language of colour and form' (my emphasis). Evidently, Grishchenko saw his task as presenting the medieval Russian icon from the perspective of pure art, which he himself strove for in his own 'Cézanne-inspired' works. This is why reproductions of Ostroukhov-collection icons such as the *Saint George and the Dragon*, the *Elijah the Prophet*, the *Descent from the Cross* and the *Lamentation* were set beside the works of Fra Angelico, Paul Cézanne (1839–1906) and Pablo Picasso (1881–1973) in the pages of his book; the intention was to evaluate the quality of Ostroukhov's collection in purely artistic terms. Ostroukhov was, the author was firmly persuaded, 'the first to begin collecting icons as artworks'.[179] In the book The Russian Icon as the Art of Painting, special attention was given to the collection of the famous collector Aleksei Morozov, which was also presented at the exhibition.[180] In fact, this was the first overview of Morozov's collection, which – like the collection of Ostroukhov – was at one point housed in a special annexe to the collector's personal mansion, in Vvedenskii Lane in Moscow. The annexe was designed in 1914 by architect Ilya Bondarenko (1867–1947). Unfortunately, the collection as displayed in the annexe (like those of Ostroukhov, Riabushinskii and many others) has not been preserved, so Grishchenko's work can also be considered the earliest publication of individual monuments of this collection. The overhead lighting of the three large halls, which housed about 220 works of Old Russian painting, clearly brought their display closer to the exposition of the art gallery, emphasizing the works as pure art.

The 1913 *Old Russian Art* exhibition thus proved to be closely connected with the Modern era's general frame of mind, and constituted one of the most significant events in the history of European culture during the *Belle Époque*. Ostroukhov, who consistently appears whenever the discovery of the medieval Russian icon as a genuine work of elevated

---

178 A. Grishchenko, *O sviaziakh russkoi zhivopisi s Vizantiei i Zapadom. XIII–XX vv.* (Moscow: A. A. Levenson, 1913), p. 17; Grishchenko, *Russkaia ikona*, pp. 243–44.
179 Grishchenko, *Russkaia ikona*, p. 153.
180 Ibid., pp. 173–206.

and unique art is discussed, played a special role in this vivid, artistic event.[181] It was Muratov who, after Ostroukhov's death in 1929, wrote the most sincere and accurate words about him, characterizing the Moscow collector as one of 'the most wonderful people', and 'the most important participant' of the era in which medieval painting was rediscovered. 'One only had to step into Ostroukhov's house to find oneself alongside eighteenth-century portraits, Italian "primitives", Dutch artists and Manet', wrote Muratov, 'the Russian icon could enter the European circle of comparison and evaluation'. Another of Muratov's estimations is worthy of note here: 'Icon collecting was now taken up with a passion by a fine, sensitive artist who had seen much, an enthusiast, collector, who knew Paris, Germany, Italy extremely well, who every year travelled to study now Velasquez in Madrid, now Rembrandt in Amsterdam, now Gainsborough in London, a great booklover, moreover, of entirely European tastes, who spent nights reading Goethe, Stendhal, Balzac'.[182] Muratov further remembered Ostroukhov in his essays 'Otkrytiia drevnego russkogo iskusstva' ['Discoveries in Russian Medieval Art'] (1923) and 'Vokrug ikony' ['Around the Icon'].[183] Muratov's letters from the first half of the 1920s also testify to Ostroukhov's role and significance in Muratov's creative output.[184]

Muratov began to actively promote medieval Russian painting, including the icons from Ostroukhov's collection, in the West in precisely this period. As observed above, Muratov's book *La pittura russa antica* came out in Italian in 1925, with reproductions of many of the Moscow

---

181 After the October Revolution (1917) and the nationalization of the collection (1918), Ostroukhov not only continued to add to a collection which no longer belonged to him at his own expense, but worked on a guidebook for the icon gallery of his museum. Documents preserved in the archives clearly reveal Muratov's influence on this – their relationship continued after the latter's emigration in 1922. Notions of the Hellenistic foundations of the medieval Russian icon and the national characteristics of its drawing and colouring may all be found on the pages of the famous collector's draft (RGALI, f. 822, ed. khr. 76. Katalog ikon I. S. Ostroukhova [1919], ll. 1–4).

182 P. P. Muratov, 'I. S. Ostroukhov', in Muratov, *Russkaia zhivopis' do serediny XVII veka*, p. 382.

183 Muratov, *Russkaia zhivopis' do serediny XVII veka*, pp. 333–34, 358–63, 366–68, 374–75.

184 In one of them, Muratov wrote to the Moscow collector from Germany: 'I have thought about you a lot recently because I have been preoccupied with the treatment of the Russian publication "Old Russian Primitives" [...] I plan to publish in Russian, French, English'. OR GTG, f. 10, ed. khr. 4448 (Letter from P. P. Muratov to I. S. Ostroukhov, 16 January 1923).

collector's icons.[185] In the sixth volume of Grabar's edited series on the history of Russian art, by contrast, Ostroukhov's icons appeared amongst various icons and frescos discovered in the early Soviet period and, in particular, alongside the oldest Russian icons from the Moscow Kremlin cathedrals (twelfth to the fourteenth century), and the wall paintings in Vladimir's Cathedral of St Demetrius (dating from the twelfth century) and the Dormition Cathedral (from the beginning of the fifteenth century).[186] Muratov's *Les icones russes* [*The Russian Icons*] also contained a refinement of his theory of the origins of medieval Russian painting, and greatly prepared a western audience for the first major exhibition of medieval Russian icons in the West, which toured Austria, Germany, Britain and the USA between 1929 and 1932.[187]

The exhibition was a particular success in Britain. Held in the halls of the Victoria and Albert Museum in London from 18 November until 14 December 1929, it attracted a huge number of visitors and glowing commentaries in the English press.[188] The exhibition was accompanied

---

185 Muratov, *La pittura russa antica*, trans. Lo Gatto; E. Lo Gatto, *I miei incontri con la Russia* (Milan: Mursia, 1976), pp. 56–59.

186 From 1919 to 1921, Muratov worked at the Commission for the Preservation of Cultural Heritage, and therefore witnessed the first discoveries of the oldest Russian icons from the twelfth to the fourteenth centuries.

187 This exhibition was a grandiose artistic and commercial enterprise organized by the Soviet government in order to obtain foreign currency funds for the industrialization of the country. The special catalogues in English and German released for the exhibition laid the foundations for the widespread commercialization of Russian icons in the West, thereby creating serious competition in the international market for Western European 'primitives'. Paradoxically, it was precisely this intervention by the Soviet state in the western antiques market that contributed to introducing medieval Russian art to a broader western audience. See Russian Icon Exhibition, *Ancient Russian Icons. From the XIIth to the XIXth Centuries*, 2nd ed. (London: Russian Icon Exhibition Committee, 1929); *Denkmäler altrussischer Malerei. Russische Ikonen vom 12.–18. Jahrhundert* (n.a.) (Berlin: Ost-Europa-Verlag, 1929); *Denkmäler altrussischer Malerei. Russische Ikonen vom 12.–18. Jahrhundert* (n.a.) (Vienna: Hagenbund, 1929);Museum of Fine Arts, *Russian Icons* [*Catalogue of Exhibition*]. *Museum of Fine Arts, Boston. October 14–December 14* (Boston, MA: Museum of Fine Arts, 1930); Art Institute of Chicago, *Catalogue of Russian Icons* (Chicago, IL: Metropolitan Museum of Art, 1931).

188 See E. H. Minns, 'The Exhibition of Icons at the Victoria and Albert Museum', *Slavonic and East European Review*, 8 (1930), 627–35. Minns was also the English-language translator of N. P. Kondakov's book *The Russian Icon* (Oxford: Clarendon Press, 1927). See W. Salmond, 'Ellis H. Minns and Nikodim Kondakov's "The Russian Icon" (1927)', in *Modernism and the Spiritual in Russian Art. New Perspectives*, ed. L. Hardiman and N. Kozicharow (Cambridge: Open Book Publishers, 2017), pp. 165–92, https://doi.org/10.11647/OBP.0115.08

by a special album entitled *Masterpieces of Russian Painting*, which included magnificent illustrations and overview articles, amongst which those by Martin Conway (1856–1937) and the famous British artist and critic Roger Fry had particular significance for the medieval Russian icon's reception by a western audience.[189] Moreover, if Conway's article solely addressed the history of Russian icon-painting, then Fry's aesthetic approach to the perception of medieval painting was entirely in accord with the new theory of artistic form. His attentive reading of the characteristic elements of the medieval Russian icon's artistic language was clearly reminiscent of observations made by Muratov, Shchekotov, and Grishchenko. Using the methods of stylistic analysis and oriented on that same Symbolist tradition of visual-aural parallels as Russian authors, the British critic was, it seems, one of the first western researchers to observe that special rhythmic composition which has always distinguished the Russian icon from Byzantine and Balkan works. Viewing the Russian icon as a work of art, Fry emphasized its unique harmony of colours and shapes. He also highlighted the 'extraordinary perfection' of the copy Chirikov made of Rublev's *Trinity*, the 'melodious colour rhythms' of which reminded him of the best work of early Italian art and, in particular, of the works of Martini.[190] As a critic, Fry paid tribute to the new theory of artistic forms, calling Russian icons 'masterpieces' and viewing them as part of a continuum with Byzantine and early Italian painting. As an artist, Fry also seems to have penetrated the very essence of the Russian icon, stressing its particular endeavour to convey the ideal sphere of the surrounding reality. In this sense, then, the exhibition of medieval Russian painting in the halls of the Victoria and Albert Museum in London played as important a role as the 1913 exhibition in Moscow. This understanding of medieval Russian icons and the Sienese Madonnas as masterpieces of painting clearly corresponded with a new perception of European culture as an entire and indivisible unity.

---

189 M. Conway, 'The History of Russian Icon Painting', in *Masterpieces of Russian Painting*, ed. M. Farbman (London: Europa Publications, 1930), pp. 13–34; R. Fry, 'Russian Icon Painting from the West European Point of View', in *Masterpieces of Russian Painting*, ed. Farbman, pp. 35–58.

190 According to Fry, the icon – like music – directly appealed to a person's spiritual nature. He compared the icon painter's inspiration with that of a composer and musician. See Fry, 'Russian Icon Painting', pp. 36, 56.

4. Florenskii, Metaphysics and Reverse Perspective

> Icon-painting is a visual manifestation of the metaphysical essence of that which it depicts.
>
> —Pavel Florenskii (1882–1937)[191]

In philosophy, the modern age represents a period of transition from Classical to non-Classical knowledge. That the medieval Russian icon began to be interpreted as a 'masterpiece of art' at the beginning of the twentieth century was an achievement not just of the Formalist School of art history, but of Postclassical philosophy and theology. The famous Russian philosopher and art historian Pavel Florenskii played a key role in this process, arguing that the pictorial art of the medieval icon aimed to present us with the invisible, noumenal structures of the world around us (see Fig. 4.1). It was, in fact, Florenskii who discovered a fundamentally new approach to conceptualizing the pictorial forms of the medieval icon, not Pavel Muratov (1881–1950) and other art critics who switched from iconographic research to formal analysis in the second decade of the twentieth century. In sum, Florenskii's interpretation of reverse perspective was based on a new way of seeing the world: the Patristic tradition of the theology of the icon was advanced amid a characteristically modern convergence of diverse types of knowledge. Moreover, the revelation of the authentic painted form of medieval icons discussed in Chapter Three could not but influence the philosopher's views. This discovery prompted the philosopher (like members of the Russian avant-garde) to ponder the 'painterly meaning' of the icon as the artist's way of understanding the world: 'We started to

---

[191] P. A. Florenskii, 'Ikonostas', in P. A. Florenskii, *Istoriia i filosofiia iskusstva. Sbornik tekstov* (Moscow: Akademicheskij proekt, 2017), pp. 9–118 (p. 61).

understand, *having only just touched upon the icon'*, Florenskii wrote, 'the absolute seriousness of the task of art – not the applied use of art in the sphere of morals, community, ornamentation and so forth, but in and of itself, as *manifesting a new reality'*.[192]

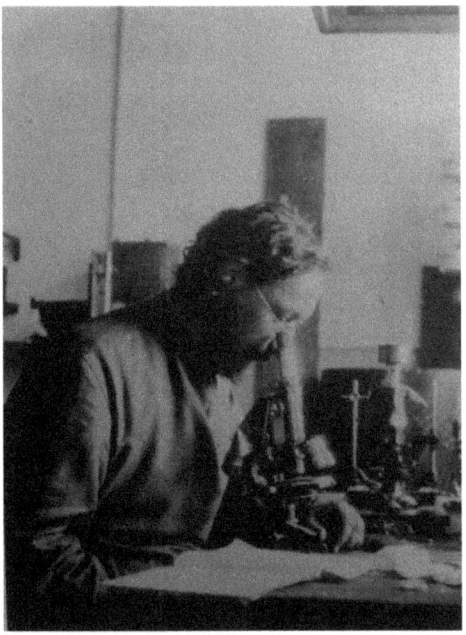

Fig. 4.1 Pavel Florenskii (1882–1937) in a State Experimental Electrotechnical Institute Laboratory, Moscow, 1925. Public domain.

As a religious philosopher, Florenskii started from Pseudo-Dionysius the Areopagite's (fifth to sixth century) famous definition of the icon: the icon is a 'visible image of mysterious and supernatural visions'.[193] This informed Florenskii's understanding of the icon as a spatial boundary

---

192 P. A. Florenskii, 'Molennye ikony prepodobnogo Sergiia', in Florenskii, *Istoriia i filosofiia iskusstva*, pp. 145–63 (p. 145) (my emphasis).
193 See Florenskii, 'Ikonostas', pp. 29–30. The theological meaning of the Orthodox icon is also explored in E. N. Trubetskoi, *Umozrenie v kraskakh* (Paris: YMCA Press, 1965); S. Bulgakov, *Ikona i ikonopochitanie* (Moscow: Russkii put', 1996); L. Uspenskii, *Bogoslovie ikony pravoslavnoi tserkvi* (Paris: Izd-vo Zapadno-evropeĭskogo Ekzarkhata, Moskovskiĭ patriarkhat, 1989) and L. Uspenskii, *La teologia dell'icona. Storia e iconografia* (Milan: La Casa di Matriona, 1995); P. N. Evdokimov, *Teologia della bellezza. L'arte dell'icona* (Milan: Edizioni San Paolo, 2017); L. Uspenskii and V. Losskii, *The Meaning of Icons* (Boston, MA: Boston Book and Art Shop, 1952). In contrast to all these works, Florenskii's theology of the icon is clearly determined by the distinctive features of his cosmogony.

between the earthly and the heavenly, the visible and the invisible. He saw the icon precisely as the metaphysical border between two worlds. Wielding his colossal erudition in many spheres of knowledge, from mathematics and physics to theology and languages, Florenskii launched a comprehensive effort to substantiate this boundary. The metaphysics of the icon clearly occupied a special place in the thinking of this 'Russian Leonardo'.

A Copy of Andrei Rublev's *Trinity*

Florenskii's fundamentally new approach to the medieval icon was largely shaped by the peculiarities of his creative trajectory. After graduating from Moscow University's Faculty of Physics and Mathematics in 1904, Florenskii entered the Moscow Spiritual Academy at the Trinity Lavra of St Sergius, and became a priest in 1911. As a student, he was attracted by Vladimir Soloviev's (1853–1900) philosophy, published in the journals *Vesy* [*The Scales*] and *Novyi put'* [*New Path*]. He moved in literary circles, and, through the poet Andrei Bely (1880–1934, a fellow student at Moscow University), was introduced to the Symbolist poets Alexander Blok (1880–1921), Zinaida Gippius (1869–1945), Dmitrii Merezhkovskii (1866–1941) and Valerii Briusov (1873–1924). From 1912 to 1917, Florenskii headed the journal *Bogoslovskii vestnik* [*The Theological Herald*], concurrently holding a professorship at Moscow Spiritual Academy. During this period, he established a series of original courses on the philosophy of the cult, Kantian problematics and the history of ancient philosophy. After the 1917 October Revolution, he worked in the Commission for the Preservation of Monuments of Art and Antiquities at the Trinity Lavra of St Sergius, compiling an inventory of its artistic valuables – the medieval icons and cult items made from precious metals. Consequently, his *Opis' panagii Troitse-Sergievoi Lavry XII–XIX vekov* [*An Inventory of the Panagias of the Trinity Lavra of St Sergius*] was published in 1923. A small (26.4 x 18.1 cm) copy of Andrei Rublev's (1360–1428) *Trinity* icon (1411, or 1425–27, Tretyakov Gallery, Moscow) dates from this period, and can be found among the few icons owned personally by Florenskii and preserved in the Moscow house of his heirs. Florenskii ordered this from a young icon painter and restorer, Vasilii Kirikov (1900–78). The copy was evidently made at the beginning of the 1920s, in other words, at a time when further restoration work was being carried out on Rublev's *Trinity*, at that point in the iconostasis of the Lavra's Trinity Cathedral. It appears to be the earliest surviving copy made of Rublev's properly cleaned icon, which has been gracing the walls of the Tretyakov Gallery since 1929 and has been returned to the Russian Orthodox Church for safekeeping today (see Fig. 4.2). These restoration works were undertaken by order of the Commission for the Discovery of Early Paintings, composed of Igor Grabar (1871–1960), Alexander Anisimov (1877–1937), Aleksei Grishchenko (1883–1977) and Konstantin Romanov (1858–1915), and also the Commission for the Preservation of the Trinity Lavra of St Sergius' Monuments of Art and Antiquity, in which Florenskii served alongside Count Yurii Aleksandrovich Olsuf'ev (1878–1939). Kirikov worked as an assistant to Grigorii Chirikov (1891–1936), who completed the copy of Rublev's *Trinity* icon for the exhibition of Old Russian painting in Western Europe and the United States of America from 1929 to 1932 (see Chapter Three).[194]

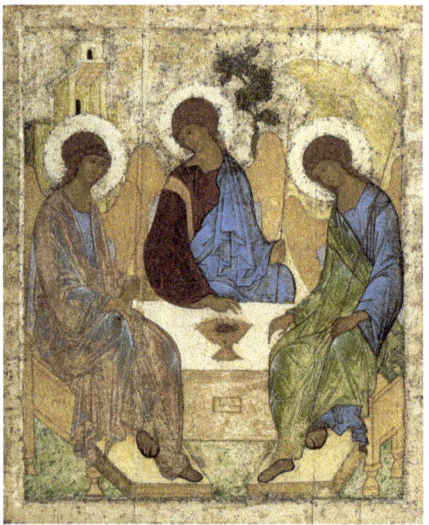

Fig. 4.2 Andrei Rublev (1360–1428), *The Holy Trinity* (1411, or 1425–27), tempera on wood, 141.5 x 114 cm. Tretyakov Gallery, Moscow. Wikimedia, public domain, https://commons.wikimedia.org/wiki/File:Andrey_Rublev_-_%D0%A1%D0%B2._%D0%A2%D1%80%D0%BE%D0%B8%D1%86%D0%B0_-_Google_Art_Project.jpg

---

194 In 1929 G. O. Chirikov's copy replaced Andrei Rublev's original icon in the iconostasis of the Holy Trinity-St Sergius Lavra's Trinity cathedral. On the restoration history of Rublev's *Trinity* icon see: L. Nersesjan and D. Suchoverkov, *Andrej Rublev. L'icona della Trinità. A lode di san Sergio* (Rome: Orizzonti Edizioni, 2016).

The *Trinity* in Florenskii's collection was placed in a *kiot* [icon-case], which gives some indication of the religious and aesthetic relationship the philosopher had with this devotional image. Kirikov endeavoured to convey the most important characteristics of colour and composition of Rublev's masterpiece. On the icon are three angels painted in a circle, symbolizing that the three persons of the Trinity are one in essence. In Florenskii's words: 'Rublev's *Trinity* exists, so God exists' – the whole point of his symbolism and metaphysics of the icon.[195] Rublev's icon is 'Russian icon-painting's most beautiful image'. Absorbing the world of human culture, it is, itself, 'absolute reality'. There are therefore grounds to suppose that this copy of the icon was connected not just with Florenskii's prayer life, but also with his famous characterization of the original, which so clearly reveals a mystical perception of the celebrated icon: 'In Rublev's work it is not the subject, not the number "three", not the chalice on the table, and not the wings that move, astound, and almost set us afire, but the sudden lifting of the *veil of the noumenal world* before us, and it is not aesthetically important to us how the icon painter achieves this laying bare of the noumenal, and whether they would be the same colours and the same devices in some other hands, but that he has truly conveyed to us the revelation he saw'.[196] In other words, Florenskii's icon-copy suggests that Rublev's *Trinity* played a special role in his creative laboratory, set as it was before the philosopher's eyes while he was creating that 'concrete metaphysics' of the justification of man (anthropodicy) – a system within which the reinterpretation of the medieval icon's artistic form came to be of primary significance.[197] A substantial part of Florenskii's main work, *Stolp i utverzhdenie istiny* [*The Pillar and Foundation of the Truth*], published in 1914, was dedicated to clarifying the symbolic meaning of the icon.[198] In the period from

---

195 Florenskii, 'Ikonostas', p. 31.
196 Florenskii, 'Troitse-Sergieva lavra i Rossiia', in Florenskii, *Istoriia i filosofiia iskusstva*, pp. 139–40 (my emphasis).
197 Rublev and literature about him feature prominently in Florenskii's drafts and preparatory notes; works on Rublev by Vasilii Uspenskii (1870–1916), Nikolai Likhachev (1862–1936), Muratov, Vasilii Gur'ianov (1867–1920), Nikolai Punin (1888–1953) and Vasilii Georgievskii (1861–1923) are all mentioned (see 'Skhema opisaniia ikon', in Florenskii, *Istoriia i filosofiia iskusstva*, pp. 112–13).
198 In *Stolp i utverzhdenie istiny. Opit pravoslavnoi teoditsei*, Florenskii scrutinizes the iconography of icons of the Mother of God and of Sophia, the Wisdom of God, in particular. While working on the book, he ordered a small icon of the Mother of

1918 to 1925, however, his creative legacy was enhanced by a string of works which revealed a new approach to the language of medieval art: 'Obratnaia perspektiva' ['Reverse Perspective'] in 1919, 'Ikonostas' ['Iconostasis'] in 1921–22, 'Molennye ikony prepodobnogo Sergiia' ['Devotional Icons of St Sergius'] in 1918–19, *Mnimosti v geometrii* [*The Imaginary in Geometry*] in 1922, and several others. Florenskii originally prepared some of these works ('Reverse Perspective' and 'Devotional Icons of St Sergius') as papers for sessions of the Commission for the Preservation of the Trinity Lavra of St Sergius' Monuments of Art and Antiquities.

The scholar's religious experience greatly shaped his perception of Rublev's *Trinity* and his understanding of its particular metaphysical meanings. According to Russian philosopher Aleksei Losev's (1893–1988) memoirs, Florenskii's study of the icon 'was combined with a state of religious reverence'; therefore 'ritual, the icon, and in general everything that was external in the church was illuminated with inner feeling and infused with deep intimacy for Florenskii.[199] It is also clear that Florenskii drew upon the icon collection at the Trinity Lavra of St Sergius in his constructions of the icon's metaphysics, and above all on the iconostasis of the Trinity Cathedral, which was, at that time, the

---

God with rare iconography (of the *Blagodatnoe nebo* [*Heaven Full of Grace*] type), which is now – like his copy of Rublev's *Trinity* – on display at the Pavel Florenskii house-museum in Moscow. Florenskii's description of another rare icon, *The Annunciation with Cosmic Symbolism*, and the circumstances in which he discovered it, testifies to a sustained and intense interest in the symbolic system of Orthodox icons: 'Addressing the cosmic aspect of the Mother of God', he writes, 'we cannot pass over in silence a rather puzzling icon of the Annunciation, "found" by me in a church in the village of Novinskii, in the Nerekhtskii district (*uezd*) of Kostroma region (*guberniia*). I say "found", because this icon was in a state of neglect, and was lying around somewhere on a windowsill, covered with such a layer of dust and dirt that the image could not be seen at all. It caught my eye during confession, and for reasons I can't explain, attracted my attention and as soon as I was able I went back to this village and set about cleaning the icon. After about two hours an image stood out against the recessed golden background, which proved to be a really fine work with a multitude of minute details and figures, painted with painstaking care; I think there must be over 150 figures. Judging from the composition, this icon either dates to the end of the seventeenth or to the end of the eighteenth century'. See P. A. Florenskii, *Stolp i utverzhdenie istiny. Opit pravoslavnoi teoditsei* (Moscow: Izdavitel'stvo pravda, 1990), p. 540. See also the Italian publication: P. A. Florenskii, *La colonna e il fondamento della verità*, ed. N. Valentini and C. Balsamo (Milan: Edizioni San Paulo, 2010).

199 'P. A. Florenskii po vospominaniiam A.F. Loseva' (n.a.), *Kontekst* (1990), 6–24 (p. 21).

only early fifteenth-century iconostasis preserved within the church for which it was created.²⁰⁰ Painted 'in praise of Sergius of Radonezh', Rublev's *Trinity* was set to the right of the central, Holy Doors in the 'local row' (that is, the first tier of the iconostasis). This tier also included a fifteenth-century *Hodegetria Mother of God*, a hagiographical icon of St Sergius of Radonezh from the end of the fifteenth century, a sixteenth-century icon of the Dormition, and a *Saviour* in the style of Simon Ushakov (c. 1626–86), amongst others. The icons above – depicting the feasts of the Lord, the apostles and the prophets – all date from the golden age of medieval Russian painting, their colours and refined shapes captivating the imagination. The long services in the Trinity Cathedral, which the philosopher attended often while he was teaching at the Spiritual Academy, were clearly distinguished by a special mysticism and reverence. Rays of softly diffused light, emanating from windows under the dome, allowed for the unhurried contemplation of an iconostasis made between 1425 and 1427 by a group of master painters headed by Rublev and Daniil Chernyi (c. 1360–c. 1430). The monastery also housed the grave of its founder, St Sergius (c. 1314–92), above which were two devotional icons traditionally believed to have belonged to the saint. Florenskii dedicated a special essay to these fourteenth-century icons (the *Hodegetria Mother of God* icon and the *St Nicholas* icon). The historical and cultural significance of this famous Russian monastery as a whole is reflected in his article entitled 'Troitse-Sergieva Lavra i Rossiia' ['The Trinity Lavra of St Sergius Monastery and Russia'].²⁰¹

Florenskii's active participation in the work of academic research institutes such as the Moscow Institute of Art Historical Research and Museum Studies (MIKhM), the Institute of Artistic Culture (INKhUK) and the Higher Art and Technical Studios (VKhUTEMAS)

---

200 Florenskii was also able to participate in compiling an inventory of the Holy Trinity-St Sergius' Lavra's icons (see Y. A. Olsuf'ev, *Opis' ikon Troitse-Sergievoi lavry* (Sergiev: Tipografia Ivanova Publ., 1920). It is no accident that particular icons which were found within the monastery are analyzed in his texts (see, for example P. A. Florenskii, 'Obratnaia perspektiva', in P. A. Florenskii, *Istoriia i filosofiia iskusstva. Sbornik tekstov* (Moscow: Akademicheskij proekt, 2017), pp. 181–236 (p. 225)).

201 The article was written for the 1919 guide *Troitse-Sergieva lavra*, prepared by the Commission for the Preservation of the Trinity Lavra of St Sergius' Monuments of Art and Antiquities.

played a crucial role in the early 1920s. These institutions, which brought together leading lights in the theory and practice of visual arts, including representatives of the avant-garde, were instrumental in advancing innovative approaches to the study of icons. According to Florenskii's own memoirs, his paper 'Reverse Perspective' was prepared in October 1919 and, for some reason, not delivered before the Commission for the Preservation of the Trinity Lavra of St Sergius. Instead, it was read on 29 October 1920 at a meeting of the Byzantine section of the MIKhM, at the Narkompros (People's Commissariat for Education) Institute of Art Historical Research and Museum Studies, Russian Academy of Sciences. Amongst those who discussed the paper were Muratov (at that point, director of the Institute), Boris Kuftin (1892–1953), Nikolai Romanov (1867–1948), Aleksei Sidorov (1891–1978) and Nikolai Shchekotov (1884–1945). 'The liveliness of the debate convinced me yet again', Florenskii wrote about this meeting, 'that the question of space is one of the most fundamental in art and, I would go so far as to say, in understanding the world in general'.[202]

The work of the Physico-Psychological Department of the Russian Academy of Artistic Sciences (GAKhN), headed by Wassily Kandinsky (1866–1944) until he emigrated to Germany in December 1921, attracted special interest at this point in time. This department was addressing, in part, the same problems of the 'language of things' and 'synthesis of the arts' broached by Florenskii. Anatolii Bakushinskii (1883–1939) (who replaced Kandinsky as the head of the department) gave a paper on 'Linear and Reverse Perspective in Art and Perception' on 25 August 1921, as part of a series of lectures on 'Elements of Art'. The paper was later published as a stand-alone article, which included criticism of Florenskii's 'mystical' approach to reverse perspective.[203] At

---

[202] Florenskii, 'Obratnaia perspektiva', p. 225. If P. Muratov sought to capture a 'visual impression shared' with the medieval Russian icon in the Hellenistic landscape, Florenskii saw in the icon the roots of linear perspective and the illusionism of artistic thinking. See also the discussion on Florenskii's 'Reverse Perspective' paper: 'Kratkaia zapis' obsuzhdeniia doklada P. A. Florenskogo "Ob obratnoi perspective", prochitannom na Vizantiiskoi sektsii MIKhM 29 oktiabria 1920', in Florenskii, *Istoriia i filosofiia iskusstva*, pp. 228–29.

[203] A. V. Bakushinskii, 'Linear perspektiva v isskustve i zritel'nom vospriiatii real'nogo prostranstva', *Iskusstvo*, 1 (1923), 213–63. For further detail on the work of the Physico-Psychological Department of GAKhN, see N. P. Podzemskaia,

a meeting of the Physico-Psychological Department in 1924, papers on the significance of dreams in academic and artistic works were also discussed; for example, Sidorov's contribution on 'Artistic Creativity during a Dream' and Pavel Karpov's (1873–c. 1932) on 'The Dream as a Research Method between Consciousness and the Subconscious'. In this same period, in establishing the metaphysical essence of the sacred image, Florenskii was also comparing the icon with the dream, as discussed further below.

In the first half of the 1920s, as well as actively participating in numerous conferences and debates, Florenskii was also a member of GAKhN's Figurative Arts sector and closely connected with the Physico-Psychological Department. In 1921–23, he lectured on spatial composition in painting at the faculty of Printing and Graphics at VKhUTEMAS. Florenskii developed and instructed his audience and students on various subjects, including the theory of perception, issues of space and time in works of ancient and medieval art, and the symbolism of rhythm, colour and line in the icon. These topics also formed the basis of his new key work *U vodorazdelov myslii* [*At the Watersheds of Thought*], which was published considerably later.[204] The lectures contained the most vital theoretical material; they elaborated on the problem of vision and the interrelation between the human eye and the object it observes. Within this discourse, a Modernist aesthetic was clearly discernible, laying the foundation for a fundamentally new phenomenological approach to art criticism. For Bernard Berenson (1865–1959) and Muratov, sight and connoisseurship (discussed in Chapter One) were still privileged forms of knowledge; for Florenskii, sight itself became an object of intense scrutiny and philosophical interpretation. In this respect, his lectures shared affinities with the works of GAKhN's philosophers, who were directly addressing questions of the philosophy of art. They particularly resonated with the phenomenological theories of Gustav Shpet (1879–1937), who viewed art as a form of applied philosophy.

'Nauka ob iskusstve v GAKhN i teoreticheskii proekt V.V. Kandinskogo', in *Iskusstvo kak iazyk – iazyki iskusstva. Gosudarstvennaia Akademiia khudozhestvennykh nauk i esteticheskaia teoriia 1920-x godov*, ed. N. S. Plotnikov and N. P. Podzemskaia, 2 vols. (Moscow: NLO, 2017), I, 203–05.

204 The first collection came out in France in 1985 with the YMCA Press. P. A. Florenskii, *U vodorazdelov mysli. T. 1. Stat'i po iskusstvu* (Paris: YMCA Press, 1985).

The Book Cover

Florenskii found kindred spirits amongst artists within the walls of VKhUTEMAS too: Vladimir Favorskii (1886–1964), Lev Zhegin (1892–1969), Aleksandr Shevchenko (1883–1948), Vasily Chekrygin (1897–1922), Nikolai Chernyshev (1885–1973) and others. Some of them belonged to the Makovets Society of artists (1921–27), the eponymous publication of which reflected the ideological and artistic position of Florenskii and his group. The Society was named after the Makovets hill on which St Sergius of Radonezh had founded the Trinity Lavra of St Sergius.[205] The artist Favorskii's book cover for Florenskii's *The Imaginary in Geometry* (1922) (see Fig. 4.3) served as clear testimony to the fact that developing new approaches to understanding the icon resonated with the Florenskii's *mathematical* interests. Above all, it aligned with his *theory of discontinuity*, a concept he acquired from his mathematics teacher, Professor Nikolai Bugaev (1837–1903), while still in Moscow University.[206] This cover, he wrote, 'is art saturated with mathematical thinking': it reveals the meaning of the theory of the imaginary as applied to art.[207] In essence, however, the cover drawing leads us to an understanding of the *twofold and self-contained* space of the Orthodox icon on the basis of the theory of discontinuity. In this period, Florenskii links the metaphysical properties of the artistic space of the medieval icon specifically with the concept of discontinuity (discreteness), and contrasts this concept with the *endless and singular nature* of the Renaissance painting's space.

---

205 The *Makovets* journal (1922, 1–2) reflected the artists' programme (which brought them closer to Florenskii in terms of their views). See N. Misler, 'Il rovesciamento della prospettiva', in P. A. Florenskii, *La prospettiva rovesciata e altri scritti*, ed. N. Misler (Rome: Casa del libro, 1983), pp. 5–17.

206 See L. Grekhem, *Imena beskonechnosti: pravdivaia istoriia o religioznom mistitsizme i matematicheskom tvorchestve*, trans. Kantor Zh. M. (St Petersburg: European University at St Petersburg, 2011), pp. 70, 88. See also L. Graham and J.M. Kantor, *Naming Infinity. A True Story of Religious Mysticism and Mathematical Creativity* (Cambridge, MA: Harvard University Press, 2009).

207 P. A. Florenskii, *Mnimosti v geometrii* (Moscow: Lazur' Publ., 2004), p. 61 (the appendix entitled 'Explanation of the Cover'). See the Italian translation of this text in P. A. Florenskii, 'Spiegazione della copertina', in Florenskii, *La prospettiva rovesciata e altri scritti*, ed. Misler, pp. 136–43.

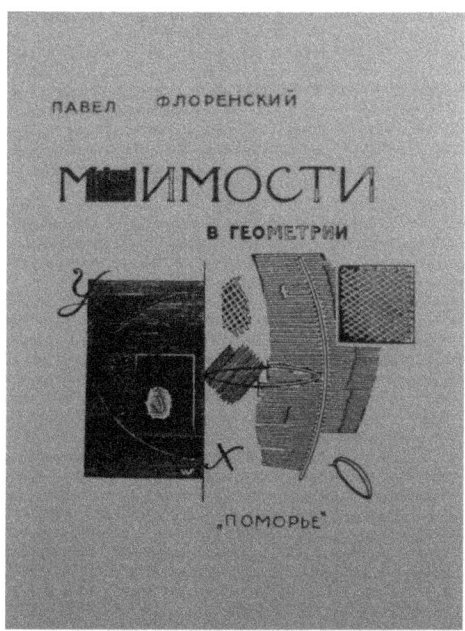

Fig. 4.3 Vladimir Favorskii (1886–1964), book cover for Pavel Florenskii's *Mnimosti v geometrii* [*The Imaginary in Geometry*] (Moscow: Pomorye, 1922). Public domain.

On Favorskii's cover the reader saw an original typeface composition, differently shaded planes, geometric figures and separate letters, inclining and foreshortened in various ways. In his 'Explanation of the Cover', which was included within the book, Florenskii wrote: 'A large rectangle, shaded with black hatching, provides the image of the front-facing side of the plane, and the sections hatched in white depict the imaginary side of the plane'.[208] In this way, the artist revealed how the imaginary breaks through into reality and vice versa. As is well known, Florenskii's mathematical theory (or the so-called 'visual model of the imaginary') was intended to prove the duality of visible reality. This model consisted of two planes, one of which is regarded as material (visible) and the other as imaginary (virtual). A transition to the sphere of virtual reality with the help of the symbol (the icon) was entirely possible, according to the philosopher, but only 'through the *breaking* of space and the body *turning* itself *inside out*'.

According to this analogy, Florenskii perceived the artistic space of the icon (which was only starting to be discussed in terms of the development

---

[208] Florenskii, *Mnimosti v geometrii*, pp. 53, 65.

of style) to be double and 'discontinuous', that is, like a certain spatial part of the phenomenal plane. Beyond the visible surface of this plane, its reverse, 'imaginary' surface is revealed – the immeasurable depths of the world of the noumena. Thus, in depictions of the caves and holes in the icon-type *Voskresenie Christovo* [Resurrection of Christ], for example, the philosopher perceived 'ruptures' and 'breaks' in the visible surface: in his mystical epiphanies they are apprehended as 'flickers' of the very metaphysical boundary between the two worlds (see Fig. 4.4). On Favorskii's cover, the black square with the mirror image of the letter *i* depicted on it could correspond to those kinds of black caves and holes, indicating that, in the virtual world, phenomena and objects are just as they are in the real world, but simply 'turned inside out' – in other words, represented inversely.

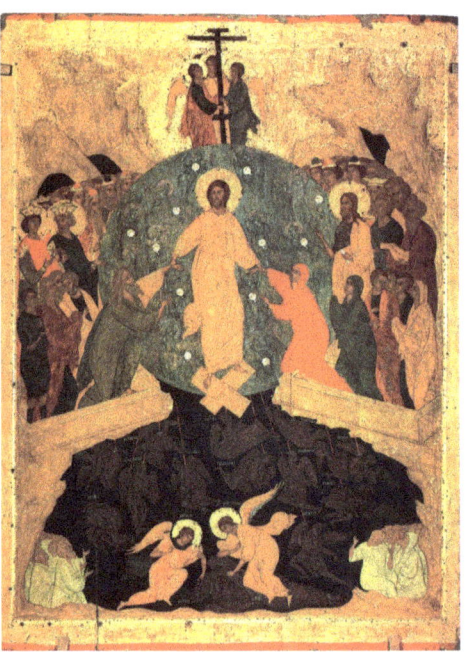

Fig. 4.4 Dionysius and workshop, *The Resurrection of Christ* (c. 1502), tempera on wood, 137.2 x 99.5 cm. State Russian Museum, St Petersburg. Wikimedia, public domain, https://commons.wikimedia.org/wiki/File:Descent_into_Hell_by_Dionisius_and_workshop_(Ferapontov_monastery).jpg

In short, it is entirely possible that Florenskii's presentation of the icon, as set out in its final version specifically in *The Imaginary in Geometry*, provided a sort of mathematical basis for the indivisibility of the real and the noumenal worlds. The Byzantine tradition of the theology of the icon was here developed not only within a context of contemporary theology and aesthetic theory, but of new advances in mathematical theory. Florenskii's diligent study of the classics of religious mysticism (above all, Plato (428/27–348 BC), Pythagoras (c. 570–495 BC) and Plotinus (c. 204/5–70 AD)) in the 1910s brought to his interpretation of reverse perspective the enthusiasm for other 'ways of knowing', embraced my mystics, and provided yet another key to decode the symbolic language of medieval art.

Investigating the Term

Medieval scholars fully understood that human beings always view things in perspective: the eye cannot see objects from different sides. However, perception of the divinely established nature of things was more important in the Middle Ages. God is present everywhere. He knows how the universe is ordered. When the medieval artist wished to create in the icon an ideal world not governed by earthly laws, he used, therefore, the so-called *perspectiva artificialis* [painterly or artificial perspective], which had forgotten about the geometry of Euclid and the spherical nature of the optical field. This allowed him to summarize different points of view in space, that is, to convey a visual impression of looking at an object from different sides. However, God is present from time immemorial. He not only sees everything, but also knows everything. This necessitated depicting events in different time dimensions. Their strict sequentiality had no significance: they were depicted and united exclusively from the perspective of eternity and the 'end times'. This spatial-temporal synthesis of different points of view (that is, the gaze of divine omnipresence) also represented a fundamental moment in the establishment of reverse perspective. Lacking any subjectivism, this perspective already appeared in Antique pictorial systems, but it entered the canon and acquired its most perfect shape in Byzantine painting.

Reverse perspective showed the phenomena and objects of the invisible world in another, 'reverse' dimension, only faintly reminiscent of their outward appearance in the reality that surrounds us. Renaissance (linear) perspective, however, served to depict the visible and earthly world, and presented an image of the reality around us for contemplation, the so-called 'retinal image' reflected (and distorted) in the spherical surface of our eye.[209] The contrast between these two perspectives reflected two opposing ways of viewing and ordering the world. A religious point of view always presupposes knowledge of how the world is ordered. Since, in the Middle Ages, that universe was perceived as divinely ordained, the medieval icon painter also depicted the world in the way that God saw it. This differed from the Renaissance artist's view, where the artist made his own gaze the centre of the entire visible universe. Reverse perspective, therefore, assumed the divine point of view, while the Renaissance perspective assigned human perception the primary role.

Oskar Wulff's (1864–1946) German-language article dedicated to reverse perspective appeared in 1907.[210] It has long been thought that Wulff himself introduced the term *die umgekehrte Perspektive* [reverse, or 'inverse', perspective] into academic circulation.[211] However, this term had already appeared in a dissertation by the Russian scholar Dmitrii Ainalov (1862–1939), *Ellinisticheskie osnovy vyzantiiskogo iskusstva* [*The Hellenistic Foundations of Byzantine Art*] (1900). Ainalov's dissertation was examined by his friend Wulff, who shared his views. A future protégée of Nikodim Kondakov (1844–1925), the founder of Byzantine Studies in Russia, Ainalov wrote and defended his dissertation at St Petersburg

---

209 See J. Frisby and J. V. Stone, *Seeing. The Computation Approach to Biological Vision* (Cambridge, MA: The MIT Press, 2010). On linear perspective, see also M. Kemp, *The Science of Art: Optical Themes in Western Art from Brunelleschi to Seurat* (New Haven, CT: Yale University Press, 1992).

210 O. Wulff, 'Die umgekehrte Perspektive und die Niedersicht. Eine raumanschauungsform der altbyzantinischen Kunst und ihre Fortbildung in der Renaissance', *Kunstwissenschaftliche Beiträge, August Schmarsow gewidmet zum fünfzigsten Semester seiner akademischen Lehrtätigkeit*, ed. H. Weizsäcker (Leipzig: K. Hiersemann, 1907), pp. 3–42, https://archive.org/details/bub_gb_oJjpAAAAMAAJ

211 See, for example, C. Antonova, 'On the Problem of "Reverse Perspective": Definition East and West', *Leonardo*, 43.5 (2010), 464–69 (pp. 464, 468). Nicolletta Misler, for example, suggests that Florenskii appropriated the term 'reverse perspective' directly from Wulff. She demonstrates that although Florenskii does not cite Wulff, he uses the very same examples from the history of reverse perspective that Wulff does, in particular Raphael's *Ezekiel's Vision* and Michelangelo's *The Last Judgement* (see P. A. Florenskii, *Beyond Vision. Essays on the Perception of Art*, ed. N. Misler, trans. W. Salmond (London: Reaktion, 2002), p. 199). However, it is entirely possible that Florenskii knew of the existence of this term from other works.

University. Wulff maintained the closest links with this academic community. Demonstrating that reverse perspective developed in the first- and second-century art of Syria and Persia, and from there spread to Byzantine art, Ainalov noted in his conclusion that

> *one discerns a reverse perspective* in depictions of figures, buildings, various architectural shapes; knowledge of foreshortening is lost, reliefs become flat [...] All these changes comprise the distinguishing features present in later Byzantine artworks of the so-called mature style. One must credit their appearance to the art of Syria and Persia. *Reverse perspective*, archaic figures, flat reliefs indicate the transfer of eastern artistic techniques into the sphere of Antique art. In the east, foreshortening, *correct perspective* and high relief were unknown.[212]

As can be seen, Ainalov gives no definition of reverse perspective, and refers to it as if it is already common knowledge.[213] Reverse perspective suggests that objects are depicted in reverse order from 'one-point perspective', in other words that the objects get bigger rather than smaller the further away they are. This gives us grounds to argue that the term 'reverse perspective' was in circulation before 1900, and that Ainalov and Wulff were well acquainted with it. One could say the same of both Florenskii and Muratov. Thus, during discussion of the

---

212 D. V. Ainalov, *Ellinisticheskie osnovy vyzantiiskogo iskusstva* (St Petersburg: n.p., 1900), p. 219 (my emphasis). See the English edition, D. V. Ainalov, *The Hellenistic Origins of Byzantine Art*, ed. C. Mango, trans. E. Sobolevitch and S. Sobolevitch (New Brunswick, NJ: Rutgers University Press, 1961).

213 This suggests that the term 'reverse perspective' may be a translation from a foreign language – most likely German. This, incidentally, calls into question Kurt Nyberg's conjecture (and that of Charles Lock, who followed him) that the term 'reverse perspective' was the invention of Ainalov, and the German term *die umgekehrte Perspektive*, used by Wulff, is a direct translation from the Russian. Wulff clearly used the term 'reverse perspective' alongside other conventional terms of the time – 'spatial perspective', 'linear perspective', 'central perspective' – using these to characterize Byzantine art of the ninth to the eleventh century, and the 'Greek' manner of early Italian artists. He also mentions a 'bird's-eye' view in characterizing ancient Assyrian images. Moreover, nowhere does he discuss Ainalov's antecedence in the creation of the term 'reverse perspective', and he only cites him in discussions of eastern influence on Byzantine art (see Wulff, 'Die umgekehrte Perspektive und die Niedersicht', fn. 35). Cf. K. W. Nyberg, *Omvänt perspektiv i bildkonst och kontrovers: En kritisk begreppshistoria från det gångna seklet* (Uppsala: Uppsala Universitet, 2001); C. Lock, 'What is Reverse Perspective and Who Was Oskar Wulff?', *Sobornost/Eastern Christian Review*, 33.1 (2011), 60–89. See also O. Tarasov, 'Florensky and "Reverse Perspective": Investigating the History of a Term', *Sobornost/Eastern Churches Review*, 43.1 (2021), 7–37.

abovementioned 'Reverse Perspective' paper that Florenskii delivered on 29 October 1920 at a meeting of the Byzantine section of the Moscow Institute of Art Historical Research, Muratov noted: 'Elements of reverse perspective are also found in antiquity. Reverse perspective moved from the Hellenistic world to the Byzantines'.[214] This observation suggests that Muratov was familiar with the term 'reverse perspective' from Ainalov's book, amongst others, which he drew on (as demonstrated above) for the characterization of Byzantine art's 'Hellenistic foundations'.

Wulff's article provided a groundbreaking explanation of the construction of medieval images. Instead of attributing it to a failure to create correct linear perspective (as had been suggested earlier), the article portrayed it as an elaborated system designed to reflect the worldview of the era. Wulff suggested that the forms of reverse perspective are predicated upon an *internal* viewpoint; in other words, the icon is drawn from the point of view of an internal observer, as it were. Moreover, the 'bird's-eye' view was also important for him, as seen in the title of his article 'Die umgekehrte Perspektive und die Niedersicht' ['Reverse Perspective and Bird's-Eye View'].[215]

---

214 See 'Kratkaia zapis' obsuzhdenii doklada P. A. Florenskogo "Ob obratnoi perspektive", prochitannogo v Vizantiiskoi sektsii MIKhM 29 oktiabria 1920 goda', in Florenskii, *Istoriia i filosofiia iskusstva*, p. 229.

215 Notes made by participants in the discussion of Florenskii's paper 'Reverse Perspective', delivered on 29 October 1920, suggest that Russian scholars were well aware of Wulff's article, although Florenskii himself did not refer to it. Romanov, in particular, observed: 'That which is called reverse perspective is that same linear perspective but, as Wulff said, not formed from the point of view of the main person. Reverse perspective is formed from ornamental devices and the artist's psychological-religious impressions...' (see 'Kratkaia zapis' obsuzhdenii doklada', pp. 228–29). The concept of the internal point of view in the formation of the icon was subsequently supported in the works of Boris Uspenskii, in particular. The position of the artist-observer within the picture ('divine perspective') was convincingly demonstrated by the semantics of 'right' and 'left' in the icon painter's image. That which from a 'human perspective' (from the point of view of an external observer) seems to be on the left, seems from the divine point of view (the position of an internal observer, located as it were on the other side of the image) to be on the right – implying that it holds greater significance (see B. A. Uspenskii, '"Pravoe" i "levoe" v ikonopisnom izobrazhenii', in *Sbornik statei po vtorichnym modeliryiushchim sistemam*, ed. J. Lotman (Tartu: Tart. un-t, 1973), pp. 137–45). Uspenskii gives further weight to the symbolic meaning of the reference point in the construction of a picture in his analysis of the composition of Jan van Eyck's (1390–1441) *Ghent Altarpiece* (fifteenth century) (B. A. Uspenskii, *Gentskii altar' Iana van Eika. Bozhestvennaia i chelovecheskaia perspektiva* (Moscow: zdate'skii dom 'Rip-Kholding', 2013), pp. 38–40; see also the Italian translation B.

A. Uspenskii, *Prospetiva divina e prospetiva umana: La pala di van Eyk a Grand* (Milan: Mondadori Università, 2010); see also O. Tarasov, 'Retsenziia na knigu: Uspenskii B. A. *Gentskii altar' Iana van Eika. Bozhestvennaia i chelovecheskaia perspektiva.* Moscow 2013', *Toronto Slavic Quarterly*, 50 (2014), 280–91; *Voprosy iskusstvoznaniia*, 3–4 (2014), 641–49). Moreover, Uspenskii was the first to clearly distinguish the internal – in relation to the depicted space – position of the viewer (the artist is situated in the depicted space, and is, in other words, depicting the world around himself) from the dynamic of the viewer's position inside the space depicted (which determines all sorts of ruptures and combinations). Both of these are characteristic of the pre-Renaissance system of representation, which is altogether lacking in the illusionism and subjectivism present in linear perspective. This system of representation appears most vividly and consistently in icons, but it is not confined to icon-painting. As we have already observed in the Introduction, Uspenskii was also the first to publish the text of Florenskii's 'Reverse Perspective' article, which was discovered in one of the Moscow collections. The article appeared in 1967 in *Trudy po znakomym sistemam*. My work on later Russian icon-painting of the seventeenth to nineteenth centuries also reveals that changes in the system of reverse perspective were related to a change in perspectives in man's religious view of the world. Changes to the medieval canon – such as cases of reverse and linear perspective being combined, areas of landscape widening and incorporating elements of the real world, and also the appearance of all sorts of poetic texts in Baroque-era icons – testified to the increasing significance of personal piety and the value of earthly actions in the economy of salvation. Concrete historical facts may also be explained by the combination of reverse and linear perspectives (in the eighteenth-century Russian icon *Procopius of Ustiug, Fool for Christ*, for example, elements of Western European landscape introduced into the system of representation narrate St Procopius's arrival in Rus from the West). In other words, the very nature of the changes to the medieval canon proves that the medieval icon was composed from an internal (divine) point of view. In the modern era, these changes were by no means connected to changes in the psychology of perception (human eyes, as before, continued to see the world via the system of *perspectiva naturalis*), but were dependent upon changes in the system of piety and articles of faith. The coexistence of old ritualist icons (created in accordance with the medieval canon) and new-rite religious images aligned with the new rules of church life in Russian culture testifies to this. These new rules were firmly established from the mid-seventeenth century and impacted the artistic system of the Russian icon itself, as well as impacting the system of supervision over icon-painting, and the manufacture and trade in icons. My monograph *Icon and Devotion* was the first to apply the approach of cultural studies to researching Russian icon-painting of the seventeenth to the nineteenth century. As we know, the semiotics of the icon directs our focus towards the symbolic language of reverse perspective as an exclusive system. It emphasizes the detection of internal, regular patterns which relate to the inherent rules of this language (B. A. Uspenskii, *Semiotics of the Russian Icon* (Lisse: Peter de Ridder Press, 1976), https://archive.org/details/semioticsofrussi0000uspe). Cultural studies of the icon (also using semiotic approaches) are already scrutinizing changes in the system of reverse perspective influenced by other cultural phenomena – paintings, religious engravings, popular devotional literature and so forth. Cultural studies of the icon also draw on the sociology of art and the anthropology of religion, and this approach allows the distinctive characteristics

In a 1924 essay entitled 'Perspektive als symbolische Form' ['Perspective as Symbolic Form'], Erwin Panofsky (1892–1968) criticized Wulff's position on the internal point of view in the construction of the medieval image without reference to reverse perspective as such. He characterized perspective, as a whole, as a projection on the *spherical* surface of the visual field, and explained changes in this system via historical conceptions of space. Panofsky influenced many working on perspective in the twentieth century, and, of course, he himself was influenced by the neo-Kantian ideas of Ernst Cassirer (1874–1945), who understood the graphic form as a symbol incorporating spiritual and sensible principles into a unified entity.[216] Defining perspective as a symbolic form, therefore, Panofsky analyzed the philosophical

---

of collective religious experience to be discerned in later icons (O. Tarasov, *Icon and Devotion. Sacred Spaces in Imperial Russia*, trans. R. Milner-Gulland (London: Reaktion, 2002)). Conceiving of the internal viewpoint as the 'gaze of God' prompted stern criticism from Soviet historians, especially in the works of the academic and mathematician Boris V. Rauschenbach (1915–2001). Rauschenbach suggested that reverse perspective should be understood as a graphic plan for conveying objective information ('objective perspective'). 'The concept of "a point of view" or of "multiple points of view"', he wrote, 'is, as a rule, meaningless, if the geometry of objective space is being depicted' (B. V. Rauschenbach, *Prostranstvennye postroeniia v zhivopisi. Ocherk osnovnykh metodov* (Moscow: Nauka, 1980), pp. 3, 19–20, 32; cf. B. A. Uspenskii, 'O semiotike ikony', *Trudy po znakovym sistemam*, 5 (1971), 178–222 (pp. 197–98)). The space in medieval Russian icons may thus be interpreted as 'a real perception of space', moreover, 'as far as is possible, undistorted'. In other words, Rauschenbach's construct related to the specificities of the psychology of visual perception, not to the particularities of a religious view of the world. The Soviet academic attempted to prove, via mathematical calculations, that medieval Russian icon painters had 'intuitively' discovered the laws governing the artistic space of the icon, thereby anticipating the individual postulates of Lobachevskian geometry (see B. V. Rauschenbach, *Prostranstvennye postroeniia v drevnerusskoi zhivopisi* (Moscow: Nauka, 1975)). Cf. C. Antonova, *Space, Time and Presence in the Icon: Seeing the World with the Eyes of God* (Farnham: Ashgate, 2010), pp. 29–62.

216 On the influence of neo-Kantianism in the academic work of Panofsky, see S. Ferretti, *Cassirer, Panofsky and Warburg: Symbol, Art and History* (New Haven, CT: Yale University Press, 1989); M. Holly, *Panofsky and the Foundation of Art History* (Ithaca, NY: Cornell University Press, 1984), pp. 114–57. In western historiography, of course, the concept of 'reverse perspective' has not been addressed in systematic fashion; even major works have passed over it (see, for example, J. White, *The Birth and Rebirth of Pictorial Space* (London: Faber and Faber, 1957)). In short, western audiences first encountered Florenskii's notion of reverse perspective via Uspenskii's book in English (Uspenskii, *Semiotics of the Russian Icon*). Florenskii's article 'Reverse Perspective' was published in Italian translation, with commentary by N. Misler, by Casa del libro (Rome) in 1983 (*La prospettiva rovesciata e altri*) and in English by the London publisher Reaktion Books in 2002 (*Beyond Vision*).

theories and metaphysics of light in pagan and Christian Neoplatonism, which lead him to a deeper understanding of the meaning of the Renaissance painting. In Antiquity, theoreticians did not perceive space as a relationship between height, width and depth. Their emphasis was not on representing space in a system of coordinates, but rather on portraying the object itself. The world was perceived as *discrete* and devoid of continuity. Moving into the medieval period, according to Panofsky, the artistic space within medieval images continued to be characterized by a 'closed interior' and a 'closed window', with figures and objects in medieval depictions appearing necessarily as if glued onto a bare wall. Panofsky argued that artists learnt to order space as a whole only in the Renaissance era. In comparison with space in medieval images, therefore, the space of a Renaissance painting is uniform (homogenous) and measurable. It displays the capacity to stretch on forever and appears inseparably connected with bodies and objects. Space was now understood as a system in which height, width and depth relate to each other, and, accordingly, the world in Renaissance art also seemed measurable. Moreover, according to Panofsky, such an understanding of space was already developing in the Gothic era, evidenced by the Naumburg Cathedral relief depicting the Last Supper (c. 1240–42). The deep arches framing the scene create a deep spatial zone, as it were, carved into the wall, reminiscent of a theatre stage; the relief reveals an effort to unify the figures with the environment they inhabit. The view through the window, which had been closed since Antiquity, was once again opened and the picture became 'a segment carved from endless space'. Panofsky also identified the significance of the painting revolution instigated by Giotto (c. 1267–1337) in the artist's groundbreaking re-evaluation of the picture plane. Henceforth, the picture was no longer perceived as a 'wall' or 'board', as non-existent forms of unconnected figures and things. Its surface took on the nature of transparent glass. Revealing the influence of Cassirer's understanding that our perception is always limited, Panofsky underlined the functional nature of linear perspective: a Renaissance picture only ever reflected a system of geometric calculations, not reality itself.[217] At the same time, considering the history of the origin of the *artistic idea* over centuries and

---

217 E. Panofsky, *Perspective as Symbolic Form*, trans. C. S. Wood (New York: Zone Books, 1997), pp. 30, 43, 51, 53–56, fig. 6.

agreeing that this idea is found (as an artistic design) only in the soul of the artist, Panofsky was essentially defending Renaissance aesthetics and Western European anthropocentrism. His criticism of the concept of the internal point of view advanced by Wulff also testifies to this.

In contrast to Wulff and Panofsky, Florenskii firstly explained reverse perspective as a *synthesis* of different points of view. Secondly, he established the *metaphysical* meaning of this perspective. Thirdly, he revealed its inseparable links with the distinct features of *Orthodox ritual*. According to Florenskii (who was following the dogma of icon veneration and developing the Byzantine tradition of the theology of the image), the artistic idea belongs to God; it is transcendental and bestowed through revelation. Consequently, his view of the artistic space of the medieval icon was grounded in *non-Euclidian geometry*, and he conceptualized it as a 'living organism' – he envisioned artistic space not merely an artistic representation, but as 'a window' and 'a door' through which Christ himself is manifested in the world.

Considering the composition of a Byzantine or medieval Russian icon in more concrete terms, Florenskii explained reverse perspective as a special construction of the world of angels and saints, which appears before the viewer through the *mobile gaze* of the artist projected onto a flat surface. A *synthesis of points of view* is thus created in the composition of the drawing, and the viewer can see objects represented on the icon from different sides: 'As the closest arrangement of devices of reverse perspective', Florenskii wrote,

> we should note the multicentredness in images: a drawing is composed as if the eye looked at various parts of it from different vantage points. Here single parts of a chamber, for example, are drawn more or less in accord with the demands of ordinary linear perspective, but each one from its own special point of view, in other words from its *special* centre of perspective; and occasionally also with its own special horizon, and other parts, moreover, are depicted also using reverse perspective. This complex elaboration of perspectival foreshortenings is found not only in the depiction of architecture [*palatnoe pis'mo*], but also in countenances...[218]

As a result of this dynamic gaze, the icon is perceived as an exclusive space composed of separate fragments, in which now a *roundedness* of form arises, now a representation of *supplementary planes* appears, now all sorts of *distortions* of space and 'errors' in draftsmanship stand out

---

218 Florenskii, *Istoriia i filosofiia iskusstva*, p. 482.

sharply. It is also due to these 'errors' that the 'wonderful expressiveness' – to quote Florenskii – of the iconic image is achieved. He demonstrated this via the example of the sixteenth-century *Spas Vsederzhitel'* [*Christ Pantocrator*] from the sacristy of the Trinity Lavra of St Sergius.[219] In other words, the icon appears to us as an image of Christ himself and of the heavenly world in its ontology; whilst linear perspective such as that used by Antonello da Messina (c. 1425/30–79) to construct his well-known painting *Christ Blessing* (c. 1465, The National Gallery, London), presents us with an individual, *concrete image* of the God-man. The Renaissance painting is *part of the world*, a geometric 'cut out' from the surrounding reality, since the composition of its picture space proposes only an external point of view and the illusion of looking through a window. And if linear (Renaissance) perspective created a correlation between bodies and objects in the space of the painting and revealed the world in its details, then reverse perspective – owing to its multiplicity of points of view – creates the world in its integrity.

Likewise, Florenskii demonstrated that linear perspective allotted to the viewer the role of a merely passive observer: he could occupy only one fixed place in the given moment in time. Reverse perspective – which, in the construction of the icon, presupposed a mobile gaze – already implied an *active* viewer. The space created by reverse perspective (the magnification of objects with distance) was oriented precisely on the viewer, since, from any perspective, the vanishing point of the optical rays falls upon the one standing before the icon. The invention of the icon as a cult image in Byzantium, therefore, may also have facilitated a profound experience for the person praying before it – an experience involving physical actions such as approaching the icon, making the sign of the cross and bowing before it, kissing and decorating it. We may cautiously suppose that Florenskii discovered the 'mobile gaze' in the construction of the icon not only within the theoretical frameworks of the philosophy of mathematics, Modernist aesthetics and theology, but also within the context of his personal religious experience, during his participation as a priest in liturgical life and his experience of long church services held before icons. A mystical perception of early icons could also be a significant factor here.[220]

---

219 Florenskii, 'Obratnaia perspektiva', pp. 183–84, 225.
220 Florenskii's thesis on the internal and mobile position of the artist-observer in the construction of the icon found support in the 1920s and 1930s in the works

of Zhegin and Nikolai Tarabukin (1889–1956), an art historian and member of the State Academy of Artistic Sciences (GAKhN). Moreover, Zhegin provided detailed evidence for the dynamics of the observer's position, in particular, which stood out most clearly to him in the composition of the icon's landscape (the hills of the icon) with its distorted horizon. Influenced by Florenskii, Zhegin also paid attention to 'ruptures' in the lines of the icon's drawing overall, as a result of which he drew conclusions about the various types of *dislocation, fracture* and *distortion* in the icon's space (see L. F. Zhegin, *Iazykh zhivopisnogo proizvedeniia (Uslovnost' drevnego iskusstva). Predislovie i kommentarii B. A. Uspenskogo* (Moscow: Iskusstvo, 1970), p. 29). Florenskii's notion of Greco-Roman landscape painting was apparently based on detailed research by Mikhail Rostovtsev (1870–1952) (see M. Rostovtsev, *Ellinistichesko-rimskii arkhitekturnyi peizazh* (St Petersburg: n.p., 1908)), testified to by the extensive citation of this book in Florenskii's article 'Reverse Perspective'. Florenskii's views were entirely shared by Tarabukin. The first version of Tarabukin's 'Philosophy of the Icon' was written in 1916 and he continued working on it right up until the mid-1930s. The author gave a brief, condensed definition of reverse perspective, explained the dynamic position of the internal viewer and the characteristics of the medieval worldview, and also discussed new methodological approaches to the study of the icon. 'Reverse perspective', he wrote, 'is a depiction of space beyond the bounds of the visible world and represented in a way other than (that is, inverse to) the usual mode for the here-and-now. Reverse perspective is a visual representation of a notion of the "other world"'. Florenskii's ideas were most clearly evinced in Tarabukin's conception of the medieval icon's picture space: 'The icon painter does not think in Euclidean terms', Tarabukin noted, 'he rejects perspective as a form expressing infinite space. The world of icon-painting is finite. Instead of the fathomless azure "heavens", there is a golden background, which symbolizes that the events contemplated in the icon are taking place beyond the fixed limits of earthly time and space, and are depicted *sub specie aeternitatis* [under the aspect of eternity]. If one perceives it from the perspective of the viewer, too, the space of the icon is imagined as finite because, unfolding in so-called "reverse perspective", it must end somewhere beyond the frame of the icon, in the viewer's eyes [...] In icon-painting, space is finite and dynamic, endowed with multiple horizons and *multiple points of view, which is possible only with a rotating orientation* in similar space and subject to there being several moments in time combined into one. Hence the spatial and temporal "dislocations" in icon-painting, the multilocality and multi-temporality of the illustration of events in the unity of their unifying super-spatial (in the sense of locus) and super-temporal (in the sense of pragmatic) meaning' (my emphasis). The icon's connection with religious experience and the medieval worldview are especially emphasized in grasping its deep meaning: 'One may and even should talk about the aesthetics of the icon, but this is an insignificant element of the innermost content of the icon's challenge as a whole [...] and the whole is the religious meaning of the icon'. At the same time, the author emphasized that the icon 'constitutes a visually expressed representation of the medieval conception of the world, and its images vividly articulate the most complex religio-philosophical and cosmological ideas' (N. M. Tarabukin, *Smysl ikony* (Moscow: Pravoslavnogo bratstva Sviatitelia Filareta, 1999), pp. 128, 124, 82, 130). In contrast to Florenskii, Zhegin and Tarabukin, Bakushinskii did not connect reverse perspective with a religious view of the world, explaining it via the laws of the psychology of perception and, above all, via binocular vision. According to his conception, reverse perspective is achieved as a result of the

The synthesis of points of view in the creation of the iconic image is especially visible in the depiction of architecture and various types of objects. Florenskii's archive in Moscow contains an exercise book entitled 'Reverse Perspective and the Like. Materials and Comparisons. Moscow 1921'. In the drawings and their accompanying inscriptions (which Florenskii may also have done for his lectures in VKhUTEMAS), spread across the unlined pages, we find a heightened focus on the internal position of the artist-observer, and also on the geometry of architecture, holy books and ecclesiastical furniture. We may cautiously suppose that Florenskii made these sketches not only to demonstrate the meaning of reverse perspective's foreshortenings but also to understand and feel the very metaphysics of the construction of early icons.

His sketch of an Assyrian depiction of a camp is especially interesting, specifically representing – I would argue – an internal point of view, one that is moving around a circle (see Fig. 4.5). In this regard, Florenskii indicated that the sketch was 'very important' for the theory and history of perspective.

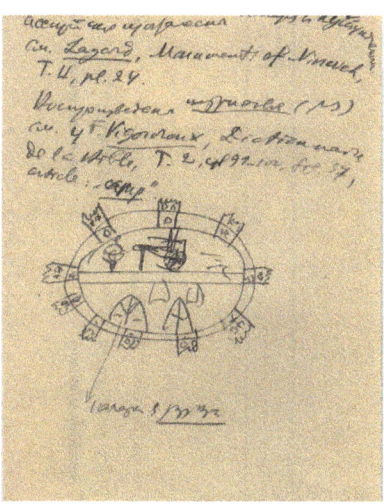

Fig. 4.5 Pavel Florenskii (1882–1937), drawing with the caption 'The Assyrian depiction of a camp is very important for the theory and history of perspective', pencil on paper. Archive of Florenskii's family, Moscow. Printed with the permission of the heirs. All rights reserved.

---

overlapping of two reflections of reality, since each eye sees the world ordered in linear perspective. In essence, Bakushinskii's theory was a defence of linear perspective and Renaissance-era anthropocentrism with its 'solely correct' point of view (see Bakushinskii, 'Linear perspektiva').

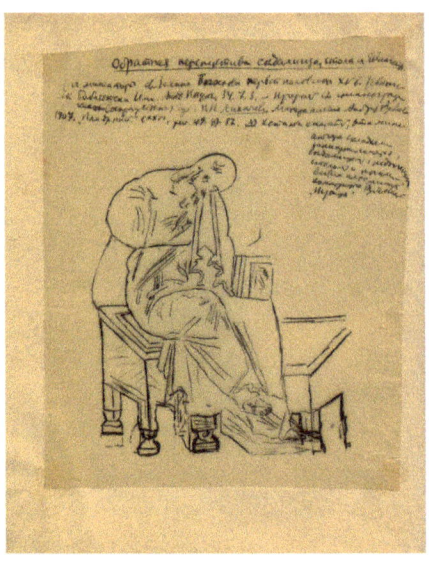

Fig. 4.6 Pavel Florenskii (1882–1937), drawing with the caption 'Reverse perspective of sedilia [clergy seating], table and Gospel, from a miniature of St John the Theologian [from the] first half of the fifteenth century', pencil on paper. Archive of Florenskii's family, Moscow. Printed with the permission of the heirs. All rights reserved.

In copying a miniature of John the Theologian from the first half of the fifteenth century (reproduced in Nikolai Likhachev's (1862–1936) *Manera pis'ma Andreia Rubleva* [*Andrei Rublev's Style of Painting*], published in 1907 in St Petersburg), the philosopher primarily focused on the composition of the *clergy stalls*, *table* and *Gospel* (see Fig. 4.6). Moreover, the special symbolic weight of the Gospels, as the artistic centre of the icon, was highlighted. Holy books are almost always magnified and turned towards the viewer in icons.[221] As a result of the mobile gaze of the internal observer, in the drawing of the Gospel there are additional planes while the figure of the apostle himself is depicted in unusually rounded fashion. Florenskii also detected correspondences with Rublev's *Trinity*, a copy of which – we may recall – was constantly before the philosopher's gaze. Florenskii's caption on this very sketch testifies to this: 'By the way, the folds of the draped himatia, the clergy stall, the pedestal, the table and legs in this miniature are strongly reminiscent of the composition of Rublev's *Trinity*'. In turn, one may

---

221 Florenskii, 'Obratnaia perspektiva', pp. 182–83.

observe that the way the architecture is depicted in Rublev's icon also suggests a view from several positions (a mobile gaze), as a result of which we find additional planes and niches, which transform the architectural background into a clear, graphic symbol, striving to fuse with the Bible story's meaning.

Florenskii examined how depictions of architecture are directly connected with worldview using the example of the drawing of St Melania of Rome in the Vatican Library's Menologion (MS Vat. gr. 1613, compiled c. 1000) in particular, and also through Giotto's work. A 'contradictoriness' of points of view was observed in the composition of the Menologion's drawings of walls and the pedestals of columns. Giotto's perspectival constructions, according to Florenskii, signified the start of a new era. He detected in them the beginnings of linear perspective and the imitation of nature, and even called Giotto 'the father of contemporary landscape painting', citing Giorgio Vasari (1511–74) in support. Giotto's innovations are especially clear in the frescos of the Upper Church of St Francis of Assisi, in which complex perspectival challenges are set: their retreating parallels converge at one point on the horizon, in which the beginnings of illusory decoration may also be discerned. Florenskii suggested that the artist may have found these examples of 'trompe l'oeil' precisely in the scenery of medieval *mystery plays* with their flat, side-scene houses and pavilions.[222] Much as Dante (c. 1265–1321) and Petrarch (1304–74) introduced the language of the common people into poetry, Giotto drew inspiration from applied and vernacular artistic culture.

In lectures analyzing spatial-temporal relationships in painting, Florenskii used the example of the icon-type *Sv. Ioann Bogoslov I uchenik Prokhor na ostrove Patmos* [St John the Theologian with his Disciple Prochoros on the Island of Patmos] to observe the mobile gaze and synthesis of points of view as a special artistic device. The viewer sees both the spine and chest simultaneously in the depiction of the figure of Prochoros. His face is turned towards both the Evangelist and the

---

222 Ibid., p. 197. Here, Florenskii follows a long tradition of attributing the Franciscan cycle of frescos in the Upper Church of St Francis of Assisi to Giotto. It should be noted that Giotto's authorship has been questioned in contemporary scholarship, and these frescos are now attributed to 'Giotto and his workshop' (see A. Smart, *The Assisi Problem and the Art of Giotto: A Study of the 'Legend of St. Francis' in the Upper Church of San Francesco, Assisi* (Oxford: Clarendon Press, 1971)).

viewer. Ideally, such 'anatomical contradictions' are able to reflect the main idea of the icon – that of Prochoros' mediation between the Evangelist and the text of the Gospel. This is convincingly illustrated by an icon from Ilya Ostroukhov's (1858–1929) former collection (c. 1500, Tretyakov Gallery, Moscow), in which the figure of John the Theologian is depicted appealing to the heavens in such a way as to convince the viewer of the divine revelation of his Book. The stooping figure of Prochoros tells of this humble and modest disciple's service. 'The meaning of the figure of Prochoros', Florenskii noted, 'is specifically in his mediation, in his service as an instrument, and therefore the movement *towards* the Evangelist and *towards* the paper are both entirely necessary in order to convey the significance of this figure through the medium of graphic art'. Moreover, Florenskii uses the concept of 'artistic perception' (sometimes called 'synthesizing vision'), through which a visual synthesis is accomplished, removing anatomical contradictions in the drawing of a figure. It is precisely this visual synthesis which allows the artistic and theological meaning of the medieval icon to be discerned.

Florenskii detected similar compositional devices in the Deesis tier of the Russian iconostasis. The upper part of the figures of the apostles was often depicted turned towards the central figure of Christ, while the lower part of the same figures might be turned towards the viewer. (A typical example of this is the Deesis tier of the iconostasis of the Trinity Cathedral of the Trinity Lavra of St Sergius.) By this composition, the medieval artist conveyed a spiritual movement towards Christ, as a journey towards the centre, rather than as a mere mechanical movement through space: 'The movement of those coming to the Saviour is a spiritual one, not a mechanical displacement in space, and the merging of their verticals with the first principle has nothing in common with a rejection of physical impenetrability of bodies'. Through these 'anatomical contradictions' of reverse perspective and through the vertical, rhythmical repetitions, the Almighty is perceived not as an emperor among his subordinates but precisely as the 'axis of the world', showing the believer 'the possibility of being sanctified and made straight by the Divine Logos'.[223]

---

223 P. A. Florenskii, 'Analiz prostranstvennosti i vremeni v khudozhestvenno-izobrazitel'nykh proizvedeniiakh', in Florenskii, *Istoriia i filosofiia iskusstva*, pp.

At first glance, Florenskii's 'synthesizing vision', which explains all these perspectival contradictions, bears a resemblance to the concept of 'unmediated perception' discussed by representatives of the German Formalist School, which – we may recall – regarded such perception as inherently 'objective'. However, in the thinking of both pioneers of the formal study of art (Heinrich Wölfflin (1864–1945)) and the new generation of art critics (Berenson, Muratov), 'intelligent vision' was supposed to reveal the uniqueness of an artwork's artistic form. For Florenskii, 'synthesizing vision' was devoted to recognizing the metaphysics of the object contemplated.

The synthesis of points of view in time and space stands out especially clearly in the case of *hagiographical* (or *vita*) *icons*. Florenskii was one of the first to pay attention to the significance of the pictorial frame, with scenes from the *vita* of the saint, in shaping the unique spatial and temporal organization of the hagiographical icon. According to Florenskii, the margins of the icon form that boundary which also makes the depiction conventional. The devices of reverse perspective here accord with the specificities of the icon's frame.[224] Due to its margins and indentation in the board (the ark, which recalls the classical niche in a wall), the icon 'is a special world enclosed within itself in the limits of the frame'. Moreover, the frame of a *vita* icon constitutes not only the margins and the 'ark', but also the pictorial setting of the figure of the saint represented in the centre. In this sense, the pictorial frame acquired additional significance, since, on the one hand, the scenes depicting historical episodes from the life of the saint were closely connected with the real world (historical time), and, on the other hand, were related to the sacred time of the centrepiece (the 'end times'). *Time* is thus understood as the most important organizational principle of the *vita* icon's artistic space, imparting a hidden theological dimension to it: taken as a whole, the entire construct clearly answers to the *two natures* of Christ (divine and human) and was intended to represent events in the real life of a person as the successive changes in their spiritual condition on the road to sanctity.

237–520 (pp. 358–59).
224 For further detail on the icon's frame, see O. Tarasov, *Framing Russian Art: From Early Icons to Malevich*, trans. R. Milner-Gulland and A. Wood (London: Reaktion, 2011), pp. 27–29.

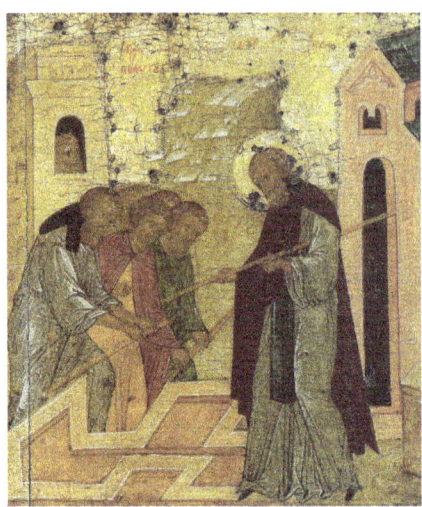

Fig. 4.7 Dionysius (1444–1502) and workshop, *The Miraculous Building of the Church*, detail from the hagiographical icon of *St Dimitrii Prilutskii* (c. 1503), tempera on wood. Vologda State Museum-Reserve. Wikimedia, public domain, https://commons.wikimedia.org/wiki/File:Dimitry_Prilutsky_Icon_stamp_15.jpg

Thus, historical time is arranged in the panels on the frame – scenes of the saint's birth, their ascetic feats, miracles and also their death and burial as moments of transition from this world to the next (see Fig. 4.7). As a rule, a frontal portrait of the saint was placed in the centre. Here, the time of their actual historical life led to their perfection, and the saint, crossing the frontier, finds themselves in a different dimension – one they have already visited, but not inhabited. And if the central representation of the saint enabled prayerful and metaphysical contact with the viewer, then the surrounding panels were meant for sequential reading and scrutiny, reminiscent of illustrations and approximating frescos and miniatures in illuminated manuscripts.

We encounter a frontal image of the saint in the centre of the earliest surviving *vita* icon of St Sergius of Radonezh (end of the fifteenth century), from the iconostasis of the Trinity Cathedral in the Trinity Lavra of St Sergius. (The icon is located in the low row on the left.) The frame incorporates eighteen episodes from his former, historical life, selected for their significance in terms of experience and repetition in the present, as 'models' for the acquisition of sanctity; for example, the birth of the infant saint, his monastic tonsure, the founding of the Trinity

Lavra of St Sergius monastery, his receiving of the cenobitic Rule from the Ecumenical Patriarch of Constantinople. In following the pattern, in other words, a person ordered their inner image according to the icon's scheme. Miracle-working scenes were especially significant for changing a person's inner nature. Thus, the panel depicting the healing of Zakhar Borozdin illustrated the tale of how St Sergius appeared in a dream to Zakhar Borozdin, a prominent Tver noble, and led him to his reliquary in the monastery. As a result of this encounter with St Sergius's relics, the sick man was cured, and woke up healthy. Through miraculous, divine intervention, a real, historical event from the life of a Tver nobleman acquired a cosmological dimension. Moreover, this event happened in a dream, which further complicates the interaction between the real and the metaphysical planes. According to Florenskii, a dream is the first step into another world, it is the 'sign' of a crossing from one sphere to another. Representing an elemental, metaphysical experience, the dream unites two worlds – the visible world, and the invisible world.[225] Thence, as a *borderline* state the *dream* reminds Florenskii of the *icon*. Positing the hypothesis of time 'turned inside out' in dreams (that is, time moving backwards), the Florenskii identified the most important moments in perceiving and reading the *vita* image.[226] When subject to the main event – the 'awakening' in other time and space – the events from the real life of the saint depicted on the frame could be picked out in random order (akin to the montage technique in cinematography). In other words, they acquire significance only in divine perspective. Therefore, the central position of the saint's portrait (their transfigured state) in the *vita* icon may serve as further evidence that reverse perspective in medieval icons was conceived as a reflection of the divine point of view.

---

225 Florenskii, 'Ikonostas', pp. 9–7. Florenskii's interest in dreams is reflected in his article 'Predely gnoseologii', *Bogoslovskii vestnik*, 1.1 (1913), 170–73. The third edition of Sigmund Freud's *Interpretation of Dreams* was published in Russian translation that very same year (*Tolkovanie snovidenii*, trans. M. Kotik (Moscow: N. A. Stollyar, 1913)). Florenskii's thinking about dreams also appears to have drawn on the work of du Prel (K. du Prel, *Filosofiia mistiki ili dvoistvennost' chelovecheskogo sushchestva*, trans. M. S. Aksenov (St Petersburg: n.p., 1895)) and on Classical authors, particularly Plutarch and Plato, who also found in dreams an analogy for death.

226 For an interesting meditation on the perception of history, dreams and the *vita* icon, see B. A. Uspenskii's article 'Istoriia i semiotika', in *Pavel Aleksandrovich Florenskii*, ed. A. N. Parshin and O. M. Sedykh (Moscow: ROSSPEN 2013), p. 207.

Meanwhile, methods of depicting the human *face* and *body* also reveal, according to Florenskii, the metaphysical qualities of the icon. The figures of St Sergius of Radonezh on the *vita* icons just discussed, or on the sixteenth-century icon *Christ Pantocrator* from the sacristy of the Trinity Lavra of St Sergius which Florenskii mentions in his research, are examples of this. The depiction of the face and its orientation are, for Florenskii, ways of perceiving the world, fixed by language in the grammatical persons: *Ya* [I], *On* [He] and *Ty* [You]. The frontal depiction of the first person (I), changes into a *lik* [countenance] that expresses the deified state of the saint. 'This ideal appearance, considered in and of itself as an object of veneration', Florenskii stressed, 'of course cannot be presented in any position [*povorot*], except straight'.[227] This same law of frontality is seen in Ancient Greek and Egyptian art, and similarly in the Buddhist tradition. The human face represented frontally always harbours magical agency. In contrast, images in profile always convey a *volevoi povorot* [volitional turn], which indicates the ancillary *function* of the person depicted within the scene. This is why saints are depicted as forward-facing on icons, while ordinary individuals are portrayed in profile. Saints, for example, are depicted facing us in the middle of a *vita* icon; figures such as magi, shepherds or servants are depicted in profile in the surrounding panels, since they fulfil a secondary function in the narrative of holy events. Another example is how the countenance of the Christ child is usually depicted frontally on *Theotokos Hodegetria* [*The Mother of God Who Shows the Way*] icons, while the countenance of the Mother of God is painted slightly *turned*, which indicates the greater sacred status of the former in relation to the latter.

By the same token, the semantically important figure was also depicted larger in relation to the less important. This can be seen in the example of the Novgorodian icon *The Divine Fatherhood* (*Paternitas*) *with Saints* (late fourteenth century, Tretyakov Gallery, Moscow), which was held in Botkin's house-museum in St Petersburg (mentioned in Chapter One) at the beginning of twentieth century. This same semantic emphasis concerns the *objects* and *gestures* of holy people depicted on icons. Semantically important gestures and objects, as a rule, are presented in *close-up* shots, a departure from the laws of linear

---

227 Florenskii, 'Analiz prostranstvennosti i vremeni', pp. 305–06.

perspective. This may be seen in the Archangel Gabriel's gesture of blessing in icons of the Annunciation, or images of the scroll St John of Damascus holds in medieval Russian *O Tebe raduyetsya* [*In You Rejoices*] icons, with the opening words of the hymn in honour of the Mother of God. This emphasis shows that the text of the song composed by St John of Damascus was at the very heart of the icon's composition. The same may be said of depictions of the outer clothing (the 'mantle') which the prophet Elijah leaves to his disciple Elisha on icons of the *Ognennoye vozneseniye Ilyi Proroka* [*Fiery Ascent of the Prophet Elijah*]. The materiality and the miraculous power of the 'mantle' turns it into the central device of the composition, uniting heaven and earth (see Fig. 4.8).

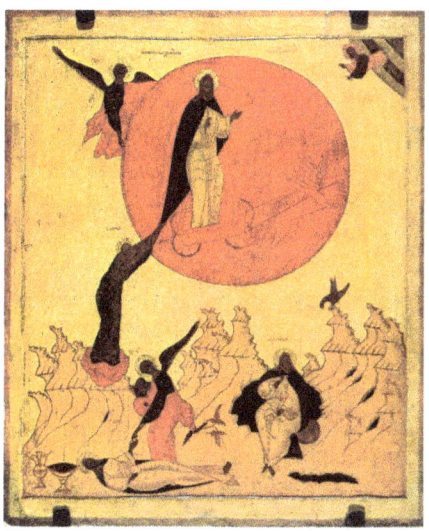

Fig. 4.8 *The Fiery Ascent of the Prophet Elijah* (sixteenth century), tempera on wood, 124 x 107 cm. State Historical Museum, Moscow. Reproduced in Mikhail Alpatov, *Early Russian Icon Painting* (Moscow: Moscow Iskusstvo, 1978), p. 86. Wikimedia, public domain,
https://commons.wikimedia.org/wiki/File:Elie_with_the_firey_wagon.jpg

Florenskii also linked the absence of *shadows* in the artistic space of the icon with the system of reverse perspective: 'The absence of a definite focus of light, the contradictory nature of illumination in different places of the icon, the effort to bring forward masses which should have been overshadowed – yet again, this is neither coincidence nor a blunder by a naive craftsman, but artistic calculation, which imparts maximum artistic expressiveness'.²²⁸ Florenskii clearly follows Plato and his symbol of the Cave in the determination of people's knowledge, since, in his works, *light* and *shade* acquire gnoseological meaning in the context of the metaphysics of reverse perspective. Platonic Ideas are 'shadows', 'the negative of things', 'intaglio experiences'; *a turn towards the light* is a transition to a new level of cognition, and symbolizes our drawing closer to the truth.²²⁹ From any viewpoint, therefore, iconic images exclude shadow; when perceiving *inscriptions*, *figures*, *architecture* and *landscape* depicted on the icon, *a turn* (which also suggests a mobile gaze) may well convey gnoseological meaning (see Fig. 4.9). The icon is a transfigured reality, which knows no shadow.

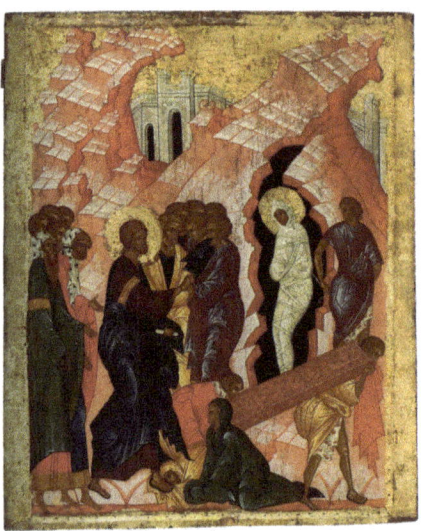

Fig. 4.9 Novgorod School, *The Raising of Lazarus* (c. 1497), tempera on wood, 71.5 x 58 cm. State Russian Museum, St Petersburg. Wikimedia, public domain, https://commons.wikimedia.org/wiki/File:Lazarus,_Russian_icon.jpg

Broaching the topic of the symbolics of *line* and *light* in the icon, Florenskii pointed out that – in contrast to the painting, where the

---

228 Florenskii, 'Obratnaia perspektiva', p. 184.
229 In Plato's Cave, people (freed from their fetters) turn towards the light and perceive the world unmediated rather than via a reflection. The turn here is understood as a transition to a new level of cognition, which may be brought about by a reflection. The historico-cultural meaning of the shadow in Western European painting is explored, in particular, in V. Stoichita, *A Short History of the Shadow* (London: Reaktion, 2018).

draftsmanship is of primary importance – it is specifically light which has most significance in an icon. The lines of the drawing are the contours of a spiritual object, a sort of enclosing of the noumenon. The golden and coloured lines of architecture and the clothes of the saints are therefore lines intensifying and directing mystical contemplation – they are understood as the sum total of the beholding eye's task. They thus reveal and refer the gaze to the space of the invisible world. (Florenskii relates lines, unlike composition, to the 'internal construction' of the icon.) However, it is light, specifically, which amplifies the influence of the general drawing of the icon on a person's spiritual sight. Light tunes the inner pitch of the religious image.

Florenskii's formulation of the question of the *anthropology of the religious image* was of particular interest in connection with the mobile gaze. Discussing the relationship between the subject and object of sight, Florenskii emphasized a person's 'psychophysiological space'; in particular, their field of vision, which is connected to the body. In his opinion, the forms of reverse perspective must not, therefore, be regarded as separate from human corporality – from that 'psychophysiological space' of religious experience which the philosopher conceives as discontinuous and finite. After all, this space is filled with sensations, and within the realm of sensations, the concept of infinity becomes nonsensical.[230] Therefore a person's very sight, as a continuation of their body, indicates to us that aesthetic analysis of the icon cannot and must not be restricted to geometrical analysis alone. The movement of the perceiving eye is also the movement of the perceiving body, its position on the vertical or horizontal plane. Specific elements of icon veneration, such as bowing, making the sign of the cross and kissing, may therefore have a direct relationship with how an icon's composition and colour are perceived. In other words, 'really, experientially perceived' space must become the starting point for analysis of the icon, rather than the 'Kantian-Euclidian' space that represents one possible abstract, intellectual formula. *Sounds, scents, sensations of warmth* and even the

---

230 Florenskii, 'Analiz prostranstvennosti i vremeni', p. 398. In elaborating the concept of psychophysiological sight, Florenskii touched on a broad range of texts, including works on the psychology of perception by Ernst Mach and Hermann von Helmholtz, citing, in particular: E. Mach, *Poznanie i zabluzhdenie. Ocherki po psikhologii issledovaniia* (Moscow: Skirmunta, 1909); E. Mach, *Analiz oshchushchenii* (Moscow: Skirmunta, 1908).

geometrical measurements of an icon – all these signify the heterogeneity of the psychophysiological space, its discontinuity and finiteness, highlighting how the icon (like any other work of art) reflects the very essence of a human being and their place in the world. Hence, aesthetic analysis of the artistic space of the icon is conceived as additional analysis of unmediated visual perception, the ultimate aim of which is to understand the inner world of the human being. Only then will the particular features of the icon's artistic language, inseparably connected with a person's psychophysiological makeup, reveal to us the particular features of the religious experience of the person who prayed before that icon.

In his detailed investigation of the artistic language of icons once belonging to Sergius of Radonezh – a fourteenth-century *Theotokos Hodegetria* icon, and the *St Nicholas* icon (first quarter of the fourteenth century, the Trinity Lavra of St Sergius Museum) – Florenskii demonstrates how an attentive reading of the artistic forms of the given icons not only helps us understand the 'nature of high art' but also grants us glimpses of the individual religious psychology of one of Russia's most famous saints. If the choice of a devotional image may be shaped by spiritual and aesthetic taste, then the nobility of the artistic form may entirely respond to the nobility of a person chosen for salvation: 'For the fourteenth-century person, the icon was a spiritual mould for their own self', Florenskii reflected,

> evidence of their inner life. In this case, the spiritual heights of St Sergius help us to understand that which was acknowledged as supreme art by the universal consciousness of humanity, in other words, namely that which corresponded precisely to the meaning of the dogma of icon veneration; and conversely, the nature of the icon-painting chosen by a great bearer of the Holy Spirit, *personally* chosen for his own devotions, in his own hermitage cell, helps us to understand the formation of his personal spirit, his inner life, those spiritual powers by which the forefather of Rus nourished his own spirit. Attention to the two cell icons of St Sergius allows us to simultaneously and deeply delve into two questions which complement and supplement each other: namely the question of the nature of great art and the question of the character of the elevated spirit – art of dogmatic importance and a spirit of historical Russian universality. These two icons are not only two monuments,

authentically testifying to an elevated spirit, but also two ideas, which have themselves directed early Russian history.[231]

Within his metaphysics of the icon, Florenskii also paid particular attention to the mystical nature of the *word* written on the icon, whether that be the name of the image, or the words of prayers or hymns in honour of the saints. Questions which he dealt with in the realm of linguistics and the theory of the symbol clearly spilled over into research of iconographical language, including the metaphysics of letters and names.[232] The name is a word, and the first line of St John's Gospel declares: 'In the beginning was the Word, and the Word was with God, and the Word was God' (John 1:1). For Florenskii, the *name of God* on an icon therefore was *God Himself*, together with the sounds and the letters. In this, Florenskii paid tribute to patristic tradition, on the one hand (in accord with the dogma of icon veneration, since the *name* icons 'are full of holiness and grace'), and, on the other, to 'name glorification [*imiaslavie*]', the Athonite mystical current which appeared in 1913 and consisted of a special veneration of the name of God.[233] Name glorifiers were convinced that in glorifying the name of God, they rendered God real. Hence, Florenskii's interest in 'naming' and its role in intuitively mystical cognition of the world determined his heightened attention

---

231 Florenskii, 'Molennye ikony prepodobnogo Sergiia', p. 147. See also the Italian edition: P. A. Florenskii, 'Icone di preghiera di san Sergio', in P. A. Florenskii, *La mistica e l'anima russa*, ed. N. Valentini and L. Zak (Milan: Edizioni San Paolo, 2006), pp. 157–88). On the basis of these observations, one may also raise the issue of the detection of distinct traits of religious psychology in the language of the popular, mass-produced icon. This type of icon, as dedicated works have demonstrated, was entirely able to retain the important meanings of various historico-cultural and religious experiences (see Tarasov, *Icon and Devotion*, p. 351; compare Vladimir Toporov's (1928–2005) observations on how icon-painting is capable of 'most precisely capturing the sphere of the ideal, and of the deepest penetration into the mystery of religious consciousness' (V. N. Toporov, 'Ob odnom arkhaichnom indoevropeiskom elemente v drevnerusskoi dukhovnoi kul'ture - *svet-', in *Iazyki kul'tury i problemy perevodimosti*, ed. B. A. Uspenskii (Moscow: Nauka, 1987), pp. 184–252 (p. 231)).
232 Florenskii also commented especially on the style of inscriptions in the aforementioned 'Explanation of the Cover' in his work *The Imaginary in Geometry* (Florenskii, *Mnimosti v geometrii*, p. 64).
233 For Florenskii, therefore, the icon as a whole is also 'the Name of God inscribed in paints' (Florenskii, 'Ikonostas', p. 31). In his work 'Imena' ['Names'] (1922–25), Florenskii revealed the spiritual significance of naming as revealing the essence of a personality and phenomenon. See also P. A. Florenskii, 'Stroenie slova', *Kontekst* (1972), 348–55.

also to the *appellation* of the icon. In Florenskii's work, the *word* written on the icon proves to be mystically connected with the act of creation, which found its analogy, for example, not only in the biblical tradition (in naming a thing, God created it), but also in the Jewish mystical tradition of the Kabbalah (the Book of Creation, the Zohar), in which the name of God was considered sacred and the creation of a new essence by naming was emphasized.[234] This is why the distinct way a name is plotted onto an icon (using tildes), and the decoration of letters of the shortened names of Christ and the Mother of God, always had great significance and could testify to the broader cultural orientations of different epochs. If the act of naming in and of itself gave an object existence, then the icon (for example, Rublev's *Trinity*) too could serve as proof of the existence of God. The texts located in the clothes of the saints, too, could provide clear evidence of this fusion of words and images in the icon. In other words, in the context of religious revelation, all these special features in the depiction of the countenances and clothing of the saints, the borders and background, the inscription and decoration, acquired clear metaphysical meaning in Florenskii's eyes.

The Power of the Symbol

Florenskii's metaphysical interpretation of the icon was largely grounded in his era's theory of symbolism, which he was already captivated by in 1902–04. Here, the Byzantine theology of the icon was clearly combined with the latest aesthetic theory. This is most evidently expressed in Florenskii's conceptualizing of the twofold nature of the religious symbol, in which, for him, the sign and its meaning coincide to the extent of *being indistinguishable*. Hence his famous pronouncements: 'The iconostasis is the saints themselves' or 'In icon-painted images we ourselves [...] see the grace-filled and lucid countenances of the saints,

---

234 Florenskii had already begun to associate the concept of rupture in mathematics with the act of renaming in his student years, according the act of renaming with special symbolic meaning. The philosopher connected the topic of 'naming' with ideological and religious issues, endeavouring to see knowledge as an interrelated whole. Florenskii's work on the interrelation between higher mathematics (discrete set theory, discovered at this time by Dmitri Egorov (1869–1931) and Nikolai Luzin (1883–1950)) and name-glorification is scrutinized in Grekhem and Kantor, *Naming Infinity*.

and in them, in these countenances – the miraculously manifest Divine image and God Himself'.[235] Such an understanding of the symbol allowed the philosopher to combine two spaces in his particular cosmology, to include the invisible world in the visible world – in the space of the reality that surrounds us.

By Florenskii's own admission, symbolism formed the bedrock of his worldview.[236] This did not happen by chance. As a student he was already attempting to write poetry in the Symbolist spirit and fraternizing with Symbolist poets. He was well acquainted with Soloviev and Friedrich Nietzsche (1844–1900) and, of course, with the works of Symbolist artists, one of whom – Mikhail Nesterov (1862–1942) – later painted his famous portrait *Philosophers*, of Florenskii together with Sergei Bulgakov (1871–1944) (1917, Tretyakov Gallery, Moscow). Florenskii's 'concrete metaphysics' therefore suggested, above all, empathy and the reading of reality with the help of elementary symbols. What was at stake was, in essence, the specific function of the religious sign, the ability of the symbol to make something invisible visible, which also underpinned Florenskii's unique symbolic theory of the icon. According to this theory (which, in its distinct theses, was clearly consonant with the theurgical symbolism of Bely[237] and the 'symbolic realism' of Vyacheslav Ivanov (1866–1949)), the world was conceived as a *many-layered reality*, and cognition of the meanings of this reality was achieved exclusively by means of *intuition* and *empathy*, that is, via recognition of the phenomenon as a symbol able to disclose its contents. And the more understandable and accessible the interpretation of symbols via this route, the deeper

---

235 Florenskii, 'Ikonostas', p. 31.
236 Recalling the mystical illuminations of his childhood, Florenskii wrote: 'But back then I also internalized an idea central to my later outlook on the world – that in a name is the thing named, in the symbol is the symbolized, in a representation of reality the represented is present, and that is why the symbol is the symbolized' (P. A. Florenskii, *Detiam moim. Vospominaniia proshlykh let* (Moscow: Moskovskii rabochii, 2000), p. 16).
237 Above all, Florenskii's and Bely's shared belief in the 'magic of words' springs to mind here: 'Language is creative work's most powerful instrument', Bely wrote. 'When I name a thing with a word, I confirm its existence' (see A. Bely, 'Magiia slov', in A. Bely, *Simbolizm kak miroponimanie. Sbornik* (Moscow: Respublika, 1994), p. 79). For his part, Florenskii laid particular stress on the connection between 'verbal magic' and metaphysical origin in his article 'The Magic of the Word' (P. A. Florenskii, 'Magichnost' slova', in P. A. Florenskii, *Sochineniia v 2-x tomakh*, 2 vols. (Moscow: Mysl', 1990), II, 252–73).

the meaning revealed, and the more questions were generated about the way spiritual and material existence was arranged. Hence, to Florenskii, the *icon* seemed precisely a *symbolic border* between two worlds. In his work, the icon constantly appears as a 'door' or 'window' through which the saints and Christ himself appear to us.[238]

Moreover, this unmediated symbolic vision provided a fundamentally new philosophical perspective not only on the artistic form of the medieval icon, but also on its *function* in the system of ecclesiastical ritual and even on the very *process* of icon-painting. It would therefore hardly be an overstatement to say that the metaphysics of reverse perspective, the metaphysics of the business of icon-making, and the religious symbolism of church ritual proved to be, in Florenskii's philosophy, extremely close and interdependent.

Various remarks indicate that Florenskii was familiar with the mass production of icons in the seventeenth to nineteenth century in the Suzdal region villages of Palekh, Mstera and Kholui, which is reminiscent of the popular icons produced by the Italo-Cretan 'madonneri'.[239] It is entirely possible that this acquaintance went further than books. The philosopher lived in a simple wooden house in Sergiev Posad, next to the Trinity Lavra of St Sergius, which had long been supplied with 'Suzdal-style' icons. Village icon painters travelled here on various commissions, and Florenskii would have been able to observe their work. Kirikov, who made the above-mentioned copy of Rublev's *Trinity*, came from Palekh. One way or another, the speed at which the village masters worked, the automatic nature of their methods, acquired symbolic significance in Florenskii's eyes. Here, the metaphysics of the icon's form corresponds not so much with the artistic quality of the work as with the canon of icon-painting and with the religious experience it evokes: 'An icon

---

238 Florenskii, 'Ikonostas', pp. 38–39. On Florenskii's philosophy of the border, see A. V. Mikhailov, 'Pavel Florenskii kak filosof granitsy. K vykhodu v svet kriticheskogo izdaniia "Ikonostasa"', *Voprosy iskusszvoznaniia*, 4 (1994), 33–71.

239 Palekh, Mstera and Kholui were the biggest centres of popular artisanal icon-painting in seventeenth- to nineteenth-century Russia. Popular icons (typologically comparable with the outputs of Italo-Greek 'madonneri' in the seventeenth to eighteenth centuries) were painted here alongside expensive, specially commissioned icons. The scale of this mass icon production business may be deduced from the fact that, in the nineteenth century, between 1.5 and 2 million icons a year were painted in one village – Kholui – alone. See Tarasov, *Icon and Devotion*, pp. 53–55.

may be of high craftsmanship or low', the philosopher explained, 'but without fail a *genuine* perception of the other world, *genuine* spiritual experience, underpins it'. Elsewhere he writes:

> Above all the icon is not a work of art, a product of self-sufficient artistry, but is a work of testimony for which artistry, along with many other things, is necessary. So that which you refer to as mass produced also relates to the essence of an icon, since testimony needs to filter through to every home, every family, to become genuinely popular, to proclaim the Kingdom of Heaven in the very thick of everyday life. The possibility of working quickly is also an essential element of icon-painting technique; icons of exceedingly fine hand, of the Stroganov School for example, are of course very characteristic of the era that reduced the holy to a luxury item, a vainglorious collectable.[240]

This revelation of the deep connection between the technical process of creating an icon and its metaphysical essence is also influenced by Symbolist theory, which Florenskii adapted in his interpretation of church tradition. In other words, the very process of icon-painting is interpreted by Florenskii on a deep philosophical and theological level; he sees it as a sort of sacred act on the metaphysical border of two worlds. The multilayered process of preparing the icon – from the preparation of the board and the choice of paint to the application of letters and words by brush (i.e., its *naming*) – proves to be an important condition for clarifying the most important function of the devotional image, that is, to serve as a window onto the other world. The production of the icon is, in essence, a path of symbolic convergence of the visible and invisible, the heavenly and the earthly, in which the icon painter's gradual 'revelation' of the image is compared with the gradual revelation of the metaphysical plane of existence. For Florenskii, then, the preparation of the board, the ways in which the drawing is applied to it, the prayers uttered by the icon painter before commencing work all represent symbolic primary elements of reality, which invariably for him have a *discrete* nature and arise from separate symbolic forms: 'the living *metaphysics is expressed* in the very methods of icon-painting', he

---

240 Florenskii, 'Ikonostas', pp. 35, 75. The expensive Stroganov icons from the end of the sixteenth to the beginning of the seventeenth centuries were famously distinguished by their miniature technique and exquisitely finished detail. They were painted on the order of the Russian aristocracy by masters (Prokopii Chirin, Stefan Aref'ev and others) who served the needs of the royal court.

stressed, 'in its techniques, in the materials employed, in icon-painting's manner of execution'.[241] Moreover, these methods and materials could express an era's feeling for the world no less clearly than the style of work.[242]

The icon painter's cast of mind was also of interest. According to church tradition, only the saints may be icon painters; the design of the icon belonged to them. The master's individuality was only made manifest, then, in implementing the canon. Florenskii therefore refused to credit even Rublev with artistic design: 'in the icon of the Trinity Andrei Rublev was not an independent creator, but merely brilliantly implemented the creative idea and basic composition gifted by Saint Sergius'.[243] In developing this position, the philosopher was not only following the dogma of icon veneration but also drawing on the text of the *Skazanie o sviatykh ikonopistsakh* [*Tale of the Holy Icon Painters*], from the second half of the seventeenth century. He also recalled the supervision of icon production, and wrote about recent miraculously-appeared icons and their mass reproduction.

Moreover, the *spatial image* of church ritual also had especial symbolic meaning for Florenskii. He discussed church ritual as a spatial icon and a *synthesis of the arts*, revealing some common ground with the work of the Symbolist poet Ivanov (who devoted particular attention to the mystery cults of the ancient world), and also to concepts developed by Richard Wagner (1818–83), who had pondered the synthesis of the arts in relation to musical drama. Florenskii's brief text 'Khramovoe deistvo kak sintez iskusstv' ['Church Ritual as a Synthesis of the Arts'], which was prepared in 1918 as a paper for the Commission for the Preservation of the Trinity Lavra of St Sergius' Monuments of Art and Antiquities and published in the second issue of the *Makovets* journal (1922), is, in essence, an interpretation of the medieval icon and ritual in the context of the theory of symbolism.[244]

---

241 Ibid., p. 52 (my emphasis).
242 The process of preparing an icon in the eighteenth and nineteenth centuries is described in detail in O. Tarasov, *Ikona i blagochestie. Ocherki ikonnogo dela v imperatorskoi Rossii* (Moscow: Progress-Kul'tura, 1995), pp. 165–81.
243 P. A. Florenskii, 'Troitse-Sergieva lavra v Rossiia', in Florenskii, *Istoriia i filosofiia iskusstva*, pp. 139–40.
244 P. A. Florenskii, 'Khramovoe deistvo kak sintez iskusstv', in Florenskii, *Istoriia i filosofiia iskusstva*, pp. 121–29 (see also the Italian edition: P. A. Florenskii, 'Il rito

Let us recall that the Lavra, founded by St Sergius of Radonezh in 1337, had grown into one of the most important centres of Russian sanctity during the period from the fourteenth to the start of the twentieth century. At the same time, it had become a centrepoint for the highest achievements of Russian art. Besides the Trinity Cathedral with its iconostasis by Rublev and Chernyi (discussed above), the foundations of its main Church of the Dormition (1559–85) were laid by Ivan the Terrible (1530–84) and contained medieval icons and frescos painted by the best masters of their day. Within the monastery's great walls and towers there were also architectural monuments from the seventeenth to the nineteenth century, and burial sites belonging to the most illustrious Russian families. Its sacristies were full of the most valuable donations and gifts from all over the Orthodox world. It is therefore no coincidence that Florenskii saw the 'historical realization' of the synthesis of the arts in the Trinity Lavra of St Sergius, with its architecture, its unique collection of medieval books and icons, its ecclesiastical plate, its system of church ritual and even the vestments of the monastic clergy – all moving to striking effect around the monastery grounds. As a 'living' museum (which, in Florenskii's words, facilitated the study of the fundamental questions of *contemporary aesthetics*), the Lavra stood in contrast to what he referred to as a 'dead' museum, that is, a traditional archaeological museum housing a collection of rarities and individual ecclesiastical objects, or a museum of medieval Russian icons as artworks such as that of Ostroukhov. Here, Florenskii followed the path of famous critics of the museum such as Georg Wilhelm Friedrich Hegel (1770–1831) and Nietzsche (whose ideas were subsequently developed by Martin Heidegger (1889–1976) and Maurice Merleau-Ponty (1908–61)), who, in their time, asserted that museums aestheticized the perception of cultural monuments, cut art off from life and imposed a passive attitude towards it.[245] In proposing 'the taking of the museum out to life and the bringing of life into the museum', Florenskii therefore indicated, in one stroke, the most important conditions for the perception of such a highly complicated artistic creation as the *medieval icon*.

---

ortodosso come sintesi delle arti', in *Bellezza e liturgia. Scritti su cristianesimo e cultura*, trans. C. Zonghetti (Milan: Mondadori, 2010), pp. 27–38).

245 Notably, Florenskii also sees Muratov as a kindred spirit in the 'saturation of museum business with life', quoting extensively from *Images of Italy*. See Florenskii, 'Khramovoe deistvo kak sintez iskusstv', p. 123.

Thus, for example, in the context of a church synthesis of the arts, the metaphysical qualities of the medieval icon's reverse perspective could be revealed, according to Florenskii's observations, exclusively through the soft and natural *light* provided by lit candles and burning lamps. In essence, the multiple points of view involved in creating the artistic space of the icon (the curvature of its shapes, the supplementary and vivid planes of the architectural backdrop, the recesses and exaggerated proportions of particular items) were all conceived in relation to the flickering tones of uneven lighting. This glimmering light, then, was needed to establish metaphysical contact with the images of the saints: flame 'animated' the symbols and allowed the countenances, and the golden clothes and attributes of sanctity, to be perceived strictly as phenomena belonging to a different, invisible world. Moreover, this *art of flame* was directly connected with the *art of smoke*, the translucent veil of incense creating that special aerial perspective, which supplemented the reverse perspective and yet further dematerialized the form of the medieval icon. 'And the many special features of the icon', Florenskii concluded, 'which tantalise the sated gaze of our times: the exaggeration of some proportions, the emphasis of lines, the abundance of gold and semi-precious stones, *basma* [decorative strips of fine metal] and halos, pendants, brocade and velvet cloths embroidered with pearls and stones, all this, in the conditions proper to the icon, exists not as piquant exoticism by any means, but as the necessary, certainly, irremovable, and only way to convey the spiritual contents of the icon...'.[246]

In other words, with its reverse perspective, colouring, distinctive graphic features and visually musical correspondences, the medieval icon here proved inseparably correlated with other symbolic forms of church ritual – the art of fire, the art of aromas, singing and even the rhythm of the priest's movements during the liturgy.[247] All these elements contributed to creating that special sacred atmosphere of an Orthodox church, which was conceived, felt and experienced almost simultaneously. Here, as may be imagined, in their nobility and clarity

---

246 Ibid., p. 126.
247 A little later, Tarabukin – developing Florenskii's thinking – dedicated a special paper to the rhythmic composition of the icon. He delivered 'Ritm i kompozitsiia v drevnerusskoi zhivopisi' ['Rhythm and Composition in Medieval Russian Painting'] on 22 December 1923 at the Institute of Art History in Petrograd (see Tarabukin, *Smysl ikony*, pp. 204–06).

the forms of the language of icon-painting answered to the forms of the ecclesiastical decoration overall, exemplified, for instance, in the Trinity Cathedral of the Trinity Lavra of St Sergius, with its icons by Rublev and his workshop. In its entirety, this reminded Florenskii of that 'musical drama' which, in Wagner's conception of *Gesamtkustwerk* [synthesis of the arts] was viewed as the chief form of 'the art of the future', and which for Nietzsche, for example, offered access to metaphysical eternity. In his *Die Geburt der Tragödie* [*The Birth of Tragedy*] (1872), Nietzsche wrote: 'art is not merely an imitation of the reality of nature, but in truth a *metaphysical* supplement to the reality of nature, placed alongside thereof for its conquest'.[248] Florenskii also developed the notion of 'musical drama' in relation to church ritual:

> We recall the rhythm and tempo of the clergy's movements while censing, for example, the play of overflowing folds of rich fabrics, the fragrances, the special atmosphere winnowed by fire, ionized by thousands of burning flames; we remember, moreover, that the synthesis of temple action is not restricted to the sphere of the figurative arts, but embraces vocal art and poetry too – poetry of all kinds – being itself, on the level of aesthetics, *musical drama*. Here everything is subordinate to a single aim, to the supreme effect of this musical drama's catharsis, and thus everything, here mutually coordinated, when taken separately either does not exist or, at any rate, pseudo-exists.[249]

Yet again it is impossible to miss the influence of Platonism in Florenskii's musings on ecclesiastical ritual and the synthesis of the arts. This is no coincidence. Plato is clearly Florenskii's favourite philosopher, from whom he adopted concepts including the idea (*eidos*, in the Greek), the image (*lik*, in the Russian) and the unity of multiplicity. Moreover, it is in Plato, specifically, that consciousness approaches the comprehension of existence through the visual (sensory) understanding of things. This clearly resonates in Florenskii's reflections on understanding the

---

248 F. Nietzsche, 'Rozhdenie tragedii iz dukkha muzyki. Predislovie k Richardu Vagneru', in F. Nietzsche, *Sobranie sochinenii v 2-x tomakh*, 2 vols. (Moscow: Khudozhestvennaia literatura, 1990), I, 57–157 (p. 153) (my emphasis). See also R. Vagner, 'Proizvedenie iskusstva budushchego', in R. Vagner, *Izbrannye raboty* (Moscow: Arts, 1978), pp. 164–95. English quotation from F. Nietzsche, *The Birth of Tragedy or Hellenism and Pessimism*, trans. W. A. Haussmann (London: George Allen and Unwin, 1910), p. 182, https://www.gutenberg.org/files/51356/51356-h/51356-h.htm

249 Florenskii, 'Khramovoe deistvo kak sintez iskusstv', p. 127 (my emphasis).

icon-painted form via the senses, the language of which appeals to both the sensory and to the extrasensory simultaneously. Following Plato in opposing imitative painting, Florenskii saw in the canonical form, specifically, the possibility of 'the emancipation of the artist's creative energy', the special conditions for attaining the 'artistically embodied *truth of things*' (my emphasis) in creative work. To accept the icon-painting canon is to feel a connection with collective religious experience; the canon is 'the concentrated intellect of humankind'. Furthermore, we can also see canons of the oldest cultures in the icon-painting canon: 'The stabler and firmer the canon, the deeper and more purely it expresses the spiritual need of humankind as a whole: canonical is ecclesiastical, ecclesiastical is conciliar, and conciliar, then, embraces all of humankind'.[250] In his day Losev rightly observed that, for Florenskii, 'the Platonic idea is expressive, it has a distinct living countenance'.[251] Florenskii related this 'living countenance' of the Platonic idea not only to the decisions of the Seventh Ecumenical Council (787 AD) that affirmed the dogma of icon veneration: his observations and analyses of church ritual and icons are full of clear evocations of the Classical world. To a great extent, his Orthodox symbolism proceeded specifically from Classical symbolism. And here, once again, we cannot fail to observe a point of commonality with the theories of the Russian Symbolist poet Ivanov.[252] In discussing the indissoluble connection between the icon's artistic system and other types of art, Florenskii detected the heritage of Antiquity in the very spatial image of Orthodox ritual: 'I cannot but recall', he noted,

---

250 Florenskii, 'Ikonostas', p. 43.
251 A. F. Losev, *Ocherki antichnogo simbolizma i mifologii* (Moscow: Mysl', 1930), p. 680. The preparatory materials for *Iconostasis* point to the text 'Platonizm i ikonopis'' ['Platonism and Icon-Painting']. In the text of *Iconostasis* itself, the Platonic idea is compared with the icon-painted countenance (Florenskii, *Istoriia i filosofiia iskusstva*, pp. 22, 523). Many of Florenskii's contemporaries noted the 'Hellenic source' in the stamp of Florenskii's personality. According to Zhegin's memoirs, a copy of an Antique bas-relief with an image of Aphrodite hung next to a crucifix in Florenskii's office. See L. Zhegin, 'Vospominaniia o. P. Florenskom', *Vestnik russkogo khristianskogo dvizheniia*, 135 (1982), 60–71.
252 'Ivanov is all about Antiquity and all about art', the famous Russian theologian Georges Florovskii (1893–1979) wrote about these ideas. 'He comes to Christianity from the cult of Dionysius, from the ancient "Hellenic religion of the suffering god" [...] and the Christianity he misinterprets in a Bacchic and orgiastic spirit creates a new myth'. See G. Florovskii, *Puti russkogo bogosloviia* (Moscow: Institut russkoi tsivilizatsii, 2009), p. 582.

those more ancillary arts forgotten or half-forgotten today, which are nevertheless wholly essential elements of temple action: the art of fire, the art of aroma, the art of smoke, the art of clothing and so on, up to and including the absolutely unique Trinity prosphora, with the secret of their baking unknown, and the idiosyncratic choreography revealed in the rhythmic churchly movements of the clergy's entrances and exits [through the doors of the iconostasis], in the descending and ascending of countenances, in the circumambulation of the altar and church, and in church processions. He who has tasted the cup of Antiquity well knows the extent to which this is all ancient and lives as the heritage and a direct scion of the ancient world, in particular of the sacred tragedy of Hellada.[253]

The article 'Church Ritual as a Synthesis of the Arts' also discusses the *mystical* significance of the pale blue curtain of incense, which brings a special 'deepening' of aerial perspective to contemplation of the icon: in the clouds of incense the countenances of the icons are transformed into the ideas of the Platonic world. Stressing the enigmatic nature of Orthodox liturgy in the spirit of symbolism, Florenskii clearly paid tribute to the mysterious dimensions of ancient religions. The Orthodox priest resembles here, at times, a Greek pagan priest versed in special formulas, diverging from the role of an Orthodox Pastor. The comparison of early Christian spirituality and the spirituality of Byzantium, along with the emphasis on the mysterious nature of the church's synthesis of the arts, constitutes the hallmarks of Florenskii's conception.

Under the influence of the 'cup of Antiquity', therefore, the philosopher also perceived traits of Zeus in images of *Christ Pantocrator*, and in the *Hodegetria* image he detected characteristics of the goddess Athena, whose divine epithets clearly – for him – corresponded with the 'ecclesiastical appellations' of the Mother of God.[254] Florenskii also revealed forms of the Greek goddess of fruitfulness Demeter, in whose image the Greeks collated all their premonitions of the Virgin Mary, in the nineteenth-century Russian icon-type of the Mother of

---

253 Florenskii, 'Khramovoe deistvo kak sintez iskusstv', p. 128.
254 Florenskii also perceived Antique traits in the above-mentioned *Hodegetria* and *St Nicholas* icons which, according to tradition, belonged to St Sergius of Radonezh: 'In relation to the character of the lines, elastic, gently undulating and never angular, very similar in both icons', he noted, 'this utter completeness gives them an air of antiquity: not Byzantine, but precisely Classical, Hellenic, and moreover not Hellenic in a [dry] academic way, but a still-warm Hellenic, full of inner awe and light'. Florenskii, 'Molennye ikony prepodobnogo Sergiia', pp. 152–153, 155.

God *Sporitel'nitsa khlebov* [*The Multiplier of Grain*]. In Florenskii's works, the medieval Russian icon was often set alongside Ancient Greek sculpture of the golden age: 'Russian icon-painting of the fourteenth and fifteenth centuries achieves an artistic perfection the equal or even the like of which has never been seen in art the world over, and which may be compared in some sense only with Greek sculpture – also the embodiment of spiritual models and also, after a bright ascendancy, degraded by rationalism and sensuality'.[255]

Florenskii's treatment of reverse perspective consequently came across as imbued with deep philosophical and culturological meanings. Constantly turning to the philosophy of the sign, of names and the ontology of existence, the philosopher made a genuine discovery in the sphere of religious art. The way Byzantine theology of the icon was interpreted in his works was unusually interesting. Noting the multiplicity of points of view in constructing the artistic space of the medieval image, Florenskii convincingly demonstrated that the icon could pose the most important existential questions. The medieval icon was deservedly key to his philosophical interpretation of the spatial boundary between the visible and the invisible.

A New Middle Ages

Florenskii, Wulff and Panofsky, who were using different approaches to the study of perspective and its connection with the distinctive worldviews of various eras, complemented one another as well as 'argued' with each other. They all concluded that reverse perspective is a *way of seeing*, and not a primitive crafts device, as had been suggested earlier. However, given that Florenskii's position was connected with his 'concrete metaphysics', it is absolutely clear that, for him, the problem of perspective was above all a philosophical question. In Florenskii's work, all the distinctive aspects of modernity's scientific worldview – individualism, the individual point of view and the mathematization of nature and appearance of a 'second nature' (a world of ideal mathematical objects) – proved inseparably connected with the analysis of the composition of paintings and icons. After all, linear perspective

---

255 Florenskii, 'Ikonostas', pp. 43–44.

set the object in a continuous and measurable space, which was one of the main subjects of Florenskii's criticism. Florenskii connected this with the evolutionary theories of the era of positivism (including that of Charles Darwin (1809–82)), which had become inimical to the new, Postclassical thinking during the *Belle Époque* (c. 1871–1914).

According to Florenskii, in the Renaissance era, linear perspective in painting became not just a new method of depiction in art, but also a new *principle of seeing* the world. The *human eye* became the gauge of the truth of this seeing, that same visual perception with all its optical distortions that medieval theologians – well acquainted with the laws of optics – had judged to be worldly and sinful. In the system of medieval values embodied in the Byzantine icon or the Gothic altar there was no place for optical illusions. Linear perspective evoked illusionism and theatricality, in other words, a 'mask' of life rather than genuine life itself. This was because, as Florenskii demonstrated, its roots lay in *Antique theatre* and *theatre décor* – in applied rather than genuine art, designed for a static point of view, aligning with the immobile gaze of a seated viewer, passively absorbing a theatrical performance.

In volume ten of *Politeia* [*The Republic*] (c. 375 BC), Plato discussed imitative painting, which aimed to reproduce not the 'real being' but the 'appearance' of things. The artist-imitator reproduces phantoms, and not reality. This is why Plato also equated the laws of linear perspective with focus, and understood illusionism in art, as a whole, as connecting 'with the element of our soul that is far removed from rationality'. Genuine art should turn a person to the contemplation of ideas (*eidos*).[256] Developing this thesis and using the image of the Platonic Cave to exemplify the position of a spectator in the ancient theatre, Florenskii convincingly showed that illusionistic painting was focused mainly on the *object*, thereby disregarding the perceiving *subject*: 'And there, I suggest, the viewer or decorator-artist is chained, verily, like the prisoner of the Platonic Cave, to the theatre seat and cannot, and equally must not, have a direct, living relationship with reality – as if separated from the stage by a glass partition and having only one motionless, seeing eye, without penetrating the very essence of life itself...'.[257]

---

256 Plato, 'Gosudarstvo', in Plato, *Sobranie Sochinenii*, trans. A. F. Losev, 3 vols. (Moscow: Mysl', 1971), III, 218, 307, 312–13.
257 Florenskii, 'Obratnaia perspektiva', pp. 189–90.

At the same time Florenskii showed that, from Antiquity onwards, the various types of perspective have been applied in art according to the needs of culture and religion. The perspectivity innate in 'normal' vision was common knowledge in the cultures of the ancient world: the human eye cannot fail to notice that the road narrows towards the horizon even though it knows this is not actually the case. Given the state of mathematical sciences in Egypt, Greece and Ancient Rome, ways of creating images within a system of linear perspective could easily have been mastered. They were, however, deliberately not used. It was more important to depict what the artist *knew* rather than what he *saw*. An image constructed according to linear perspective and imitating reality was therefore as remote from reality as any other, since mimesis is not perfect: 'The various methods of depiction', Florenskii explained, 'differ from one another not in the way that a thing differs from its depiction, but on the symbolic plane'.[258]

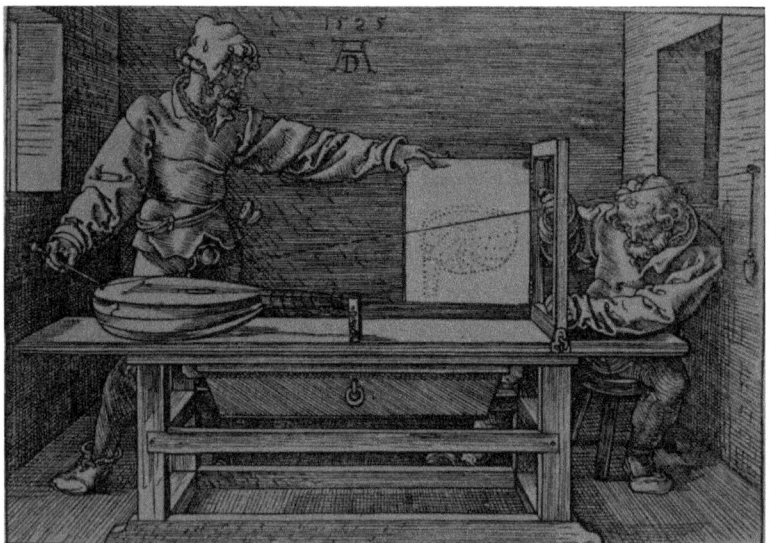

Fig. 4.10 Albrecht Dürer (1571–1528), *Man Drawing a Lute* (1525), woodcut. Metropolitan Museum of Art, New York. Wikimedia, public domain, https://commons.wikimedia.org/wiki/File:Dürer_-_Man_Drawing_a_Lute.jpg

The descriptions and images of the optical instruments Florenskii found in Albrecht Dürer's (1471–1528) *Man Drawing a Lute* (1525, Metropolitan

---

258 Ibid., p. 189.

Museum of Art) confirmed the conventional nature of the Renaissance-era perspectival construction of the world (see Fig. 4.10). Explaining the construction of these drawing machines, Florenskii strove to clarify that the image achieved with their help was not a product of visual synthesis but merely the result of a geometric calculation:

> Dürer's third device no longer had any relationship with sight whatsoever: here it is not the eye that realizes the centre of projection, although it too is artificially immobilized, but a certain point on a wall to which is fixed a ring with a long thread attached. This latter almost reaches to a glazed frame standing upright on the table. The thread is tautened, and a viewfinder attached to it which directs the 'line of sight' to the point on the object, projected from the point at which the thread is fixed to the wall. It is then not hard to mark the corresponding point of projection on the glass with a pen or brush. Taking a sight on the various points of the object one after another, the draughtsman plots the object on the glass, but from the 'wall point' rather than the 'view point'; sight, then, plays a supporting role in this case.[259]

Revealing such a drawing as merely a system of geometric calculations, Florenskii (in contrast to Panofsky) strove to connect the theory of linear perspective with criticism of the Renaissance era's anthropocentrism, and also with the 'Kantian' worldview which, for him, meant nothing other than looking at the world as if it were a site for scientific experiments.

Illusionistic painting, without doubt, accorded with the new European project of possessing nature rather than being present in that nature. And if the Antique and medieval perception of the world affirmed that every being is good, then the spirit of the modern age proposed to substitute an artificial model for reality. Florenskii's idea of a 'new Middle Ages', his defence of medieval cultural values, also becomes more understandable therefore: 'a full and rich river of true culture flows in the Middle Ages', he wrote, 'with its own science, with its own art, with its own statehood, and basically with all that comes under culture, but specifically with its own, and moreover with everything affiliated with true antiquity'. Elsewhere he writes, too, that 'the spirit of the new man is to cast off all reality [...] the spirit of the

---

259 Ibid., p. 207.

man of Antiquity, like the medieval man, is acceptance, the grateful recognition and affirmation of all reality as good...'.[260]

Linear and reverse perspectives seemed to Florenskii not only to be methods of creating images, but also to be in opposition as false and true pictures of the world. For him, the Renaissance painting is 'a screen, obscuring the light of existence', while the icon is a window open wide onto reality, that is, onto a world of essences and values that are genuine rather than imaginary.[261] It is quite clear that in Florenskii's work, the contrast between reverse and one-point perspective is polemical. Posing the question 'is deeming the icon naïve not in itself a naïve judgement?' and – entirely in the spirit of the times, when Berenson and Muratov were defending the value of 'the early masters' – answering in the affirmative, Florenskii went a great deal further. He demonstrated that the technique of linear perspective was merely an artistic device that reflected a worldview peculiar to the modern age, with its emphasis on comprehending nature through science.

In Florenskii's thinking, the *icon*, as genuine art always speaks to man's image of the world, to Platonic ideas (*eidos*) and the essence of things. Even those great artists who applied the rules of linear perspective (Giotto, Raphael (1483–1520), El Greco (1541–1614)) occasionally broke them and depicted the world from various points of view, and not by accident. Since the law of reverse perspective is characteristic precisely of 'spiritual space', this immediately made their compositions more expressive and inspired. This is why the *Last Supper* (c. 1495–98, Santa Maria delle Grazie, Milan) as painted by Leonardo da Vinci (1452–1519) – an artist who epitomized the spirit of the modern age for Florenskii – invited one into the picture space, while Michelangelo's (1475–1564) *Last Judgement* (1536–41, Sistine Chapel, Vatican City) – composed from several points of view – held the onlooker at a respectful distance. Elements of reverse perspective are clearly visible in the composition of this famous fresco: 'This is seen, by the way, from the fact that the lower figures obscure the upper ones', Florenskii noted. 'But as far as sizes are concerned, the figures *increase* in size the higher up the fresco they are – in other words, according to their distance from the viewer. This is characteristic of that spiritual space: the further away something

---

260 Ibid., pp. 193–94.
261 Ibid., pp. 196–203.

is in it, the larger it is, and the nearer, the smaller it is. This is *reverse perspective*'. In this respect, Michelangelo seemed to Florenskii 'either in the past, or perhaps in the future Middle Ages, a contemporary of and in no way contemporary to Leonardo'.[262] In other words, the world's most expressive works of painting generally contained perspectival irregularities. This is also why later Italo-Greek and Russian icons from the seventeenth to nineteenth centuries, which might be painted in accordance with the laws of Renaissance perspective and depict the objects represented in a naturalistic manner, also seemed to Florenskii less expressive than Byzantine and medieval Russian icons.

Since Florenskii explored the icon's laws of spatial-temporal relations in relation to cultural space as a whole, he may be considered the founding father of contemporary cultural studies of the icon. The philosopher continually drew comparisons with other cultural phenomena – Greek statues, the theatre of Antiquity, Egyptian burial masks – in discussing perspective. Hellenistic landscapes and portraiture, Renaissance architecture, painting and engraving were also key foci. In Florenskii's work (as in Muratov's, incidentally), the Byzantine and medieval Russian icon therefore featured as an integral part of world culture. In contrast to Muratov, however, Florenskii simultaneously addressed the issue of the icon's reception.

Florenskii's consideration of the essence of linear perspective was clearly connected with his reflections on the crisis of academic thinking in the modern era, on the inability of science to respond to contemporary challenges regarding questions about the history and meaning of human existence. These questions would later be thoroughly analyzed in Edmund Husserl's (1859–1938) famous work *Die Krisis der europäischen Wissenschaften und die transzendentale Phänomenologie* [*The Crisis of European Sciences and Transcendental Phenomenology*] (1936). Florenskii's 'concrete metaphysics', and his commentary on the icon, were also influenced by the neo-Kantianism of the Marburg School. They were also close to Cassirer's philosophy of symbolic forms, in which we also encounter in the symbol a unified spiritual and sensuous principle. Researchers have also identified links between Florenskii's metaphysics and astrology, with the constructs of Kabbala and with occultism: 'The

---

262 Ibid., pp. 203, 508.

Romantic tragedy of western culture is closer and more understandable to Florenskii than the problematics of Orthodox tradition', Georgii Florovskii noted, 'and true to form, he went decidedly backwards in his work, beyond Christianity, to Platonism and the religions of Antiquity, or slipped off sideways to the study of occultism and magic'.[263] Interesting connections between Florenskii's concepts and the phenomenology of Merleau-Ponty are also being discovered.[264]

Since Florenskii critiqued one-point perspective in the context of criticism of the anthropocentrism and naturalism that emerged from the Renaissance era, at times, his theoretical positions in the sphere of the theory of art converged with those of his opponents, the avant-garde artists who – almost at the same time as Florenskii – had turned their attention to the methods conventionally used in the medieval icon to convey spatial-temporal relations. These representatives of the Russian avant-garde were, like Florenskii, primarily interested in the arrangement of the medieval icon's artistic text: reverse perspective, line and light, acute foreshortening, the dynamics of gesture and the combining of several points of view. For the Russian avant-garde (and above all, for Kazimir Malevich (1879–1935)), the icon made it possible to escape into a sphere of 'pure painting', into the sphere of metaphysical essences and realities.[265] Taking the icon as a starting point, Malevich's Suprematism gave it a contemporary shape: 'I have one bare [icon], without a frame [...] an icon of my times', Malevich wrote in 1916.[266] Icons and folk pictures served the founders of Neoprimitivism and Abstractionism – Mikhail Larionov (1881–1964), Natalia Goncharova (1881–1962) and

---

263 Florovskii, *Puti russkogo bogosloviia*, p. 630.
264 T. Shteler, 'Obratnaia perspektiva: Pavel Florenskii i Moris Merlo-Ponti o prostranstve i lineinoi perspective v iskusstve Renessansa', *Istoriko-filosofskii ezhegodnik*, ed. N. V. Motroshilova and M. A. Solopova (Moscow: Nauka, 2006), pp. 320–29.
265 O. Tarasov, 'Florenskii, Malevich e la semiotica dell'icona', *Nuova Europa*, 1, (2002), 34–47; C. Carboni, *L'ultima icona: arte, filosofia, teologia* (Milan: Jaca Book, 2019).
266 *Otdel rukopisei Gosudarstvennogo Russkogo* [*State Russian Museum, Manuscript Division, St Petersburg*] (henceforth OR GRM), f. 137, ed. khr. 1186, l. 2 ob. (Letter from K. S. Malevich to A. N. Benois). The letter was written in response to Alexandre Benois' (1870–1960) criticism of the *0.10* Futurist exhibition held in Petrograd in 1915. For Benois, the Suprematist *Black Square* (1915, Tretyakov Gallery, Moscow) evoked associations with the icon, which Malevich also commented on (see also A. Benois, 'Poslednaiai futuristicheskaia vystavka', *Rech'* (9 January 1916), n.p.).

Kandinsky — as models for surmounting the naturalistic language of representation.[267] In essence, we witness the parallel discovery and application of a set of archetypal symbols in the fields of linguistics, the theory of artistic forms and the visual arts, including new directions in painting. Noteworthy examples include Kandinsky's theoretical works, dedicated to the problems of colour and point to plane; Florenskii's musings on the significance of texture, colour and line in the icon; and Florenskii's *Symbolarim* project, the first article of which was entitled 'Tochka' ['Point'].[268]

The particular proximity of Florenskii's concept of the mobile gaze in the icon to the theory of synthetic Cubism, which had proposed a synthesis of several viewpoints in the construction of the object in the painting, is worthy of attention. According to the theory of Cubism promulgated by Georges Braque (1882–1963) and Pablo Picasso (1881–1973), a view of an object not from one but from *several viewpoints* placed visible reality in a new perspective, which allowed access to another dimension of existence. Discussing Picasso's creativity in 'Smysl idealizma' ['The Meaning of Idealism'] (a detailed commentary on Platonism) (1914), Florenskii cited a work by the artist Grishchenko, 'Russkaia ikona

---

267 On the Russian avant-garde's discovery and reinterpretation of the artistic language of the icon, see O. Tarasov, 'Russian Icons and the Avant-Garde: Tradition and Change', in *The Art of Holy Russia. Icons from Moscow, 1400–1600*, ed. R. Cormack and D. Gaze (London: Royal Academy of Arts, 1998), pp. 93–99; A. Spira, *Avant-Garde Icon: Russian Avant-Garde Art and the Icon Painting Tradition* (Aldershot: Lund Humphries, 2008); O. Tarasov, 'Spirituality and the Semiotics of Russian Culture: From the icon to Avant-Garde Art', in *Modernism and the Spiritual in Russian Art: New Perspectives*, ed. L. Hardiman and N. Kozicharow (Cambridge: Open Book Publishers, 2017), pp. 115–28, https://doi.org/10.11647/OBP.0115.05

268 Florenskii's plan for *Symbolarium* dates from the 1920s (see E. A. Nekrasov, 'Neosushchestvlennyi zamysel 1920-x godov sozdaniia "Symbolarium"a' (Slovaria simbolov) i ego pervyi vypusk "Tochka"', *Pamiatniki kul'tury. Novye otkrytiia. Ezhegodnik 1982* (1984), 99–115). Kandinsky developed a theory of colour back in 1910–11, when he moved from figurative to abstract painting. His work *Über das Geistige in der Kunst* [*On the Spiritual in Art*] was written and first published in German in 1911. That same year, it was presented as a paper to the All-Russian Congress of Artists in St Petersburg (December 1911) (see W. Kandinsky, *O dukhovnom v iskusstve* (Moscow: Arkhimed, 1992)). Kandinsky's *Punkt und Linie zu Fläche* [*Point and Line to Plane*] was first published in German in Munich, 1926 (for the Russian publication, see W. Kandinsky, *Tochka i liniia na ploskosti*, trans. E. Kozina (Moscow: Azbuka, 2003)). Florenskii nowhere mentions Kandinsky's theory of colour, although he addresses the very same issues in regard to the artistic space of the icon. See P. A. Florenskii, 'Segni celesti. Riflessioni sulla simbologia dei colori', in *La prospettiva rovesciata e altri scritti*, ed. Misler, pp. 68–71.

mezhdu Vizantiei i Zapadom' ['The Russian Icon between Byzantium and the West'] (1913), in which the Cubist canvases of Picasso were compared with Russian icons.[269] Florenskii simultaneously addressed the Theosophist problem of the 'fourth dimension', which at that time was being developed in the works of Peter Uspenskii (1878–1947). In this regard, Florenskii's reasoning about art as a special form of knowing the world also found parallels in the theory and practice of the avant-garde. Much of the Modernist-era thinking about the special meaning of the artwork and the ways it influences the receiving consciousness followed on from here.

---

269 See P. A. Florenskii, 'Smysl idealizma (metafizika roda i lika)', in P. A. Florenskii, *Sochineniia v 4-x tomakh*, 4 vols. (Moscow: Mysl', 2000), III, 101–03. Cf. N. Berdiaev, 'Pikasso', *Sofiia*, 3 (1914), 57–62; P. D. Uspenskii, *Chetvertoe izmerenie. Obzor glavneishikh teorii i popytok issledovaniia oblasti neizmerimogo* (Petrograd: Iz. M. V. Pirozhkova, 1918).

Conclusion

The chapters in this book have endeavoured to show that the way we see and understand the medieval Russian icon today is largely a legacy of the culture of the *Belle Époque* (c. 1871–1914). The German Formalist School of art criticism, above all, shaped the discovery of the medieval icon's aesthetic significance. The re-evaluation of Byzantine and early Italian art that took place in Western European academia was also a key factor. However, the local, historical context of medieval icon collection within Old Believer communities in Russia, and the specific ways in which these communities understood the medieval icon, was also important. A unique body of connoisseur knowledge was amassed over the course of the eighteenth and nineteenth centuries, which included not only the skill of identifying icons as medieval, but also being able to associate them with particular 'Schools' according to their specific artistic features and place of production. This Old Believer expertise featured not only in the academic works of Nikodim Kondakov (1844–1925) and Nikolai Likhachev (1862–1936), but even informed the works of the new generation of art critics, Pavel Muratov (1881–1950), Nikolai Shchekotov (1884–1945), Nikolai Punin (1888–1953) and others. It was Muratov, above all, who combined Old Believer connoisseurship with Western European Formalism and new aesthetic theory in his study of the artistic form of medieval Russian painting from the fourteenth to the sixteenth centuries. He was one of the first to demonstrate that the medieval Russian icon ranked among the highest achievements of European culture.

It is Pavel Florenskii (1882–1937), however, who must be credited with a genuinely revolutionary discovery of the medieval icon's artistic meaning. I have argued that it was he, rather than Oskar Wulff (1864–1946) and Erwin Panofsky (1892–1968), who managed to reveal the true, eschatological meaning of reverse perspective. The icon is a symbolic form of transcendence. This means that its perspective leads the viewer's gaze beyond the bounds of the surrounding world and opens a person's 'inner eyes'. As I have shown, Florenskii ushered icon-painting into the realms of philosophical thought specifically in works written at the beginning of the 1920s, thereby inaugurating a fundamentally new era of thinking about and studying the religious image. He understood painting as a special kind of metaphysical activity, and developed his own theory of the icon within the framework of a conception of the metaphysics of religion. In his work 'Ikonostas' ['Iconostasis'], the philosopher demonstrated clearly and convincingly that the Renaissance painting did not set the essence of Christian symbolism before the viewer, but only a façade and a multiplicity of meanings. The underlying rationale for this thesis was also revealed in his article 'Obratnaia perspektiva' ['Reverse Perspective'], which advanced the fundamental difference between theatrical stylization and an understanding of painted forms as inseparable from ethics and religion. Florenskii contrasted the search for the ontological nature of the very language of art with the subjectivism of Renaissance perspective. Something much greater than craftsmanship stood behind iconographic schemas. That special authenticity, shaped by the skill of the anonymous master to elicit the deep meanings of a Christian symbol, is always present in a medieval icon.

A whole series of works (including, in particular, Francis Haskell's (1928–2000) research) has convincingly shown how changes in the cultural system itself resulted in the discovery of new names (Titian (c. 1488/90–1576), Johannes Vermeer (1632–75), Caravaggio (1571–1610)) in the nineteenth century. For my part, I have highlighted how, at the twilight of the modern age (the end of the nineteenth and beginning of the twentieth century), the concept of the new masterpiece abandoned the narrow confines of Classical taste and was steadily transferred to a system of values of autonomous art. New theory led to a new art and antiques market, and raised questions relating to the work of connoisseurs: what is a masterpiece? What is unique about it? Why is preservation of the original artistic form important? And who should determine all this: the scholar-connoisseur, the art critic or the collector? Prioritizing the analysis of artistic form, and interpreting it on the basis of neo-Kantian aesthetics, allowed (after Friedrich Schelling (1775–1854)) the masterpiece to be defined as an autonomous work of art in possession of objective artistic truth. Armed with artistic intuition and visual memory, a small circle of specialists (Bernard Berenson (1865–1959), Max Friedländer (1867–1958) and others) attested to this truth. The new masterpiece was viewed in the broad context of world art's historical development, facilitated by the emergence of new art journals, exhibitions and advertising.

There are clear parallels between the collection and study of medieval painting in Russia and the history of collecting Byzantine icons and Western European (especially Italian) 'primitives' in Western Europe and the United States of America. My examination of the academic study and new collecting of medieval Russian painting in the *Belle Époque* era reveals that the notion of the medieval icon as a masterpiece was not only theoretically grounded by the new art critics but also commercially driven by the new wave of collectors. The medieval icon entered the sphere of institutionally recognized art with the creation of Ilya Ostroukhov's (1858–1929) private Museum of Medieval Russian Painting in Moscow (1911) and the new display in the Russian Museum in St Petersburg (1913–14). In other words, for the first time in the upper echelons of Russian culture, the medieval Russian icon was recognized as both a great artistic achievement and a valuable work of art in the broader art market. The preservation of the genuine artistic form of the medieval Russian icon has been considered in a new light in this book, precisely in connection with these developments. It is no coincidence that the idea of the new restoration work was first raised in mass-circulation print by the Old Believer banker and collector Stepan Riabushinskii (1874–1942). It was in the chapel of his Moscow mansion that the essence of the medieval Russian icon as a genuine religious event was fully blended with its preservation as an authentic aesthetic object. How authentically an icon was preserved became, for Riabushinskii, also a question of the identity of a religious message in the context of national tradition. Before this, icons that had been overpainted or renovated – especially the valued miniatures of the Stroganov School – were generally used in Old Believer rituals. Now the symbolic value of the original painting of fourteenth- to sixteenth-century Muscovite and Novgorodian art became of primary importance.

On display in Ostroukhov's Museum of Medieval Russian Painting, as opposed to Riabushinskii's chapel, the icon's aesthetic value as a masterpiece of medieval painting replaced its religious purpose. Russia's new critics (Muratov, Shchekotov) were especially drawn to reflections of the traditions of Classical art in the medieval Russian icon, which enabled them to view the icon as an integral part of the wider culture of Byzantium and Western Europe. The same may be said about research by Berenson, Frederick Mason Perkins (1874–1955) and others on early Italian painting: the Italian 'primitives', like medieval Russian icons, were described as the work of artists identifiable by their distinct artistic style and as possessing a unique aura of lived aesthetic experience. Moreover, the attentive gaze of connoisseur collectors (such as Herbert Horne (1864–1916) or Ostroukhov), whose artistic instinct – according to new Formalist thinking – allowed them to understand the techniques used to create a work of art, could also reveal the true value of a masterpiece. And who was the consumer of these new masterpieces during the *Belle Époque*? Without doubt it was the aesthete and the affluent gentleman. Well-educated antiquarian restorers and commissioners, likewise in possession of that corpus of Old Believer expertise on the medieval Russian icon that was actively applied not only in academia but amongst collectors too, were also prominent players.

The art of the medieval Russian icon was first put before a mass audience in 1913. I have endeavoured to show that contemporary aesthetic theories and the new collecting, thoroughly permeated by a 'Modernist' style of thinking, lay behind the façade of the famous *Vystavka drevne-russkogo iskusstva* [*Old Russian Art*] exhibition in Moscow. It was after this particular exhibition that the medieval Russian icon became tangibly present in the cultural consciousness of an entire generation of artists. The icon's lines and pure colour helped the Russian avant-garde to regain painting's independence as a special way of understanding the world (see, especially, Kazimir Malevich (1879–1935) and Wassily Kandinsky (1866–1944)). In his books, the Russian artist Aleksei Grishchenko (1883–1977) articulated the endeavour to discover the meanings contained in the very language of medieval Russian art.

At the same time, documents clearly convey that the new collections were also significantly shaped by financial considerations. Conceiving of the icon as art immediately turned it into a commodity in the international art market. From 1929 to 1932, the Soviet state organized a grandiose exhibition and sale of 'medieval Russian primitives' in

Western Europe and the USA, and only international intervention (and the opposition of western art dealers) ensured the preservation of many prominent masterpieces of medieval Russian painting in Russian museum collections. Due to historical reasons, therefore, the medieval Russian icon did not capture the attention of the European art market, which continued to develop around the concept of authorial uniqueness. Western European reviews of the exhibition, moreover, confirmed that the search for the transcendent and the irrational in artistic forms was increasingly aligned with the general intellectual and spiritual mood of *modernity*.

Today, the concept of a 'masterpiece' is a matter of faith. The favourite topic of Postmodern theory – that of the non-specialist and the ordinary – essentially elides the difference between a masterpiece and any other artistic work, even those produced for a mass audience. The same applies to the difference between an artist and not-an-artist, in other words, ordinary individuals who paste their texts on social media platforms, such as Facebook, YouTube and X (formerly, Twitter). What we are talking about here is the art market's global domination, which governs each and all with its sign system and codes of behaviour. Moreover, sources detailing the initial discovery and collecting of medieval Russian icons and Italian 'primitives' have already revealed this system in its infancy, showcasing its evolution as it began to incorporate what had previously not been regarded as 'art'. However, the concept of a 'masterpiece' as applied to a work of art has continued to exist because museums, with their permanent exhibitions, continue to exist. The medieval icon (as a historically determined way of artistically interpreting the world) occupies a most honourable place in such exhibitions. The icon, like the abstract paintings of the twentieth century, steadfastly highlights the unreliability of the reality around us. And in this regard, for the most serious research on the limits of visibility in the era of Modernism, the icon was, and is, entirely contemporary.

Bibliography

Archives

Berenson Library Archive, Villa I Tatti, The Harvard University Center for Italian Renaissance Studies, Florence.

Biblioteka i archive doma-muzeia svaschennika Pavla Florenskogo v Moskve [*Library and Archive of the House-museum of the Priest Pavel Florenskii, Moscow*].

Otdel rukopisei Gosudarstvennogo Russkogo Muzeia (OR GRM) [*State Russian Museum, Manuscript Division, St Petersburg*], fonds 137.

Otdel rukopisei Gosudarstvennoi Tretiakovskoi Gellerei (OR GTG) [*State Tretiakov Gallery, Manuscript Division, Moscow*], fonds 10.

Rossiiskii gosudarstvennyi arkhiv literatury i iskusstva (RGALI) [*Russian State Archive of Literature and Art*], fonds 822.

Secondary Sources

Acheimastou-Potamianou, M., *Icons of the Byzantine Museum of Athens* (Athens: Ministry of Culture, Archaeological Receipts Fund, 1998).

Agosti, G., M. E. Manca and M. Panzeri, eds., *Giovanni Morelli e la cultura dei conoscitori, Atti del convegno internazionale, Bergamo, 4–7 June 1987* (Bergamo: P. Lubrina, 1993).

Ainalov, D. V., *Ellinisticheskie osnovy vyzantiiskogo iskusstva* (St Petersburg: n.p., 1900).

Ainalov, D. V., *The Hellenistic Origins of Byzantine Art*, ed. C. Mango, trans. E. and S. Sobolevitch, (New Brunswick, NJ: Rutgers University Press, 1961).

Alpatov, M., 'K voprosu o zapadnom vliianii na drevnerusskoe iskusstvo', *Slavia*, 3 (1924), 94–113.

Anisimov, A. I., 'Tserkovnaia starina na vystavke XV arkheologicheskogo s'ezda v Novgorode', *Starye gody* (October 1911), 40–47.

Anisimov, A. I., *The Vladimir Icon of Mother of God* (Prague: Seminarium Kondakovianum, 1928).

Anisimov A. I., and P. P. Muratov, *Novgorodskaia ikona Feodora Stratilata* (Moscow: K. F. Nekrasov, 1916).

Antonova, C., 'On the Problem of "Reverse Perspective": Definition East and West', *Leonardo*, 43.5 (2010), 464–69.

Antonova, C., *Space, Time and Presence in the Icon: Seeing the World with the Eyes of God* (Farnham: Ashgate, 2010).

Antonova, C., *Visual Thought in Russian Religious Philosophy: Pavel Florensky's Theory of the Icon* (New York: Routledge, 2020), https://doi.org/10.4324/9780429262890

Art Institute of Chicago, *Catalogue of Russian Icons* (Chicago, IL: Metropolitan Museum of Art, 1931).

Babelon, J.-P., M. Laclotte, N. S. F. Garnot and N. Volle, eds., *Primitifs italiens du Musée Jacquemart-André* (Paris: Editions Noesis, 2000).

Bakhrakh, A., '"Evropeets" s Arbata', in *Vozvrashchenie Muratova. Ot 'Obrazov Italii' do 'Istorii kavkazskikh voin'. Po materialam vystavki 'Pavel Muratov – chelovek Serebrianogo veka' v Gos. Muzee izovrazitel'nykh iskusstv imeni A. S. Pushkina 3 marta–20 aprelia 2008 goda*, ed. G. I. Vzdornov and K. M. Muratova (Moscow: Indrik, 2008), pp. 158–59.

Bakushinskii, A. V., 'Linear perspektiva v isskustve i zritel'nom vospriiatii real'nogo prostranstva', *Iskusstvo*, 1 (1923), 213–63.

Baldassari, A., *Icones de l'art moderne. La collection Chtchoukine* (*Livres d'art*) (Paris: Fondation Louis Vuitton, 2016).

Baldry, F., 'Rooms of Taste. Houses and House Museums of Collectors and Antique Dealers in Florence between the 19th and 20th Centuries', in *Le stanze dei tesori. Collezionisti e antiquari a Firenze tra Ottocento e Novecento*, ed. L. Mannini (Florence: Polistampa, 2011), pp. 44–64.

Barchtchévski, I., and D. Laroche, *Objets d'art Russes anciens faisant partie des collections de la Princesse Marie Tenichev, exposes au musée des arts décoratifs du 10 Mai au 10 Octobre*, 1907 (Paris: Gauterin, 1907).

Barolskii, P., 'Walter Pater and Bernard Berenson', *New Criterion*, 2 (1984), 47–57.

Bazen, G., *Istoriia istorii iskusstva. Ot Vazari do nashikh dnei*, trans. K. A. Chekalov (Moscow: Progress, 1995).

Bellini, L., *Nel mondo degli antiquari* (Florence: Edizioni del Turco, 1947).

Belting, H., *Obraz i kul't. Istoriia obraza do epokhi iskusstva*, trans. K. A. Piganovich (Moscow: Progress-Traditsiia, 2002).

Bely, A., *Simbolizm kak miroponimanie* (Moscow: Respublika, 1994).

Benois, A., 'Ikony i novoe iskusstvo', *Rech'*, 93 (1913), 2.

Benois, A., *Moi vospominaniia*, 2 vols. (Moscow: Nauka, 1993).

Benois, A., 'Poslednaiai futuristicheskaia vystavka', *Rech'* (9 January 1916), n.p.

Benois, A., 'Russkie ikony i Zapad', *Rech'*, 37 (1913), 2.

Berdiaev, N., *Filosofiia tvorchestva, kul'tury i iskusstva*, 2 vols. (Moscow: Iskusstvo, 1994).

Berdiaev, N., 'Pikasso', *Sofiia*, 3 (1914), 57–62.

Berenson, B., *The Central Italian Painters of the Renaissance* (New York and London: Putnam, 1897).

Berenson, B., *Essays in the Study of Sienese Painting* (New York: Frederic Fairchild Sherman, 1918).

Berenson, B., *Florentiiskie zhivopistsy Vozrozhdeniia*, trans. with an introduction by P. P. Muratov (Moscow: S. I. Sakharov, 1923).

Berenson, B., *The Italian Painters in the Renaissance* (Oxford: Oxford University Press, 1952).

Berenson, B., *The Italian Painters of the Renaissance* (London: Phaidon, 1959).

Berenson, B., *Lorenzo Lotto* (Milan: Electa, 1955).

Berenson, B., 'Osnovy khudozhestvennogo raspoznavaniia', *Sofiia*, 1 (1914), 40–69.

Berenson, B., *Studies in Medieval Painting* (New Haven, CT: Yale University Press, 1930).

Berenson, B., *The Study and Criticism of Italian Art* (London: G. Bell and Sons, 1902).

Berenson, B., *Zhivopistsy ital'ianskogo Vozrozhdeniia* (Moscow: Iskusstvo, 1965).

Bernabó, M., 'Pavel Muratov sull'arte bizantina e russa e sui primitivi italiani (1924–1928)', in *Letture Muratoviane III. Atti del Colloquio Internazionale (Napoli, 28–30 settembre 2017). Studi in memoria di Xenia Muratova*, ed. R. Giuliani (Rome: Lithos, 2021), pp. 257–69.

Bernardi, G., ed., *Bernard Berenson and Byzantine Art. Correspondence, 1920–1957*, with a contribution by S. Koulouris and preface by M. Bernabò (Turnhout: Brepols, 2023).

Bode, W. von, *Die Anfänge der Majolikakunst in Toskana* (Berlin: Julius Bard, 1911).

Bulgakov, S., *Ikona i ikonopochitanie* (Moscow: Russkii put', 1996).

Buslaev, F. I., 'Moi vospominaniia', *Vestnik Evropy*, 5 (1891), 171.

Buslaev, F. I., *Moi vospominaniia* (Moscow: Tipografiia G. Lessnera i A. Geshel'ia, 1897).

Buslaev, F. I., 'Moskovskie molel'ni', in F. I. Buslaev, *Sochineniia F. I. Buslaeva*, 3 vols. (St Petersburg: V Tipografii Tovarishchestva 'Obschestvennaia pol'za', 1908), I, 252–53.

Bychkov, V., *The Aesthetic Face of Being: Art in the Theology of Pavel Florensky* (Crestwood, NY: St. Vladimir's Seminary Press, 1993).

Deonna, W., 'Iskusstvo i deistvitel'nost'. Voprosy arkheologicheskogo metoda', *Sofiia*, 5 (1914), 22–48.

Du Prel, K., *Filosofiia mistiki ili dvoistvennost' chelovecheskogo sushchestva*, trans. M. S. Aksenov (St Petersburg: n.p., 1895).

Durand, J., ed., *Byzance. L'art byzantine dans les collections publiques françaises* (Paris: Éditions de la Réunion des musées nationaux, 1992).

Calo, M. A., *Bernard Berenson and the Twentieth Century* (Philadelphia, PA: Temple University Press, 1994).

Camporeale, E., 'On the Early Collections of Italian Primitives', in *Le stanze dei tesori. Collezionisti e antiquari a Firenze tra Ottocento e Novecento*, ed. L. Mannini (Florence: Polistampa, 2011), pp. 29–43.

Carboni, C., *L'ultima icona: arte, filosofia, teologia* (Milan: Jaca Book, 2019).

Carr, A. W., ed., *Imprinting the Divine. Byzantine and Russian Icons from the Menil Collection* (New Haven, CT: Yale University Press, 2011).

Chalpachcjan, V., 'Il destino della collezione romana del Conte Grigorij S. Stroganoff (1829–1910) dopo la scomparsa del collezionista', *Rivista d'arte*, 5.2 (2012), 446–73.

Chatzidakis, M., 'Le peintures des madonneri ou Veneto cretoise et sa destination', in *Venezia centro di mediazione tra Oriente e Occidente*, ed. H.-G. Beck, M. Manoussacs and A. Pertusi, 2 vols. (Florence: 1977), II, 675–90.

Chatzidakis, N., *Icons. The Velimezis Collection* (Thessaloniki: The Benaki Museum, 1997).

Cohen, R., *Bernard Berenson: A Life in the Picture Trade* (New Haven, CT: Yale University Press, 2013).

Cohen, R., *Bernard Berenson: da Boston a Firenze*, trans. M. Gini (Milan: Adelphi, 2017).

Cole, B., *Sienese Painting from its Origins to the Fifteenth Century* (New York: Harper and Row, 1980).

Conti, A., *A History of the Restoration and Conservation of Works of Art*, trans. G. Glanville (Oxford: Oxford University Press, 2007).

Conticelli, V., and D. Parenti, *Icone russe in mostra alla Galleria degli Uffizi. Catalogo* (Florence: Sillabe, 2014).

Conway, M., 'The History of Russian Icon Painting', in *Masterpieces of Russian Painting*, ed. M. Farbman (London: Europa Publications, 1930), pp. 13–34.

Cormack, R., *Icons* (London: The British Museum Press, 2007).

Cormack, R., *Painting the Soul: Icons, Death Masks, and Shrouds* (London: Reaktion, 1997).

Corrado, R., *La mostra dell'antica arte senese. Aprile–Agosto 1904. Catalogo generale illustrato* (Siena: L. Lazzeri, 1904).

Craddock, P., *Scientific Investigation of Copies, Fakes and Forgeries* (Amsterdam: Elsevier, 2009).

Dalton, O. M., *Byzantine Art and Archaeology* (Oxford: Clarendon Press, 1911).

Danilova, I. E., ed., *Gosudarstvennyi muzei izobrazitel'nykh iskusstv im. A.S. Pushkina. Katalog zhivopisi* (Moscow: n.p., 1995).

Deotto, P., 'Pavel Muratov', in *Dictionary of Literary Biography: Russian Émigré Writers of the Twentieth Century*, ed. M. Rubins (Washington, DC: Thomson Gale, 2005), pp. 237–47.

Denkmäler altrussischer Malerei. Russische Ikonen vom 12.–18. Jahrhundert (n.a.) (Berlin: Ost-Europa-Verlag, 1929).

Denkmäler altrussischer Malerei. Russische Ikonen vom 12.–18. Jahrhundert (n.a.) (Vienna: Hagenbund, 1929).

Diaghilev, S., and A. Benois, *Salon d'automne. Exposition de l'art Russe* (Paris: Moreau frères, 1906).

Diehl, C., *Manuel d'art Byzantin* (Paris: A. Picard, 1910).

Douglas, R. L., ed., *Exhibition of Pictures of the School of Siena, and Examples of the Minor Arts of that City* (London: Burlington Fine Arts Club, 1904).

Dzhotto I dzhotisty (n.a.) (Moscow: n.p., 1881).

Efros, A. A., 'Peterburgskoe i moskovskoe sobiratel'stvo (Paralleli)', *Sredi kollektsionerov*, 4 (1921), 13–20.

Evdokimov, P. N., *Teologia della bellezza. L'arte dell'icona* (Milan: Edizioni San Paolo, 2017).

Ferrazza, R., *Palazzo Davanzati e le collezioni di Elia Volpi* (Florence: Centro Di, 1994).

Ferretti, S., *Cassirer, Panofsky and Warburg: Symbol, Art and History* (New Haven, CT: Yale University Press, 1989).

Fiorin, M. F., *Catalogo della Pinacoteca Vaticana. Vol. 4: Icone della Pinacoteca Vaticana* (Vatican City: Edizioni Musei Vaticani, 1995).

Florenskii, P. A., 'Analiz prostranstvennosti i vremeni v khudozhestvenno-izobrazitel'nykh proizvedeniiakh', in P. A. Florenskii, *Istoriia i filosofiia iskusstva. Sbornik tekstov* (Moscow: Akademicheskij proekt, 2017), pp. 237–520.

Florenskii, P. A., *Bellezza e liturgia. Scritti su cristianesimo e cultura*, trans. C. Zonghetti (Milan: Mondadori, 2010).

Florenskii, P. A., *Beyond Vision. Essays on the Perception of Art*, ed. N. Misler, trans. W. Salmond (London: Reaktion, 2002).

Florenskii, P. A., *Detiam moim. Vospominaniia proshlykh let* (Moscow: Moskovskii rabochii, 2000).

Florenskii, P. A., *Iconostasis*, trans. D. Sheehan and O. Andrejev (Crestwood, NY: St. Vladimir's Seminary Press, 1996).

Florenskii, P. A., 'Ikonostas', in P. A. Florenskii, *Istoriia i filosofiia iskusstva. Sbornik tekstov* (Moscow: Akademicheskij proekt, 2017), pp. 9–118.

Florenskii, P. A., *Istoriia i filosofiia iskusstva. Sbornik tekstov*, ed. Andronik Trubachev et al. (Moscow: Akademicheskij proekt, 2017).

Florenskii, P. A., *La colonna e il fondamento della verità*, ed. N. Valentini and C. Balsamo (Milan: Edizioni San Paulo, 2010).

Florenskii, P. A., *La mistica e l'anima russa*, ed. N. Valentini and L. Zak (Milan: Edizioni San Paolo, 2006).

Florenskii, P. A., *Le porte regali. Saggio sull' icona*, ed. E. Zolla (Milan: Adelphi, 1977).

Florenskii, P. A., *La prospettiva rovesciata e altri scritti*, ed. N. Misler (Rome: Casa del libro, 1983).

Florenskii, P. A., 'Magichnost' slova', in P. A. Florenskii, *Sochineniia v 2-x tomakh*, 2 vols. (Moscow: Mysl', 1990), II, 252–73.

Florenskii, P. A., *Mnimosti v geometrii* (Moscow: Lazur' Publ., 2004).

Florenskii, P. A. 'Molennye ikony prepodobnogo Sergiia', in P. A. Florenskii, *Istoriia i filosofiia iskusstva. Sbornik tekstov* (Moscow: Akademicheskij proekt, 2017), pp. 145–63.

Florenskii, P. A., 'Obratnaia perspektiva', in P. A. Florenskii, *Istoriia i filosofiia iskusstva. Sbornik tekstov* (Moscow: Akademicheskij proekt, 2017), pp. 181–236.

Florenskii, P. A., 'Obratnaia perspektiva', *Trudy po znakovym sistemam*, 3 (1967), 381–416.

Florenskii, P. A., 'On the Icon', *Eastern Churches Review*, 8.1 (1976), 11–37.

Florenskii, P. A., 'Predely gnoseologii', *Bogoslovskii vestnik*, 1.1 (1913), 170–73.

Florenskii, P. A., 'Smysl idealizma (metafizika roda i lika)', in P. A. Florenskii, *Sochineniia v 4-x tomakh*, 4 vols. (Moscow: Mysl', 2000), III, 101–03.

Florenskii, P. A., *Stolp i utverzhdenie istiny. Opit pravoslavnoi teoditsei* (Moscow: Izdavitel'stvo pravda, 1990).

Florenskii, P. A., 'Stroenie slova', *Kontekst* (1972), 348–55.

Florenskii, P. A., *U vodorazdelov mysli*. □. *1. Stat'i po iskusstvu* (Paris: YMCA Press, 1985).

Florovskii, G., *Puti russkogo bogosloviia* (Moscow: Institut russkoi tsivilizatsii, 2009).

Foletti, I., *From Byzantium to Holy Russia. Nikodim Kondakov (1844–1925) and the Invention of the Icon*, trans. S. Melker (Rome: Viella, 2011).

Fondazione Giorgio Chini, *L'immagine dello spirito. Icone dalle terre russe, collezione Ambroveneto* (Milan: Electa, 1996).

Freud, S., *Tolkovanie snovidenii*, trans. M. Kotik (Moscow: N. A. Stollyar, 1913).

Friedländer, M., *Der Kunstkenner* (Berlin: Cassirer, 1919).

Friedländer, M., *Ob iskusstve i znatochestve*, trans. M. I. Korenev, 2nd ed. (Moscow: Andrey Naslednikov, 2013).

Frisby, J., and J. V. Stone, *Seeing. The Computation Approach to Biological Vision* (Cambridge, MA: The MIT Press, 2010).

Fry, R. 'Russian Icon Painting from the West European Point of View', in *Masterpieces of Russian Painting*, ed. M. Farbman (London: Europa Publications, 1930), pp. 35–58.

Gasbarri, G., *Riscoprire Bisanzio. Lo studio dell'arte bizantina a Roma e in Italia tra Ottocento e Novecento* (Rome: Viella, 2015).

Georgievskii, V. T., 'Kollektsiia drevnikh ikon N. P. Likhachev', *Novoe vremiia* (29 July 1913), n.p.

Georgievskii, V. T. 'Obzor vystavki drevnerusskoi ikonopisi i khudozhestvennoi stariny', *Trudy Vserossiiskogo s"ezda khudozhnikov*, 3 (1913), 163–74.

Gevaert, F., 'Vystavka "Zolotogo Runa" v Briugge', *Starye gody* (December 1907), 616–17.

Gombrich, E. H., *The Preference for the Primitive. Episodes in the History of Western Taste and Art* (London: Phaidon, 2002).

Goncharova, N., *Vystavka ikonopisnykh podlinnikov i lubkov, organizovannaia M. F. Larionovym* (Moscow: Khudozhestvennyi salon, 1913).

Grabar, I. E., ed., *Istoriia Russkogo iskusstva*, 6 vols. (Moscow: Knebel, 1910–14).

Grabar, I. E., *Moia zhizn'. Avtomonografiia. Etiudy o khudozhnikakh* (Moscow: Respublika, 2001).

Grabar, I. E., 'Glaz', *Sredi kollektsionerov*, 4 (1921), 3–5.

Grabar, I. E., *Pis'ma 1891–1917* (Moscow: Nauka, 1974).

Graham, L., and J. M. Kantor, *Naming Infinity. A True Story of Religious Mysticism and Mathematical Creativity* (Cambridge, MA: Harvard University Press, 2009).

Grekhem, L., *Imena beskonechnosti: pravdivaia istoriia o religioznom mistitsizme i matematicheskom tvorchestve*, trans. Kantor Zh. M. (St Petersburg: European University at St Petersburg, 2011).

Grigorovich, D. V., 'Dom P. S. Stroganov na Sergievskoi ulitse', *Pchela*, 1 (1875), 9.

Grishchenko, A., *Russkaia ikona kak iskusstvo zhivopisi* (Moscow: Izdanie Avtora, 1917).

Grishchenko, A., *O sviaziakh russkoi zhivopisi s Vizantiei i Zapadom. XIII–XX vv.* (Moscow: A. A. Levenson, 1913).

Grüneisen, W. de, 'Illiuzionisticheskii portret', *Sofiia*, 4 (1914), 5–59.

Grüneisen, W. de., *Sainte Marie Antique* (Rome: Bretschneider, 1911).

Hannay, H., *Roger Fry and Other Essays* (London: George Allen and Unwin, 1937).

Haskell, F., ed., *Anatole Demidoff. Prince of San Donato (1812–1870)* (London: Trustees of the Wallace Collection, 1994).

Haskell, F., *History and Its Images. Art and Interpretation of the Past* (New Haven, CT: Yale University Press, 1995).

Haskell, F., 'Les expositions des Maritres anciens et la seconde "redecouverte des primitifs"', in *Hommage à Michel Laclotte. Etudes sur la peinture du Moyen Age et de la Renaissance*, ed. F. Bologna and M. Laclotte (Milan: Electa, 1994), pp. 552–64.

Haskell, F., *Rediscoveries in Art. Some Aspects of Taste, Fashion and Collecting in England and France* (Ithaca, NY: Cornell University Press, 1976).

Haustein-Bartsch, E., and I. Bentchev, *Ikonen-Museum Recklinghausen* (Moscow: Ikonen-Museum Recklinghausen, 2008).

Hendy, P., *European and American Paintings in the Isabella Stewart Gardner Museum* (Boston, MA: Trustees of the Isabella Stewart Gardner Museum, 1974).

Hildebrand, A., *Problema formy v izobrazitel'nom iskusstve*, trans. N. B. Rozenfel'd and V. A. Favorskii (Moscow: Musaget, 1914).

Holly, M., *Panofsky and the Foundation of Art History* (Ithaca, NY: Cornell University Press, 1984).

Horne, H., *Alessandro Filipepi Commonly Called Sandro Botticelli, Painter of Florence* (London: G. Bell and Sons, 1908).

Hovey, W. R., *The Nicholas Lochoff Cloister of the Henry Clay Frick Fine Arts Building* (Pittsburgh, PA: University of Pittsburgh, 1967).

'I falsi degli Uffizi' (n.a.), *L'Antiquario*, 5 (1908), 38–39.

Ivolgin, V., 'Nravy ikonotorgovtsev', *Peterburgskii listok* (30 July 1913), n.p.

Iz kollektsii akademika N. P. Likhacheva. Katalog vystavki v Gosudarstvennom Russkom muzee (n.a.) (St Petersburg: Seda-S, 1993).

Jandolo, A., *Le memorie di un antiquario* (Milan: Ceschina, 1935).

Joni, I. F., *Le memorie di un pittore di quadri antichi. A fronte la versione in inglese 'Affairs of a Painter'*, ed. G. Mazzoni (Siena: Protagon Editori, 2004).

Kallab, W., *Die toskanische Landschaftsmalerei in XIV und XV Jahrhundert* (Vienna: Vienna Holzhausen, 1900).

Kandinsky, W., *Tochka i liniia na ploskosti*, trans. E. Kozina (Moscow: Azbuka, 2003).

Kandinsky, W., *O dukhovnom v iskusstve* (Moscow: Arkhimed, 1992).

Kantor, S. G., *Alfred H. Barr, Jr. and the Intellectual Origins of the Museum of Modern Art* (Cambridge, MA: The MIT Press, 2002).

Karakatsanis, A. A., ed., *Treasures of Mount Athos* (Thessaloniki: Museum of Byzantine Culture, 1999).

Kauchtschischwili, N., and M. Hagemeister, eds., *P. A. Florenskij e la cultura della sua epoca* (Marburg: Blaue Hörner Verlag, 1995).

Kazanaki-Lappa, M., ed., *Nasledie Vizantii: Muzei ikon Grecheskogo instituta vizantiiskikh i postvizantiiskikh issledovanii v Venetsii* (Moscow: Grand-Kholding, 2009).

Kemp, M., *The Science of Art: Optical Themes in Western Art from Brunelleschi to Seurat* (New Haven, CT: Yale University Press, 1992).

Khardzhiev, N., *K istorii russkogo avangarda* (Stockholm: Hylea Prints, 1976).

Khvoshchinskii, V. T., *Toskanskie khudozhniki. I. Primitivy* (St Petersburg: n.p., 1912).

Kieven, E., ed., *100 Jahre Bibliotheca Hertziana. Der Palazzo Zuccari und die Institutsgebäude 1590–2013* (Munich: Hirmer Verlag, 2013).

Kondakov, N. P., *Ikonografiia Bogomateri. Sviazi grecheskoi i russkoi ikonopisi s ital'ianskoi zhivopis'iu rannego Vozrozhdeniia* (St Petersburg: Tipografiia imperatorskoi akademii nauk, 1911).

Kondakov, N. P., *The Russian Icon*, trans. E. Minns (Oxford: Clarendon Press, 1927).

Kondakov, N. P., *Russkaia ikona*, 4 vols. (Prague: Seminarium Kondakovianum, 1928–32).

Kostenevich, A. G., and N. Y. Semenova, eds., *Matiss v Rossii* (Moscow: Avangard, 1993).

Kustodieva, T. K., ed., *Sobranie zapadnoevropeiskoi zhivopisi. Katalog. Ital'ianskaia zhivopis' XIII–XVI vv* (Moscow: Gosudarstvennyi Ermitazh, 1994).

Kyzlasova, I. L., *Aleksandr Ivanovich Anisimov (1877–1937)* (Moscow: Izd. Moskovskogo Gosudarstvennogo Gornogo universiteta, 2000).

Kyzlasova, I. L., ed., *Mir Kondakova. Publikatsii. Stat'i. Katalog vystavki* (Moscow: Russkii put', 2004).

Lantz, K. A., ed., *The Sealed Angel and Other Stories by Nikolay Leskov* (Knoxville, TN: University of Tennessee Press, 1984).

Lazarev, V., *L'arte russa delle icone dalle origini all'inizio del XVI secolo*, ed. G. I. Vzdornov (Milan: Jaca Book, 1996).

Lazarev, V., 'Un nuovo capolavoro della pittura fiorentina duecentesca', *Rivista d'arte*, 30 (1953), 3–63.

Lenain, F., *Art Forgery. A History of a Modern Obsession* (London: Reaktion, 2012).

Leroy, A., *Histoire de la peinture religieuse des origines à nos jours* (Paris: Amiot-Dumont, 1954).

Likhachev, N. P., *Istoricheskoe znachenie italo-grecheskoi ikonopisi. Izobrazhenie Bogomateri v proizvedeniiakh italo-grecheskikh ikonopistsev i ikh vliianie na kompozitsii nekotorykh proslavlennykh russkikh ikon* (St Petersburg: Izdanie Russkago arkheologicheskogo obva, 1911).

Likhachev, N. P., *Materialy dlia istorii russkogo ikonopisaniia: Atlas* (St Petersburg: Ekspeditsiia zagotovleniia gosudarstvennykh bumag, 1906).

Lindsay, A. W. C., *Sketches of the History of Christian Art*, 3 vols. (London: John Murray, 1847).

Lipgart, E., 'Dar grafa P. S. Stroganova Imperatorskomu Ermitazhu', *Starye gody* (April 1912), 33–45.

Lipgart, E., 'Imperatorskii Ermitazh. Priobreteniia i pereveski', *Starye gody* (January 1910), 19.

Lipgart, E., 'Kak kollektsiionirovala Velikaia kniaginia Mariia Nikolaevna', in *Nasledie Velikoi Kniagini Marii Nikolaevny*, ed. Baron N. N. Vrangel (St Petersburg: n.p., 1913), pp. 8–11.

Lo Gatto, E., *I miei incontri con la Russia* (Milan: Mursia, 1976).

Lock, C., 'What is Reverse Perspective and Who was Oskar Wulff?', *Sobornost/ Eastern Christian Review*, 33.1 (2011), 60–89.

Logan (Berenson), M., 'A Reconstructor of Old Masterpieces', *The American Magazine of Art*, 21 (1930), 628–38.

Losev, A. F., *Ocherki antichnogo simbolizma i mifologii* (Moscow: Mysl', 1930).

Mach, E., *Analiz oshchushchenii* (Moscow: Skirmunta, 1908).

Mach, E., *Poznanie i zabluzhdenie. Ocherki po psikhologii issledovaniia* (Moscow: Skirmunta, 1909).

Makovskii, S., ed., *Russkaia ikona*, 3 vols. (St Petersburg: T. Golika and A. Vilborg, 1914).

Mannini, L., 'Antique Dealer Artists Between the 19th and 20th centuries (and Paintings like Antique Shops)', in *Le stanze dei tesori. Collezionisti e antiquari a Firenze tra Ottocento e Novecento*, ed. L. Mannini (Florence: Polistampa, 2011), pp. 65–78.

Markova, V. E., *Italiia VIII–XVI vekov. Sobranie zhivopisi Gos. Muzeia izobrazitel'nykh iskusstv im. A. S. Pushkina. Katalog*, 2 vols. (Moscow: Galart, 2002).

Markova, V. E., 'Ital'ianskie "primitivy" v traditsii russkogo sobiratel'stva', in *Chastnoe kollektsionirovanie v Rossii. Materialy nauchnoi konferentsii 'Vipperovaskie chteniia-1994'*, ed. I. E. Danilova (Moscow: Gosudarstvennyĭ muzeĭ izobrazitel, nykh iskusstv im. A.S. Pushkina, 1995), pp. 186–99.

'Matiss v Moskve: V Tret'iakovskoi galeree. V krugu estetov' (n.a.), *Utro Rossii*, 248 (27 October 1911), 4.

Mavarelli, C., ed., *Museo Bandini di Fiesole. Guida* (Florence: Polistampa, 2011).

Mazzoni, G., ed., *Falsi d'autore. Icilio Federico Joni e la cultura del falso tra otto e novecento* (Siena: Protagon, 2004).

Mazzoni, G., *Quadri antichi del Novecento* (Vicenza: Neri Pozza, 2001).

Mikhailov, A. V., 'Pavel Florenskii kak filosof granitsy. K vykhodu v svet kriticheskogo izdaniia "Ikonostasa"', *Voprosy iskussvoznaniia*, 4 (1994), 33–71.

Millet, G., *Monuments byzantins de Mistra* (Paris: E. Leroux, 1910), https://bibliotheque-numerique.inha.fr/collection/item/16247-monuments-byzantins-de-mistra

Minns, E. H., 'The Exhibition of Icons at the Victoria and Albert Museum', *Slavonic and East European Review*, 8 (1930), 627–35.

Moench, E., ed., *Primitifs italiens, le vrai, le faux, la fortune critique* (Milan: Silvana Editoriale, 2012).

Moretti, S., *Roma bizantina. Opere d'arte dall' impero di Costantinopoli nelle collezioni romane* (Rome: Campisano, 2014).

Moscowitz, A. F., *Stefano Bardini 'Principe degli Antiquari'. Prolegomenon to a Biography* (Florence: Centro Di, 2015).

Muñoz, A., 'La collezione Stroganoff', *Rassegna contemporanea*, 3.10 (1910), 9.

Muñoz, A., and L. Pollak, *Pièces de choix de la collection du Comte Gregoire Stroganoff à Rome*, 2 vols. (Rome: Impr. de l'Unione editrice, 1912).

Muratov, P. P., 'Drevniaia ikonopis', *Russkoe slovo*, 36 (13 February 1913), 2.

Muratov, P. P., *Fra Angelico*, trans. J. Chuzeville (Paris: Editions G. Crès, 1929).

Muratov, P. P., *Fra Angelico. His Life and Work*, trans. E. Law-Gisiko (New York: F. Warne and Co., 1930).

Muratov, P. P., *Frate Angelico* (Rome: Valori Plastici, 1929).

Muratov, P. P., 'Ikonopis' pri pervom tsare iz Doma Romanovykh', *Starye gody* (July–September 1913), 25–33.

Muratov, P. P., *Immagini dell'Italia*, ed. R. Giuliani, trans. A. Romano, 2 vols. (Milan: Adelphi, 2019–21).

Muratov, P. P., *La peinture byzantine*, trans. J. Chuzeville (Paris: Editions G. Crès, 1928).

Muratov, P. P., *La pittura bizantina* (Rome: Valori Plastici, 1928).

Muratov, P. P., *La pittura russa antica*, trans. E. Lo Gatto (Rome: A. Stock, 1925).

Muratov, P. P., *La sculpture gothique* (Rome: Valori Plastici, 1931).

Muratov, P. P., *Les icones russes* (Paris: Schiffrin 1927).

Muratov, P. P., ed. and trans., *Novelly ital'ianskogo Vozrozhdeniia*, 2 vols. (Moscow: n.p., 1913).

Muratov, P. P., 'Novoe sobiratel'stvo', *Sredi kollektsionerov*, 4 (1921), 1–3.

Muratov, P. P., 'Novoe tondo shkoly Bottichelli', *Starye gody* (May 1911), 29–34.

Muratov, P. P., *Obrazy Italii*, 2 vols. (Moscow: Izdanie Nauchnogo Slova, 1911–12).

Muratov, P. P., 'Ocherki ital'ianskoi zhivopisi v Moskovskom Rumiantsevskom muzee. I: Sienskaia Madonna', *Starye gody* (November 1910), 605–11.

Muratov, P. P., 'Ocherki ital'ianskoi zhivopisi v Moskovskom Rumiantsevskom muzee. II: Kvatrochento', *Starye gody* (October 1910), 3–11.

Muratov, P. P., 'Otkrytiia drevnego russkogo iskusstva', *Sovremennye zapiski*, 14 (1923), 197–218.

Muratov, P. P., 'Otkrytiia drevnego russkogo iskusstva', in P. P. Muratov, *Russkaia zhivopis' do serediny XVII veka. Istoriia otkrytiia i issledovaniia*, ed. A. M. Khitrov (St Petersburg: Bibliopolis, 2008), pp. 323–24.

Muratov, P. P., 'Pereotsenki', *Sofiia*, 2 (1914), 3–4.

Muratov, P. P., 'Pol' Sezann', *Vesy*, 12 (1906), 32–42.

Muratov, P. P., 'Puti russkoi ikony', *Perezvony*, 43 (1928), 1360–67.

Muratov, P. P., 'Russkaia zhivopis' do serediny XVII veka', in *Istoriia Russkogo iskusstva*, ed. I. Grabar, 6 vols. (Moscow: Knebel, 1914–16), IV, 18–21.

Muratov, P. P., *Russkaia zhivopis' do serediny XVII veka. Istoriia otkrytiia i issledovaniia*, ed. A. M. Khitrov (St Petersburg: Bibliopolis, 2008).

Muratov, P. P., 'Shchukinskaia galereiia. Ocherki iz istorii noveishei zhivopisi', *Russkaia mysl'*, 8 (1908), 116–38.

Muratov, P. P., 'Tvorchestvo M. V. Nesterova', *Russkaia mysl'*, 4 (1907), 151–58.

Muratov, P. P., 'Vizantiiskoe mifotvorichesto', *Sofiia*, 2 (1914), 3–4.

Muratov, P. P., 'Vokrug ikony', *Vozrozhdenie* (January 1933), 2787, 2799, 2803, 2809.

Muratov, P. P., 'Vystavka drevnerusskogo iskusstva v Moskve. I: Epokhi drevnerusskoi ikonopisi', *Starye gody* (April 1913), 31–38.

Muratov, P. P., *Drevnerusskaia zhivopis' v sobranii I. S. Ostroukhova* (Moscow: K. F. Nekrasov, 1914).

Muratov, P. P., and A. I. Anisimov, *Novgorodskaia ikona Sv. Feodora Stratilata* (Moscow: K. F. Nekrasov, 1916).

Muratova, K. M., 'Ital'ianskoe iskusstvo XIII i XIV vekov v russkoi kritike: sviazi, vzaimovliianiia, sud"by', in *In Christo. Vo Khriste. Obmen khudozhestvennymi i dukhovnymi shedevrami mezhdu Rossiei i Italiei*, ed. A. Melloni (Rome: Treccani, 2011), pp. 521–68.

Muratova, K. M., 'Pavel Muratov historien d'art en Occident', in *La Russie et l'Occident. Relations intellectuelles et artistiques au temps des révolutions russes*, ed. I. Foletti (Rome: Viella, 2010), pp. 65–95.

Museo dell'Opera del Duomo, *Mostra di opere di Duccio di Buoninsegna e della sua scuola. Catalogo. Siena, Museo dell'Opera del Duomo, Settembre, 1912* (Siena: L. Lazzeri, 1912).

Museum of Fine Arts, *Russian Icons* [*Catalogue of Exhibition*]. *Museum of Fine Arts, Boston. October 14–December 14* (Boston, MA: Museum of Fine Arts, 1930).

Nekrasov, E. A., 'Neosushchestvlennyi zamysel 1920-x godov sozdaniia "Symbolarium'a" (Slovaria simbolov) i ego pervyi vypusk "Tochka", *Pamiatniki kul'tury. Novye otkrytiia. Ezhegodnik 1982* (1984), 99–115.

Nelson, R. S., 'A Painting Becomes Canonical: Bernard Berenson, Royall Tayler, and the Mellon *Madonna*', in *Renaissance Studies in Honor of Joseph Connors*, ed. M. B. Israëls and L. A. Waldman, 2 vols., Villa I Tatti Series, 29 (Florence: Villa I Tatti, 2013), I, 696–701.

Neradovskii, P., 'Boris i Gleb iz sobraniia N. P. Likhacheva', *Russkaia ikona*, 1 (1914), 63–77.

Nersesjan, L., and D. Suchoverkov, *Andrej Rublev. L'icona della Trinità. A lode di san Sergio* (Rome: Orizzonti Edizioni, 2016).

Niemeyer Chini, V., *Stefano Bardini e Wilhelm Bode: mercanti e connaisseur fra Ottocento e Novecento* (Florence: Polistampa, 2009).

Nietzsche, F., *The Birth of Tragedy or Hellenism and Pessimism*, trans. W. A. Haussmann (London: George Allen and Unwin, 1910), https://www.gutenberg.org/files/51356/51356-h/51356-h.htm

Nietzsche, F., 'Rozhdenie tragedii iz dukkha muzyki. Predislovie k Richardu Vagneru', in F. Nietzsche, *Sobranie sochinenii v 2-x tomakh*, 2 vols. (Moscow: Khudozhestvennaia literatura, 1990), I, 57–157.

Nyberg, K. W., *Omvänt perspektiv i bildkonst och kontrovers: En kritisk begreppshistoria från det gångna seklet* (Uppsala: Uppsala Universitet, 2001).

'O poddel'nikh kartinakh' (n.a.), *Starye gody* (June 1909), 339–40.

Olsuf'ev, Y. A., *Opis' ikon Troitse-Sergievoi lavry* (Sergiev: Tipografia Ivanova Publ., 1920).

Opie, J. L., *Nel mondo delle icone. Dall'India a Bisanzio* (Milan: Jaca Book, 2014).

Ostroukhov, I. S., *Alfavitnyi ukazatel' biblioteki I. S. Ostroukhova* (Moscow: n.p., 1914).

'P. A. Florenskii po vospominaniiam A.F. Loseva' (n.a.), *Kontekst* (1990), 6–24.

Panofsky, E., *Perspective as Symbolic Form*, trans. C. S. Wood (New York: Zone Books, 1997).

Parshin, A. N., and O. M. Sedykh, eds., *Pavel Aleksandrovich Florenskii* (Moscow: ROSSPEN, 2013).

Pater, W., *The Renaissance. Studies in Art and Poetry* (New York: Macmillan, 1888), https://archive.org/details/renaissancestu00pate

Pater, W., *The Renaissance: Studies of Art and Poetry* (n.p.: The Floating Press, 2010 [1873]).

Pater, W., *Renessans. Ocherki iskusstva i poezii*, trans. S. G. Zaimovskii (Moscow: Problemy estetiki, 1912).

Pater, W., *Voobrazhaemye portrety. Rebenok v dome*, trans. P. P. Muratov (Moscow: V. M. Sablin, 1908).

Pavan G., ed., *Icone dalle collezioni del Museo Nazionale di Ravenna* (Ravenna: Il Museo, 1979).

Pavlutskii, G. G., 'K voprosu o vzaimnom vliianii vizantiiskogo i ital'ianskogo iskusstva', *Iskusstvo*, 5–6 (1912), 208–20.

Pegazzano, D., *Scritti di museologia e di storia del collezionismo in onore di Cristina De Benedictis* (Florence: Edifir, 2012).

Perkins, M. F., 'Appunti sulla mostra ducciana a Siena', *Rassegna d'Arte*, 13 (1913), 5–9, 35–40.

Perkins, M. F., 'La pittura alla Mostra d'arte antica a Siena', *Rassegna d'Arte*, 4.10 (1904), 145–53.

'Peterburgskaia "Russkaia ikona"' (n.a.), *Sofiia*, 96 (1914), n.p.

Pirovano, C., ed., *Arte e Sacro Mistero. Tesori dal Museo Russo di San Pietroburgo* (Milan: Electa, 2000).

Pirovano, C., ed., *Icone russe. Collezione banca Intesa, catalogo ragionato in tre tomi* (Milan: Electa, 2003).

Pirovano, C., ed., *Icone russe. Gallerie di Palazzo Leoni Montanari* (Milan: Electa, 1999).

Pisani, R. C., *The Angeli Workshop: Federigo and the Angeli Workshop. Palazzo Davanzati. Dream and Reality* (Florence: Sillabe, 2010).

'Pis'ma P. P. Muratova (1923–1926). Publikatsiia P. Deotto i E. Garetto' (n.a.), in *Archivio russo-italiano 9: Olga Resnevic Signorelli e l'emigrazione russa: corripondenze*, ed. E. Garetto, A. d'Amelia, K. Kumpan and D. Rizzi (Salerno: Europa Orientalis, 2012), pp. 81–108.

Plato, *Sobranie Sochinenii*, trans. A. F. Losev, 3 vols. (Moscow: Mysl', 1971).

Podzemskaia, N. P., 'Nauka ob iskusstve v GAKhN i teoreticheskii proekt V.V. Kandinskogo', in *Iskusstvo kak iazyk – iazyki iskusstva. Gosudarstvennaia Akademiia khudozhestvennykh nauk i esteticheskaia teoriia 1920-x godov*, ed. N. S. Plotnikov and N. P. Podzemskaia, 2 vols. (Moscow: NLO, 2017), I, 203–05.

Praz, M., *Il patto col serpente* (Milan: Adelphi, 2013).

'Prazdnik drevnerusskogo iskusstva' (n.a.), *Tserkov'*, 8 (1913), 180.

Previtali, G., *La fortuna dei primitivi: dal Vasari al Neoclassicismo* (Turin: Einaudi, 1964).

Punin, N., 'Zametki ob ikonakh iz sobraniia N. P. Likhacheva', *Russkaia ikona* 1 (1914), 21–45.

Radnoti, S., *The Fake: Forgery and Its Place in Art* (Lanham: Rowman and Littlefield, 1999).

Rauschenbach, B. V., *Prostranstvennye postroeniia v drevnerusskoi zhivopisi* (Moscow: Nauka, 1975).

Rauschenbach, B. V., *Prostranstvennye postroeniia v zhivopisi. Ocherk osnovnykh metodov* (Moscow: Nauka, 1980).

Riabushinskii, S., 'O restavratsii i sokhranenii drevnikh sviatykh ikon', *Tserkov*, 50 (1908), 1701–05.

Richardson, J., *Two Discourses. I. an Essay on the Whole Art of Criticism as it Relates to Painting… II. An Argument in Behalf of the Science of Connoisseur* (London: W. Churchill, 1719), https://archive.org/details/twodiscoursesia00conggoog

Rostovtsev, M., *Ellinisticheski-rimskii arkhitekturnyi peizazh* (St Petersburg: n.p., 1908).

Rovinskii, D. A., *Obozrenie ikonopisaniia v Rossii do kontsa XVII veka* (St Petersburg: Izdatel'stvo A. S. Suvorina, 1856 [1903]).

Rubin, W. S., *Modern Sacred Art and the Church of Assy* (New York: Columbia University Press, 1961).

Russian Icon Exhibition, *Ancient Russian Icons. From the XIIth to the XIXth Centuries*, 2nd ed. (London: Russian Icon Exhibition Committee, 1929).

Russoli, F., ed., *The Berenson Collection* (Milan: Arti Grafiche Ricordi, 1964).

Salmond, W., 'Ellis H. Minns and Nikodim Kondakov's "The Russian Icon" (1927)', in *Modernism and the Spiritual in Russian Art. New Perspectives*, ed. L. Hardiman and N. Kozicharow (Cambridge: Open Book Publishers, 2017), pp. 165–92, https://doi.org/10.11647/OBP.0115.08

Salmond, W., *Russian Icons at Hillwood* (Washington, DC: Hillwood Museum and Gardens, 1998).

Samuels, E., *Bernard Berenson. The Making of a Connoisseur* (Cambridge, MA: Harvard University Press, 1979).

Samuels, E., *Bernard Berenson. The Making of a Legend* (Cambridge, MA: Harvard University Press, 1979).

Schapiro, M., 'Mr. Berenson's Values', *Encounter*, 16 (1961), 57–65.

Semenova, N., *Morozov: The Story of a Family and a Lost Collection*, trans. A. Tait (New Haven, CT: Yale University Press, 2020), https://doi.org/10.2307/j.ctv17z848g

Semenova, N., and A.-M. Delocque-Fourcaud, *The Collector: The Story of Sergei Shchukin and His Lost Masterpieces* (New Haven, CT: Yale University Press, 2018).

Shchekotov, N. M., 'Ikonopis' kak iskusstvo. Po povodu sobraniia ikon I. S. Ostroukhov i S. P. Riabushinskogo', *Russkaia ikona*, 2 (1914), 115–42.

Shchekotov, N. M., 'Nekotorye cherty stilia russkikh ikon XV veka', *Starye gody* (April 1913), 38–42.

Shcherbatov, S., *Khudozhnik v ushedshei Rossii* (New York: Izdatel'stvo imeni Chekhova, 1955).

Shcherbatov, S., *Khudozhnik v ushedshei Rossii* (Moscow: Soglasie, 2000).

Shmidt, D. A., 'O primitivakh. Vozrozhdenie na Severe', *Starye gody* (November–December 1908), 661–64.

Shteler, T., 'Obratnaia perspektiva: Pavel Florenskii i Moris Merlo-Ponti o prostranstve i lineinoi perspective v iskusstve Renessansa', in *Istoriko-filosofskii ezhegodnik*, ed. N. V. Motroshilova and M. A. Solopova (Moscow: Nauka, 2006), pp. 320–29.

Slesinski, R., *Pavel Florensky: A Metaphysics of Love* (Crestwood, NY: St. Vladimir's Seminary Press, 1984).

Smart, A., *The Assisi Problem and the Art of Giotto: A Study of the 'Legend of St. Francis' in the Upper Church of San Francesco, Assisi* (Oxford: Clarendon Press, 1971).

Spira, A., *Avant-Garde Icon: Russian Avant-Garde Art and the Icon Painting Tradition* (Aldershot: Lund Humphries, 2008).

Steegman, J., 'Lord Lindsay's "History of Christian Art"', *Journal of Warburg and Courtauld Institutes*, 10 (1947), 123–31.

Stoichita, V., *A Short History of the Shadow* (London: Reaktion, 2018).

Strehlke, C. B., and M. B. Israels, eds., *The Bernard and Mary Berenson Collection of European Paintings at I Tatti* (Florence: Villa I Tatti, 2015).

Strehlke, C. B., *Rediscovering Fra Angelico, a Fragmentary History* (New Haven, CT: Yale Universit Press, 2001).

Strugova, O. B., 'M. K. Tenisheva – neokonchennyi portret', in *Kniaginia M. K. Tenisheva v zerkale Serebrianogo veka. Katalog vystavki v Gos. Istoricheskom muzee*, ed. Gosudarstvennyi istoricheskii muzei (Moscow: GIM, 2008), p. 169.

Strzygowski, J., *Orient oder Rom: Beitrag zur Geschichte der spätantiken und früchristlichen Kunst* (Leipzig: Hinrichs, 1901).

Stuart, J., *Ikons* (London: Faber and Faber, 1975).

Sychev, N., 'Ikona sv. Troitsy v Troitse-Sergievoi lavre', *Zapiski otdeleniia russkoi i slavianskoi arkhitektury Russkogo arkheologicheskogo obshchestva*, 10 (1913), 1.

Symonds, J. A., *Sketches and Studies in Italy and Greece*, 3 vols. (London: J. Murray, 1907–14).

Tarabukin, N. M., *Smysl ikony* (Moscow: Pravoslavnogo bratstva Sviatitelia Filareta, 1999).

Tarasov, O., 'Florensky and "Reverse Perspective": Investigating the History of a Term', *Sobornost/Eastern Churches Review*, 43.1 (2021), 7–37.

Tarasov, O., 'Florensky, Malevich e la semiotica dell'icona', *Nuova Europa*, 1 (2002), 34–47.

Tarasov, O., *Framing Russian Art: From Early Icons to Malevich*, trans. R. Milner-Gulland and A. Wood (London: Reaktion, 2011).

Tarasov, O., *Icon and Devotion. Sacred Spaces in Imperial Russia*, trans. R. Milner-Gulland (London: Reaktion, 2002).

Tarasov, O., *Ikona i blagochestie: Ocherki ikonnogo dela v imperatorskoi Rossii* (Moscow: Progress-Kul'tura, 1995).

Tarasov, O., 'Pavel Muratov, i "primitivi" italiani e le icone russe antiche', in *Letture Muratoviane III. Atti del Colloquio Internazionale (Napoli, 28–30 settembre 2017). Studi in memoria di Xenia Muratova*, ed. R. Giuliani (Rome: Lithos, 2021), pp. 247–55.

Tarasov, O., 'Retsenziia na knigu: Uspenskii B. A. *Gentskii altar' Iana van Eika. Bozhestvennaia i chelovecheskaia perspektiva*. Moscow 2013', *Toronto Slavic Quarterly*, 50 (2014), 280–91.

Tarasov, O., 'Russian Icons and the Avant-Garde: Tradition and Change', in *The Art of Holy Russia. Icons from Moscow, 1400–1600*, ed. R. Cormack and D. Gaze (London: Royal Academy of Arts, 1998), pp. 93–9.

Tarasov, O., 'Spirituality and the Semiotics of Russian Culture: From the Icon to Avant-Garde Art', in *Modernism and the Spiritual in Russian Art: New Perspectives*, ed. L. Hardiman and N. Kozicharow (Cambridge: Open Book Publishers, 2017), 115–28, https://doi.org/10.11647/OBP.0115.05

Tarasov, O., *Ten Icons of the 15th–16th Centuries from a Private Collection: From the History of Collecting and Studying Medieval Russian Painting in Soviet Russia* (Rome: Editoriali e Poligrafici, 2023).

Tartuferi, A., *La pittura a Firenze nel Duecento* (Florence: Alberto Bruschi, 1990).

Tartuferi, A., and G. Tormen, *La fortuna dei primitivi. Tesori d'arte dalle collezioni italiane fra Sette e Ottocento. Firenze, Galleria dell'Academia, 24 giugno–8 dicembre 2014* (Florence: Giunti, 2014).

Tonini, L., *I Demidoff a Firenze e in Toscana, Atti del convegno* (Florence: Olschki, 1996).

Tonini, L., 'Nicola Demidoff collezionista russo a Firenze all'inizio del XIX secolo', in *Il collezionismo in Russia da Pietro I all'Unione Sovietica*, ed. L. Tonini (Napoli: Artistic and Publishing Company, 2009), pp. 67–88.

Toporov, V. N., 'Ob odnom arkhaichnom indoevropeiskom elemente v drevnerusskoi dukhovnoi kul'ture - *svet-', in *Iazyki kul'tury i problemy perevodimosti*, ed. B. A. Uspenskii (Moscow: Nauka, 1987), pp. 184–252.

Tormen, G., *Dipinti 'sull'asse d'oro': I primitivi nelle collezioni italiane tra Sette e Ottocento. Un itinerario, in Tesori d'arte dalle collezioni italiane fra Sette e Ottocento, Firenze, Galleria dell'Academia, 24 giugno–8 dicembre 2014* (Florence: Giunti, 2014).

Trubetskoi, E. N., *Umozrenie v kraskakh* (Paris: YMCA Press, 1965).

Uspenskii, B. A., *Gentskii altar' Iana van Eika. Bozhestvennaia i chelovecheskaia perspektiva* (Moscow: zdatel'skii dom 'Rip-Kholding', 2013).

Uspenskii, B. A., 'O semiotike ikony', *Trudy po znakovym sistemam*, 5 (1971), 178–222.

Uspenskii, B. A., '"Pravoe" i "levoe" v ikonopisnom izobrazhenii', in *Sbornik statei po vtorichnym modeliryiushchim sistemam*, ed. J. Lotman (Tartu: Tart. Un-t, 1973), pp. 137–45.

Uspenskii, B. A., *Prospetiva divina e prospetiva umana: La pala di van Eyk a Grand* (Milan: Mondadori Università, 2010).

Uspenskii, B. A., *The Semiotics of the Russian Icon* (Lisse: Peter de Ridder Press, 1976), https://archive.org/details/semioticsofrussi0000uspe

Uspenskii, L., *Bogoslovie ikony pravoslavnoi tserkvi* (Paris: Izd-vo Zapadno-evropeĭskogo Ekzarkhata, Moskovskiĭ patriarkhat, 1989).

Uspenskii, L., *La teologia dell'icona. Storia e iconografia* (Milan: La Casa di Matriona, 1995).

Uspenskii, L., and V. Losskii, *The Meaning of Icons* (Boston, MA: Boston Book and Art Shop, 1952).

Uspenskii, P. D., *Chetvertoe izmerenie. Obzor glavneishikh teorii i popytok issledovaniia oblasti neizmerimogo* (Petrograd: Iz. M. V. Pirozhkova, 1918).

Vaganova, I. V., 'Iz istorii sotrudnichestva P. P. Muratova s izdatel'stvom K. F. Nekrasova', *Litsa: Biograficheskii al'manakh*, 3 (1993), 155–265.

Vagner, R., 'Proizvedenie iskusstva budushchego', in R. Vagner, *Izbrannye raboty* (Moscow: Arts, 1978), pp. 164–95.

van Hadley, R., ed., *The Letters of Bernard Berenson and Isabella Stewart Gardner, 1887–1924* (Boston, MA: Northeastern University Press, 1987), https://archive.org/details/lettersofbernard0000bere/mode/2up

Varalis, Y. D., 'The Painter Angelos in Constantinople? Answers from the Pantokrator Icon at the State Pushkin Museum, Moscow', *The Annual Journal of the Benaki Museum*, 13–14 (2013–14), 79–88.

Velmans, T., ed., *Icone. Il grande viaggio* (Milan: Jaca Book, 2015).

Velmans, T., ed., *L'arte dell'icona* (Milan: Jaca Book, 2013).

Venturi, A., *La Galleria Sterbini a Roma. Saggio illustrativo* (Rome: Casa editrice de l'Arte, 1906), https://archive.org/details/lagalleriasterbi00vent

Venturi, L., *Il gusto dei primitivi* (Bologna: Zanichelli, 1926).

Veresova, T. V., and M. G. Talalai, *Chelovek Renessansa. Khudozhnik Nikolai Lokhov i ego okruzhenie* (Moscow: Staraya Basmannaya, 2017).

Lee, V., *Italiia. Volume 1: Genius loci. Vol. 2: Teatr i muzyka*, ed. P. P. Muratov, trans. E. S. Urenius (Moscow: n.p., 1914–15).

Vrangel, N. N., 'Sobranie I. S. Ostroukhov v Moskve', *Apollon*, 10 (1911), 5–14.

Vrangel, N. N., and A. Trubnikov, 'Kartiny sobraniia grafa G.S. Stroganova v Rime', *Starye gody* (March 1909), 115–36.

'Vystavka drevnerusskogo iskusstva' (n.a.), *Svetil'nik*, 3 (1913), 33–35.

Vystavka drevnerusskogo iskusstva, ustroennaia v 1913 godu v oznamenovanie 300-letiia Doma Romanovykh (n.a.) (Moscow: Imperatorskii Moskovskii Arkheologicheskii Institut Imeni Imperatora Nikolaia II, 1913).

Vzdornov, G. I., *The History of the Discovery and Study of Russian Medieval Painting*, ed. M. Sollins, trans. V. G. Dereviagin (Leiden: Brill, 2017).

Vzdornov, G. I., 'Nikodim Kondakov v zerkale sovremennoi vizantinistiki', in *Nauka i restavratsiia. Ocherki po istorii i izucheniia drevnerusskoi zhivopisi* (Moscow: Indrik, 2006).

Vzdornov, G. I., and K. M. Muratova, eds., *Vozvrashchenie Muratova. Ot 'Obrazov Italii' do 'Istorii kavkazskikh voin'. Po materialam vystavki 'Pavel Muratov – chelovek Serebrianogo veka' v Gos. Muzee izovrazitel'nykh iskusstv imeni A. S. Pushkina 3 marta–20 aprelia 2008 goda* (Moscow: Indrik, 2008).

White, J., *The Birth and Rebirth of Pictorial Space* (London: Faber and Faber, 1957).

Weaver, W. A., *Legacy of Excellence: The Story of Villa I Tatti* (New York: Harry N. Abrams, 1997).

Wölfflin, H., *Principles of Art History: The Problem of the Development of Style in Early Modern Art*, trans. E. A. Levy and T. Weddigen (Los Angeles, CA: Getty Research Institute, 2015).

Wulff, O., 'Die umgekehrte Perspektive und die Niedersicht. Eine raumanschauungsform der altbyzantinischen Kunst und ihre Fortbildung in der Renaissance', in *Kunstwissenschaftliche Beiträge, August Schmarsow gewidmet zum fünfzigsten Semester seiner akademischen Lehrtätigkeit*, ed. H. Weizsäcker (Leipzig: K. Hiersemann, 1907), pp. 3–42, https://archive.org/details/bub_gb_oJjpAAAAMAAJ

Wulff, O., and M. Alpatov, *Denkmaler der Ikonenmalerei* (Dresden: Avalun-Verlag, 1925).

Zabelin, I., *Domashnii byt russkikh tsarei v XVI i XVII stoletiiakh*, 2 vols. (Moscow: V. Grachev and Komp., 1862).

Zachauk, P., ed., *Icons. Icon Museum Frankfurt am Main* (Frankfurt: Ikonenmuseum der Stadt Frankfurt am Main, 2005).

Zeri, F., *Abecedario pittorico* (Milan: Longanesi, 2008).

Zeri, F., *Cos'e un falso e altri conversazioni sul'arte*, ed. M. Castellotti (Milan: Longanesi, 2011).

Zeri, F., *La collezione Federico Mason Perkins* (Turin: Allemandi, 1988).

Zeri, F., 'Qualche appunto sul Daddi', in F. Zeri, *Giorno per giorno nella pittura. Scritti sull arte Toscana dal Trecento al primo Cinquecento* (Turin: Allemandi, 1991), pp. 19–23.

Zhegin, L. F., 'Vospominaniia o. P. Florenskom', *Vestnik russkogo khristianskogo dvizheniia*, 135 (1982), 60–71.

Zhegin, L. F., *Iazykh zhivopisnogo proizvedeniia (Uslovnost' drevnego iskusstva). Predislovie i kommentarii B. A. Uspenskogo* (Moscow: Iskusstvo, 1970).

List of Figures

Fig. 1.1   Carlo Crivelli (c. 1435–95), *Poliptych of San Domenico (Pala Demidov)* (1476), tempera on wood. From the collection of Prince Anatole Demidov. National Gallery, London. Wikimedia, public domain, https://commons.wikimedia.org/wiki/File:Carlo_Crivelli_005.jpg

Fig. 1.2   Coppo di Marcovaldo (1225–76), *Madonna and Child Enthroned, with Scenes from the Life of Mary (Maestà)* (1275–80), tempera on wood, 246 x 138 cm. From the collection of Pyotr Sevast'anov. The Pushkin State Museum of Fine Arts, Moscow. Wikimedia, photograph by Sailko (2020), CC BY-SA 3.0, https://commons.wikimedia.org/wiki/File:Cerchia_di_coppo_di_marcovaldo,_maest%C3%A0.JPG

Fig. 1.3   The Italian Renaissance Hall: Italian 'primitives', medieval Greek and Russian Icons in the house-museum of Mikhail Botkin in St Petersburg. From the catalogue *Collection of M. P. Botkin* (St. Petersburg: R. Golike and A. Vilborg, 1911). Photograph by the author (2017), public domain.

Fig. 1.4   Novgorod School, *The Trinity of the New Testament, With the Chosen Saints* (the second half of the fourteenth century), tempera on wood, 113 x 88 cm. From the collection of Mikhail Botkin in St Petersburg. Tretyakov Gallery, Moscow. Wikimedia, public domain, https://commons.wikimedia.org/wiki/File:Otechestvo_ikona_Novgorod.jpg

Fig. 1.5   Cretan School, *Deesis and the Twelve Great Feasts* (c. 1540–49), tempera on wood, 50 x 80 ¾ in. From the collection of Mikhail Botkin in St Petersburg. Chazen Museum of Art, University of Wisconsin–Madison, United States of America. Wikimedia, photograph by Daderot (2014), CC0, https://commons.wikimedia.org/wiki/File:Great_Deesis_with_the_Twelve_Feasts_of_the_Church,_Greco-Byzantine,_c._1540-1549,_tempera_and_gilt_on_panel_-_Chazen_Museum_of_Art_-_DSC01943.JPG

Fig. 1.6   Duccio (c. 1255/60–c. 1318/19), *Madonna and Child ('Madonna Stroganov')* (c. 1300), tempera on wood, 23.8 x 16.5 cm. From the collection of Count Grigorii Stroganov in Rome. The Metropolitan Museum, New York. Wikimedia, public domain, https://it.wikipedia.org/wiki/File:Duccio_Di_Buoninsegna_-_Madonna_col_Bambino.jpg

Fig. 1.7 Simone Martini (c. 1284–1344), *Madonna from the Annunciation Scene* (c. 1340–44), tempera on wood, 30.5 x 21.5 cm. From the collection of Count Grigorii Stroganov in Rome. State Hermitage, St Petersburg. Wikimedia, public domain, https://commons.wikimedia.org/wiki/File:Simone_Martini_076.jpg

Fig. 2.1 Nikolai Pavlovich Ulyanov (1877–1949), *Portrait of Pavel Muratov* (1911), graphite pencil on paper, 24 x 18 cm. Private collection. Reprinted by permission of the owner. All rights reserved.

Figs. 2.2a Title page and dedication of a special copy of Pavel Muratov's book *Les icones russes*, printed for Bernard Berenson and Mary Smith (Paris: J. Schiffrin éditions de la Plèide, 1927). Villa I Tatti – The Harvard University Center for Italian Renaissance Studies, Florence. Photograph by the author (2018), public domain.

Figs. 2.2b. Title page and dedication of a special copy of Pavel Muratov's book *Les icones russes*, printed for Bernard Berenson and Mary Smith (Paris: J. Schiffrin éditions de la Plèide, 1927). Villa I Tatti – The Harvard University Center for Italian Renaissance Studies, Florence. Photograph by the author (2018), public domain.

Fig. 2.3 Novgorod School, *St Theodore Stratelates* (late fifteenth century), tempera on wood, 136.5 x 109 cm. Novgorod State Museum-Reserve. Wikimedia, public domain, https://commons.wikimedia.org/wiki/File:Theodore_Stratelates_-_hagiography_icon.jpg

Fig. 2.4 Italo-Greek School, *Mother of God of Tenderness* (fifteenth century). Plate from Nikolai Likhachev, *Materialy dlia istorii russkogo ikonopisaniia: Atlas* (St Petersburg: Ekspedisiia zagotovleniia gosudarstvennykh bumag, 1906). Photograph by the author (2016), public domain.

Fig. 2.5 Duccio (c. 1255/60–c. 1318/19), *Madonna Rucellai* (1285), tempera and gold on wood, 450 x 290 cm. Uffizi Gallery, Florence. Wikimedia, public domain, https://commons.wikimedia.org/wiki/File:Duccio_di_Buoninsegna_-_Rucellai_Madonna_-_WGA6822.jpg

Fig. 2.6 *St John Theologian with Scenes from His Life* (c. 1500). Icon detail, reproduced in Pavel Muratov, *La pittura russa antica* (Rome: A. Stock, 1925), as a characteristic example of the musical and rhythmic composition of medieval Russian icon. Photograph by the author (2020), public domain.

List of Figures

Fig. 3.1 Valentin Serov (1865–1919), *Portrait of the Artist Ilya Ostroukhov* (1902), oil on canvas, 87.5 x 78.2 cm. Tretyakov Gallery, Moscow. Wikimedia, public domain, https://commons.wikimedia.org/wiki/File:Portrait_of_the_Artist_Ilya_Ostroukhov.jpg

Fig. 3.2 Novgorod School, *Elijah the Prophet* (fifteenth century), tempera on wood, 75 x 57 cm. From the collection of Ilya Ostroukhov in Moscow. Tretyakov Gallery, Moscow. Reproduced as a color illustration in Nikolai Punin's article 'Ellinizm i Vostok v ikonopisi' ['Hellenism and the East in icon painting'], *Russkaia ikona* (1914), 3. Photograph by the author (2023), public domain.

Fig. 3.3 Constantinople School, *Christ Pantocrator* (first half of the fifteenth century), tempera on wood. From the collection of Ilya Ostroukhov in Moscow. The Pushkin State Museum of Fine Arts. Wikimedia, public domain, https://commons.wikimedia.org/wiki/File:Pantokrator_by_byzantine_anonim,_poss._by_Angelus_(15th_c.,_Pushkin_museum).jpg

Fig. 3.4 Andrei Rublev (1360–1428) School, *The Ascension of Christ* (1410–20s), tempera on wood, 71 x 59 cm. From the collection of Stepan Riabushinskii in Moscow. Tretyakov Gallery, Moscow. Wikimedia, public domain, https://commons.wikimedia.org/wiki/File:Ascension_(1410-20s,_GTG).jpg

Fig. 3.5 Novgorod School, *St Boris and St Gleb* (mid-fourteenth century), tempera on wood, 142.5 x 95.4 cm. From the collection of Nikolai Likhachev. State Russian Museum, St Petersburg. Wikimedia, public domain, https://commons.wikimedia.org/wiki/File:%D0%A1%D0%B2%D1%8F%D1%82%D1%8B%D0%B5_%D0%91%D0%BE%D1%80%D0%B8%D1%81_%D0%B8_%D0%93%D0%BB%D0%B5%D0%B1.jpg

Figs. 3.6a Novgorod School, *The Entombment of Christ* (late fifteenth century), tempera on wood, 90 x 63 cm. From the collection of Ilya Ostroukhov in Moscow. Tretyakov Gallery, Moscow. Reproduced as a color inset in Nikolai Shchekotov's article 'Ikonopis' kak iskusstvo' ['Icon Painting as Art'], *Russkaia ikona* (1914), 2. Photographs by the author (2019), public domain.

Figs. 3.6b Novgorod School, *The Entombment of Christ* (late fifteenth century), tempera on wood, 90 x 63 cm. From the collection of Ilya Ostroukhov in Moscow. Tretyakov Gallery, Moscow. Reproduced as a color inset in Nikolai Shchekotov's article 'Ikonopis' kak iskusstvo' ['Icon Painting as Art'], *Russkaia ikona* (1914), 2. Photographs by the author (2019), public domain.

Fig. 3.7 Novgorod School, *Mother of God of Tenderness* (fifteenth century), tempera on wood, 54 x 42 cm. From the collection of Ilya

Ostroukhov in Moscow. Tretyakov Gallery, Moscow. Wikimedia, public domain, https://commons.wikimedia.org/wiki/File:Mary_Mother_of_jesus1.jpg

Fig. 3.8 Novgorod School, *St George and the Dragon* (end of the fifteenth century), tempera on wood, 82 x 63 cm. From the collection of Ilya Ostroukhov in Moscow. Tretyakov Gallery, Moscow. Wikimedia, public domain, https://commons.wikimedia.org/wiki/File:Georges_icon.jpg

Fig. 3.9 Novgorod School, *Archangel Michael* (fourteenth century), tempera on wood, 86 x 63 cm. From the collection of Stepan Riabushinskii in Moscow. Tretyakov Gallery, Moscow. Wikimedia, public domain, https://commons.wikimedia.org/wiki/File:The_archangle_Michael_(Novgorod).jpg

Fig. 3.10 Photograph of *Poslednyaya futuristicheskaya vystavka kartin: 0,10* [*Last Futurist Exhibition of Painting 0,10*] (1915). Wikimedia, public domain, https://commons.wikimedia.org/wiki/File:0.10_Exhibition.jpg

Fig. 4.1 Pavel Florenskii (1882–1937) in a State Experimental Electrotechnical Institute Laboratory, Moscow, 1925. Public domain.

Fig. 4.2 Andrei Rublev (1360–1428), *The Holy Trinity* (1411, or 1425–27), tempera on wood, 141.5 x 114 cm. Tretyakov Gallery, Moscow. Wikimedia, public domain, https://commons.wikimedia.org/wiki/File:Andrey_Rublev_-_%D0%A1%D0%B2._%D0%A2%D1%80%D0%BE%D0%B8%D1%86%D0%B0_-_Google_Art_Project.jpg

Fig. 4.3 Vladimir Favorskii (1886–1964), book cover for Pavel Florenskii's *Mnimosti v geometrii* [*The Imaginary in Geometry*] (Moscow: Pomorye, 1922). Public domain.

Fig. 4.4 Dionysius and workshop, *The Resurrection of Christ* (c. 1502), tempera on wood, 137.2 x 99.5 cm. State Russian Museum, St Petersburg. Wikimedia, public domain, https://commons.wikimedia.org/wiki/File:Descent_into_Hell_by_Dionisius_and_workshop_(Ferapontov_monastery).jpg

Fig. 4.5 Pavel Florenskii (1882–1937), drawing with the caption 'The Assyrian depiction of a camp is very important for the theory and history of perspective', pencil on paper. Archive of Florenskii's family, Moscow. Printed with the permission of the heirs. All rights reserved.

Fig. 4.6 Pavel Florenskii (1882–1937), drawing with the caption 'Reverse perspective of sedilia [clergy seating], table and Gospel, from a miniature of St John the Theologian [from the] first half of the fifteenth century', pencil on paper. Archive of Florenskii's family, Moscow. Printed with the permission of the heirs. All rights reserved.

Fig. 4.7   Dionysius (1444–1502) and workshop, *The Miraculous Building of the Church*, detail from the hagiographical icon of *St Dimitrii Prilutskii* (c. 1503), tempera on wood. Vologda State Museum-Reserve. Wikimedia, public domain, https://commons.wikimedia.org/wiki/File:Dimitry_Prilutsky_Icon_stamp_15.jpg

Fig. 4.8   *The Fiery Ascent of the Prophet Elijah* (sixteenth century), tempera on wood, 124 x 107 cm. State Historical Museum, Moscow. Reproduced in Mikhail Alpatov, *Early Russian Icon Painting* (Moscow: Moscow Iskusstvo, 1978), p. 86. Wikimedia, public domain, https://commons.wikimedia.org/wiki/File:Elie_with_the_firey_wagon.jpg

Fig. 4.9   Novgorod School, *The Raising of Lazarus* (c. 1497), tempera on wood, 71.5 x 58 cm. State Russian Museum, St Petersburg. Wikimedia, public domain, https://commons.wikimedia.org/wiki/File:Lazarus,_Russian_icon.jpg

Fig. 4.10 Albrecht Dürer (1571–1528), *Man Drawing a Lute* (1525), woodcut. Metropolitan Museum of Art, New York. Wikimedia, public domain, https://commons.wikimedia.org/wiki/File:D%C3%BCrer_-_Man_Drawing_a_Lute.jpg

Index

Abstractionism 168
aesthetics 2–5, 7, 11–12, 16, 18, 20, 33–34, 37, 40–41, 46, 48, 50, 53, 61, 64, 66–67, 69, 74–75, 82–83, 86–87, 89, 92–93, 105, 116, 121, 125, 129, 136–138, 149–150, 152, 157, 159, 171–174
Ainalov, Dmitrii 61, 130–132
  Ellinisticheskie osnovy vyzantiiskogo iskusstva (The Hellenistic Foundations of Byzantine Art) 130
Akotantos, Angelos 84
Albert, Prince Consort 33
Alexander II, Emperor 33
Alexander III, Emperor 71, 76–77, 96
Alpatov, Mikhail 59, 82, 147
Altieri, Cardinal Andrea 28
America 2, 7, 9, 17, 26, 29, 38, 76, 81, 102, 115, 120, 173, 175
Amsterdam 114
Anisimov, Alexander 51, 101–102, 120
anthropocentrism 136, 139, 165, 168
Antonello da Messina 137
architecture 23, 62, 68, 136, 139, 141, 148–149, 157, 167
Aref'ev, Stefan 19, 22, 155
Arezzo 30
art and antiquities market 7, 26, 34, 41, 67, 76–77, 82, 86, 89–90, 93–96, 100, 102, 104, 110, 115, 172–175
art criticism 2, 3, 11, 12, 34, 42, 50, 66, 67, 70, 79, 82, 83, 91, 98, 101, 117, 125, 143, 171, 172, 173. *See also* Formalist School
artistic volition (*Kunstwollen*) 36
Art Nouveau 73–74

Assisi
  Basilica of St Francis of Assisi 100, 141
Assy
  Notre Dame de Toute-Grâce Church 87
Athos 60, 72
Austria 33, 115
avant-garde 3, 7, 12, 36, 42, 49, 53, 64, 87, 111–112, 117, 124, 168–170, 174

Bailo, Luigi 72
Bakst, Leon 80
Bakushinskii, Anatolii 124, 138–139
Balducci, Matteo 50
Balzac, Honoré de 67, 114
  Le Chef-d'œuvre inconnu (The Unknown Masterpiece) 67
Bandini, Angelo Maria 15
Barcelona 78
Bardini, Stefano 4, 26, 29–30, 90, 93
Bari 72
Barr, Alfred 6
Bazin, Germain 79
Beine, Karl-August 23
Belle Époque (c. 1871–1914) 2–3, 7, 9, 11, 26, 32, 38, 68, 76, 78, 82, 86, 92, 95, 110, 113, 163, 171, 173–174
Belting, Hans 76
Bely, Andrei 119, 153
Benois, Alexandre 80, 104, 110, 168
Benvenuto di Giovanni 94–95
Berenson, Bernard 2–5, 7, 32, 34, 36–42, 47–49, 52–53, 58, 65, 76, 78, 81–82, 87–88, 93–96, 98, 100, 102, 104, 109, 125, 143, 166, 173–174
Berlin 29, 37, 46, 71, 76
  Bode-Museum 29

Kunstgewerbemuseum 71
Bilibin, Ivan 47
Blok, Alexander 119
Bode, Wilhelm von 29, 32, 71, 94, 104
Bol'shakov, Sergei 83
Bonnard, Pierre 87
Borgia, Cardinal Stefano 13
Boston 29, 38
   Isabella Stewart Gardner Museum 29, 38
Botkin, Mikhail 26–28
Botkin, Piotr 70
Botkina, N. P. 70
Botticelli, Sandro 39–40, 49, 53, 82, 93
Bourget, Paul 38
Braque, Georges 87, 169
Briagin, Evgenii 85
Britain 26, 115
Briusov, Valerii 119
Broglio, Mario 47
Bruges 78
Bugaev, Nikolai 126
Bulgakov, Sergei 153
Buslaev, Fyodor 20, 22, 32
Byzantium 16, 34, 54, 56–58, 63–64, 137, 161, 170, 174
   Byzantine culture 12, 60–61
   Byzantine icon 1, 3, 9, 13, 17, 23, 31, 58–61, 63, 71–72, 76, 84, 98–100, 163, 167, 173
   Byzantine painting 2, 12, 15, 47, 56, 60, 66, 71–72, 116, 129
   Byzantine style (*maniera bizantina*) 15, 79, 98
   Byzantine tradition 53–56, 58, 66, 84, 129, 136

Cambridge, University of 48
Cannes 7
Cap Ferret 94
Caravaggio 172
Cassirer, Ernst 134–135, 167
Cavalcaselle, Giovanni 32
Cellini, Benvenuto 22
Cézanne, Paul 12, 49, 113
Chagall, Marc 87
Charlemagne 63
Chekrygin, Vasily 126
Chernyi, Daniil 123, 157
Chernyshev, Nikolai 126
China 64, 69
Chirikov, Grigorii 90–92, 116, 120
Chirikov, Mikhail 90–92
Chirin, Prokopii 19, 22, 155
Christ 18, 20–21, 61, 73, 136–137, 142–143, 146, 152, 154
Christianity 13, 16, 61, 160–161, 168, 172
Cimabue 15, 17
Cima da Conegliano 29
Clement XIII, Pope 14–15
collector 2–3, 6, 7, 11, 13, 17, 20–21, 24, 26, 28–29, 32–33, 38–40, 46, 62, 67–71, 74, 76, 78, 81–83, 87–90, 94–99, 102–103, 105, 109–110, 113–115, 172–174. *See also* Old Believers: Old Believer collections
   cabinet of curiosity (*Kunstkammer*) 21
   new collecting 7, 34, 46, 70, 83, 90, 101, 105, 173–174
   connoisseur (*conoscitore*) 2–3, 13, 33, 38, 40–41, 48–51, 66, 74, 83, 94, 110, 125, 171–172, 174
   pure visibility 33–35, 37
   visual intelligence 35
Constantinople 18, 58, 72, 84, 103, 109, 145
   Church of the Theotokos of the Pharos 18
   Kahrie Djami 58, 63
Conway, Martin 116
Coppo di Marcovaldo 24–25
Corfu 60
Cornelius, Peter von 23
Corot, Jean-Baptiste-Camille 69
Corsi, Giovacchino 94
counterfeit. *See* imitation
Couturier, Marie-Alain 87
Cozzarelli, Guidoccio 50

Crete 16, 28, 58, 60, 84, 106, 154
Cristiani, Giovanni di Bartolomeo 23–24
Crivelli, Carlo 13–14
Cubism 3, 64, 169–170
Cyprus 60

Daddi, Bernardo 33, 197
Dalton, Ormonde Maddock 47, 49, 56, 58
D'Annunzio, Gabriele 32
Dante 34, 141
Darwin, Charles 163
Davies, Joseph 28
Degas, Edgar 68–69, 80
Demidov family 26
Demidov, Nikolai 26
Demidov, Prince Anatole 14
Denis, Maurice 87
Deonna, Waldemar 65
Diaghilev, Sergei 80
Diehl, Charles 34, 47, 49, 56, 58
Dikarev, Mikhail 92
Dilthey, Wilhelm 37
Dionisii 51, 53, 144
Dossena, Alceo 94
Douglas, Robert Langton 4, 79
Duccio di Buoninsegna 3, 15, 29–30, 33, 39, 42, 50, 52, 58–59, 77, 79, 94, 97, 99, 104, 109
Dürer, Albrecht 164–165
Dusseldorf 78
Duveen, Joseph 4

Eastern Mediterranean 72
Efros, Abram 83
  'Peterburgskoe i moskovskoe sobiratel'stvo' (Petersburg and Moscow Collecting) 83
Egorov, Dmitri 152
Egypt 69, 146, 164, 167
El Greco 166
Emel'ianov, Nikolai 92
empathy (*Einfühlung*) 36–37, 40, 153
Enlightenment 1–2, 12, 21

Euclid 129, 136, 149
Eurocentrism 2, 36
Evdokiia, Princess 15
exhibition
  Early Sienese Painting (1904) 79
  Flemish Primitives and Early Art (1902) 78
  German Medieval Painting (1904) 78
  Last Futurist Exhibition of Painting 0,10 (1915) 111–112
  Manet and Postimpressionism (1910) 88
  Old Russian Art (1913) 90, 105, 112–113, 174
  Two Centuries of Russian Painting and Sculpture (1906) 80
Eyck, Jan van 78, 132

Favorskii, Vladimir 126–128
Ferapontov Monastery 51, 100
Fiedler, Konrad 35–37
Florence 4, 15, 17, 19, 21, 23, 26, 29, 32, 35, 54, 72, 76, 82, 90, 93–96
  Bandini Museum (Fiesole) 23–24
  Bardini's house-museum 26, 29, 93
  Gallery of the Academy of Fine Arts 1
  'I Tatti', Villa (The Harvard University Center for Italian Renaissance Studies) 4, 48, 81, 82, 88, 95, 100
  Palazzo Davanzati 94
  Palazzo Pitti 15, 19
  Palazzo Vecchio 21
    Cabinet of Rarities 21
  Uffizi Galleries 15, 59, 94
    Gabinetto delle pitture antiche (Cabinet of Early Paintings) 15–16
  Villa Quatro 23
Florenskii, Pavel 2, 7–8, 52, 102, 117–132, 134, 136–143, 145–172
  'Ikonostas' (Iconostasis) 8, 122, 172

'Khramovoe deistvo kak sintez iskusstv' (Church Ritual as a Synthesis of the Arts) 156, 161
Mnimosti v geometrii (The Imaginary in Geometry) 122, 126–128
'Molennye ikony prepodobnogo Sergiia' (Devotional Icons of St Sergius) 122
'Obratnaia perspektiva' (Reverse Perspective) 8, 122, 124, 132–133, 172
'Smysl idealizma' (The Meaning of Idealism) 169
Stolp i utverzhdenie istiny (The Pillar and Foundation of the Truth) 121
'Tochka' (Point) 169
'Troitse-Sergieva Lavra i Rossiia' (The Trinity Lavra of St Sergius Monastery and Russia) 123
U vodorazdelov myslii (At the Watersheds of Thought) 125
Florida 94
Florovskii, Georgii 160, 168
forgery. *See* imitation
Formalist School 2, 34–35, 37, 41, 49, 52, 117, 143, 171, 174
Fra Angelico 15, 23–24, 29, 33, 38–39, 47, 52–53, 77, 82, 113
France 7, 78, 125
fresco 23, 30, 51, 58–59, 62–63, 93, 95–96, 103–104, 109, 115, 141, 144, 157, 166
Frick, Helen Clay 4
Frick, Henry Clay 41, 81, 96
Friedländer, Max 40, 94, 104, 173
Fry, Roger 82, 88, 116
Futurism 3

Gaddi, Agnolo 32
Gaddi, Taddeo 81
Gagarin, Prince Grigorii 23
Gainsborough, Thomas 114
Galitsyn family 21
Gardner, Isabella Stewart 4, 38, 41, 81
Gaugin, Paul 87

Georgievskii, Vasilii 106, 121
Georgii Mikhailovich, Grand Prince 71, 78
Germany 26, 114, 115, 124. *See also* Formalist School
Giorgione 39–40
Giotto 17, 34, 38–39, 41–42, 50, 135, 141, 166
Gippius, Zinaida 119
Giunti, Umberto 94
Godunov, Mikhail Andreevich 15
Goethe, Johann Wolfgang von 114
Goncharova, Natalia 80, 87, 110–111, 168
Grabar, Igor 36, 46, 50, 59, 63, 74, 77, 83, 92, 97, 102, 115, 120
'Glaz' (The Eye) 83
Istoriia russkogo iskusstva (History of Russian Art) 50, 97, 101
Greece 60, 62, 69, 72, 164
Grishchenko, Aleksei 11, 53, 67, 87, 112–113, 116, 120, 169, 174
'Russkaia ikona mezhdu Vizantiei i Zapadom' (The Russian Icon between Byzantium and the West) 169
Grottaferrata 79, 98
Greek monastery 79
Gruneizen, Vladimir von 65
'Illiuzionisticheskii portret' (The Illusionistic Portrait) 65
Gur'ianov, Vasilii 92, 121

Hadrianopolis 84
Haskell, Francis 172
Hegel, Georg Wilhelm Friedrich 157
Heidegger, Martin 157
Helmholtz, Hermann von 35, 149
Hildebrand, Adolf von 35–38, 40, 49
Das Problem der Form in der Bildenden Kunst (The Problem of Form in the Fine Arts) 35
Horne, Herbert Percy 26, 32, 76, 82, 174
Humanism 21
Husserl, Edmund 167

Die Krisis der europäischen Wissenschaften und die transzendentale Phänomenologie (The Crisis of European Sciences and Transcendental Phenomenology) 167

icon. *See also* Italy: Italo-Greek icon; *See also* Novgorod: Novgorodian icon; *See also* Russia: Russian icon; *See also* Stroganov family: Stroganov icon
  as pure art 1, 13, 17–18, 21, 51–52, 68, 83, 106, 111, 113
  family icon 18
  hagiographical (or *vita*) icon 22, 54, 123, 143–146
  pilgrim icon 18
  votive icon 18
image composition
  picture space 13, 137–138, 166
  self-contained space 126
imitation 67, 92, 94–96
Impressionism 12, 35, 49, 61, 63, 87, 89
Italy 1, 5, 7, 9, 13, 16, 23–26, 29, 34–35, 40, 45–46, 50, 56–58, 60, 63, 72, 76, 78–79, 90, 93–94, 98, 100, 109, 114
  Italo-Greek icon 9, 15, 17, 23, 51, 56–57, 60, 71–72, 79, 81, 84, 98, 100, 105, 154, 167
Ivanchin-Pisarev, Nikolai 33
Ivanov, Vyacheslav 153, 156, 160
Ivan the Terrible, Tsar 157

Jacobello del Fiore 77
James, Henry 32
Japan 69, 100
Jarves, James Jackson 17
Johnson, John G. 41, 81
Joni, Icilio Federico 94–95
  Le memorie di un pittore di quadri antichi (Memoirs of an Artist of Old Paintings) 95
journal
  Apollon (Apollo) 50, 102
  Art Journal 17
  Bogoslovskii vestnik (The Theological Herald) 119
  Burlington Magazine 82
  Khudozhestvennye sokrovishcha Rossii (Artistic Treasures of Russia) 102
  L'antiquario (The Antiquarian) 93, 96
  L'Art decoratif (Decorative Art) 110
  Makovets 156
  Novyi put' (New Path) 119
  Russkaia ikona (The Russian Icon) 75, 82, 102, 104–105
  Sofiia (Sophia) 49, 53, 64–65, 105
  Sredi kollektsionerov (Among Collectors) 82
  Starye gody (Bygone Years) 49–50, 75, 77, 96, 102, 104–105
  Vesy (The Scales) 49, 119

Kallab, Wolfgang 62
Kandinsky, Wassily 124, 169, 174
Karpov, Pavel 125
Khanenko, Bogdan 102, 109
Khanenko, Varvara 87, 102, 109
Kharitonenko, Pavel 11, 70, 88, 105, 109
Kholui 71, 154
Khomiakov, Aleksei 24
Khomiakov, Dmitrii 24
Kirikov, Vasilii 119–121, 154
Kirillo-Belozerskii Monastery 51
Kiselev, Aleksandr 70
Komnenian era 60
Kondakov, Nikodim 32, 37, 56–58, 60, 70–71, 82, 89, 100, 104, 106, 130, 171
  Ikonografiia Bogomateri (Iconography of the Mother of God) 56, 71
Kuftin, Boris 124

Lanzi, Luigi 15–16
  A History of Painting in Italy 16
Larionov, Mikhail 111, 168
Lazarev, Viktor 56

Le Corbusier 87
Le Fauconnier, Henri 110
Leader, John 76
Lee, Vernon 32, 34, 46, 49
  Italy 46
Léger, Fernand 87
Lehman, Philip 4
Lehman, Robert 4
Lelli, Giuseppe 13
Lenbach, Franz von 32
Leo XIII, Pope 98
Leonardo da Vinci 39, 166
Leskov, Nikolai 33
Levitan, Isaac 70
Likhachev, Nikolai 11, 37, 56–58, 60, 70–72, 80, 82, 90–91, 100, 105–106, 121, 140, 171
  Istoricheskoe znachenie italo-grecheskoi ikonopisi (The Historical Significance of Italo-Greek Icon-Painting) 56, 72
  Manera pis'ma Andreia Rubleva (Andrei Rublev's Style of Painting) 140
  Materialy dlia istorii russkago ikonopisaniia (Materials for a History of Russian Icon-Painting) 72
Lindsay, Lord Alexander 16, 33
  Sketches of the History of Christian Art 16
Liphart, Ernst von 24
Liphart, Karl von 32
Lipps, Theodor 37
Lo Gatto, Ettore 5
Lokhov, Nikolai 96
London 13, 17, 33, 39, 46, 48, 79, 82, 88, 94, 114–115
  Burlington Fine Arts Club 79
  Courtauld Institute of Art 48
  National Gallery 14, 17, 33, 137
  Victoria and Albert Museum 115–116
Lorenzetti, Ambrogio 24, 52
Lorenzetti, Pietro 52, 94

Losev, Aleksei 122, 160
Lotto, Lorenzo 39
Luzin, Nikolai 152

Mach, Ernst 35, 149
Mackintosh, Charles Rennie 74
Madrid 114
magazine. *See* journal
Magnasco, Alessandro 12
Makovskii, Sergei 47
Malevich, Kazimir 111, 168, 174
Malyavin, Filipp 80
Mamontov, Savva 70
Manet, Édouard 68–69, 80, 88, 114
Marburg School 167
Marées, Hans von 35
Margaritone d'Arezzo 30
Maria Nikolaevna, Grand Princess 23
Mariotti, Agostino 13
Martini, Simone 25, 29–32, 38, 42, 52, 77, 104, 109, 116
Marzi, Bruno 94
masterpiece 4, 7, 13, 22, 29–31, 38, 41, 46, 49, 52–53, 55, 67–70, 79, 83, 85–86, 90, 94–97, 99, 101–102, 104–105, 107, 116–117, 121, 172–175
Matisse, Henri 5–6, 87–89, 110
Matsys, Quentin 31
Matteo di Giovanni 25, 49–50, 79, 81, 94
Matteo di Pacino 32
Medici, Duke Francesco de' 21
Medici family 15
Memmi, Lippo 38, 79
Merezhkovskii, Dmitrii 119
Merleau-Ponty, Maurice 157, 168
Michelangelo 130, 166–167
Middle Ages 129–130, 162, 165, 167
Milan 72
Millet, Gabriel 34, 47, 49, 56, 58
Mistra 58, 103
Modernism 6, 12, 35, 49, 89, 125, 137, 170, 174–175
Monet, Claude 12

Morelli, Giovanni 32, 40, 65, 94
Morozov, Aleksei 11, 51, 89–90, 105, 109, 113
Morozov family 19, 70
Morozov, Ivan 12, 89
Morris, William 34
mosaic 51, 58, 62–63, 103
Moscow
  Archaeological Society 80
  Central State Restoration Workshop 102
  Commission for the Discovery of Early Paintings 120
  Edinoverie Monastery 88
  Historical Museum 73, 147
  Institute of Artistic Culture (INKhUK) 102, 123
  Moscow Archaeological Institute 105
  Moscow Institute of Art Historical Research and Museum Studies (MIKhM) 123–124
  Moscow Spiritual Academy 119, 123
  Moscow-Tartu Semiotic School 8
  Museum of Fine Arts 6, 23–25, 29, 49, 76, 81, 84, 96, 115
  Museum of Medieval Russian Painting 6–7, 102, 173
  Novodevichy Monastery 88
  Pavel Florenskii's house-museum 122
  Rogozhskoe Cemetery 88
  Rumiantsev Museum 25, 50
  Russian Academy of Artistic Sciences (GAKhN) 124–125, 138
  Tretyakov Gallery 27, 39, 52, 68–70, 73–75, 83, 86, 88, 90–92, 101–103, 107–108, 111, 119–120, 142, 146, 153, 168
Moskowitz, Anita Fiderer 93
Mstera 71, 85, 89–90, 92, 154
Muñoz, Antonio 98–99
Muratov, Pavel 2, 4–7, 11–12, 34, 36–38, 43, 45–55, 58–66, 77, 82–83, 97–102, 104–106, 108–110, 114–117, 121, 124–125, 131–132, 143, 157, 166–167, 171, 174
Drevnerusskaia zhivopis' (Russian Medieval Painting) 5, 46, 97
La pittura bizantina (Byzantine Painting) 47, 82
La pittura russa antica (Ancient Russian Painting) 5, 64, 82, 114
Les icones russes (Russian Icons) 5–6, 47–48, 82, 115
'Novoe sobiratel'stvo' (The New Collecting) 83
Obrazy Italii (Images of Italy) 45, 50
'Otkrytiia drevnego russkogo iskusstva' (Discoveries in Russian Medieval Art) 47, 114
'Puti russkoi ikony' (Ways of the Russian Icon) 47
Russkaia zhivopis' do serediny XVII veka (Russian Painting to the Mid-Seventeenth Century) 46
'Vokrug ikony' (Around the Icon) 47, 114
'Vystavka drevnerusskogo iskusstva v Moskve' (The Eras of Medieval Russian Icon-Painting) 105
museum 3, 6, 9, 13, 15, 17, 21, 23, 26–29, 32, 38, 50, 68–70, 72, 74, 76–79, 83, 85, 88, 90, 93, 96, 99–102, 105, 111, 114, 146, 157, 175
  house-museum 26–29, 32, 93, 122, 146

Naples 6, 72
naturalism 168
Nazarene (movement) 16, 23
Nekrasov, Konstantin 64, 100, 102, 169
Nelidov, Aleksander 80
Neoprimitivism 3, 168
Neri di Bicci 32
Nesterov, Mikhail 49, 153
New York 6, 94

Metropolitan Museum of Art 29–30, 77, 164
Museum of Modern Art 6
Nicholas I, Emperor 22
Nicholas II, Emperor 73, 85
Nietzsche, Friedrich 3, 153, 157, 159
  Die Geburt der Tragödie (The Birth of Tragedy) 159
Nikon, Patriarch 13, 19–20
Novgorod 6, 20, 27, 51, 54–55, 58, 60, 62, 75, 77, 89, 91, 93, 101–103, 107–108, 112, 148
  Novgorodian icon 13, 20, 54, 56, 58–59, 63, 65, 74, 85, 93, 108, 111, 146

October Revolution (1917) 69, 96, 102, 114, 119
Old Believers 11, 13, 17–21, 33, 39, 51, 68, 70, 73, 85, 89–92, 171, 173–174
  Old Believer collections 18–19, 33, 39, 70, 73, 89
  Old Believer communities 17, 20, 73, 171
  Old Believer oratories (prayer houses) 17–21, 68, 92
  Old Believer restoration 21, 85, 92, 173
Olsuf'ev, Count Yurii Aleksandrovich 120
Orthodox Church 13, 19, 60, 118, 120, 122, 126, 157–158, 160–161, 168
  Orthodox ritual 136, 160
Ostafyevo 24
Ostroukhov, Ilya 2, 6–7, 11, 46–47, 49, 51, 62, 68–70, 74–78, 80, 82–85, 87–91, 97–103, 105, 107–115, 142, 157, 173–174
Overbeck, Johann Friedrich 23
Oxford 17
  Ashmolean Museum 17
  University of Oxford 56

Palekh 71, 154
Panofsky, Erwin 134–136, 162, 165, 171

Paris 29, 46–47, 80, 87, 110, 114
  Catholic Institute 87
  Icon Society 7, 47
  Jacquemart-André Museum 29
  Museum of Decorative Arts 80
Parsons, Harold 94
Pater, Walter 34, 39–40, 49, 53, 108
Paul III, Pope 28
Pelli, Giuseppe Bencivenni 15
periodical. *See* journal
Perkins, Frederick Mason 4, 79, 94, 100–101, 174
Persia 105, 131
perspective
  artificial perspective (*perspectiva artificialis*) 129
  linear perspective 3, 8, 124, 129–133, 135–137, 139, 141, 147, 162–167
  reverse perspective 3, 7, 21, 76, 117, 124, 129–134, 136–139, 142–143, 145, 147–149, 154, 158, 162, 166–168, 171
Petrarch 141
phenomenology 125, 168
Picasso, Pablo 64, 110, 113, 169–170
Piranesi, Giovanni Battista 100
Pisano, Nicola 94
Plato 129, 145, 148, 159–160, 163
  Politeia (The Republic) 163
Platonism 159, 168–169
  Neoplatonism 135
Plotinus 129
Pogodin, Mikhail 22, 33
Pokrovskii, Vladimir 92
Postmodernism 175
Poussin, Nicolas 12
Praz, Mario 1
Pre-Raphaelites 16
Previtali, G. 1
'primitives'
  Catalonian 'primitives' 78
  Flemish 'primitives' 12, 54, 63, 77–78, 94, 104
  French 'primitives' 78

Italian 'primitives' 1, 3–4, 12–14, 16–17, 22–28, 31, 33–35, 38, 42, 50, 54, 56, 58, 60, 63, 65, 68, 72, 76, 78, 81–82, 85–87, 89, 93–95, 99, 104–105, 114, 173–175
  origin of term 2–3, 75–76
  Russian 'primitives' 54, 80–81, 174
Primitivism 7, 87
Pseudo-Dionysius the Areopagite 118
Pskov 51, 54
Punin, Nikolai 11, 34, 75, 121, 171
Pythagoras 129

Quattrocento 13, 29, 49, 52, 54, 65, 78, 81, 93–95

Rakhmanov family 19
Raphael 3, 39, 130, 166
Rauschenbach, Boris 134
Reiman, Fyodor 31
relief 32, 62, 131, 135, 160
Rembrandt 114
Remizov, Aleksey 108
Renaissance 1–3, 5, 16, 21, 26–27, 29, 32, 34, 36, 41–42, 46, 49, 53, 64, 67, 75–76, 78, 87, 94, 96–97, 109, 126, 129–130, 133, 135–137, 139, 163, 165–168, 172
  Palaiologan Renaissance 55–56, 58–61, 65
Repin, Ilya 68, 70, 80
Riabushinskii family 19, 70
Riabushinskii, Nikolai 110
Riabushinskii, Stepan 11, 51, 59, 73, 85–86, 90, 92, 102, 105, 108–110, 112–113, 173
  'Ikonopis' kak iskusstvo' (Icon-Painting as Art) 103
  'O restavratsii I sokhranenii drevnikh sviatykh ikon' (On the Restoration and Preservation of Early Holy Icons) 85
Riabushinskii, Vladimir 47
Richardson, Jonathan 40
Riegl, Alois 36, 49

Grundlegungen zu einer Geschichte der Ornamentik (Foundations for a History of Ornament) 36
Spätrömische Kunstindustrie (The Late Roman Art Industry) 36
Rodin, Auguste 69
Romanov family 105–106
Romanov, Konstantin 120
Romanov, Nikolai 124
Romanticism 1, 12–13, 16, 33, 54, 168
  Romantic cult of art 12
Rome 7, 13, 23–24, 26, 28–30, 32, 46–47, 69, 72, 79–80, 98–99, 141
  Bibliotheca Hertziana–Max Planck Institute for Art History 32
  International 'Pavel Muratov' Study Centre 6
  Museo Sacro (Palazzo Altemps) 13
  Palazzo Barberini 31
  Palazzo Stroganov 29, 32, 99
  Palazzo Venezia 98
  Palazzo Zuccari 32
  Valori plastici (Plastic Values), publishers 47
Ronchamp
  Notre-Dame du Haut Chapel 87
Rostovtsev, Mikhail 62, 138
Rouault, Georges 87
Rovinskii, Dmiitrii 20, 33
  Obozrenie ikonopisaniia (A Survey of Icon-Painting) 20
Rublev, Andrei 6, 39, 51–53, 86, 90, 116, 119–123, 140–141, 152, 154, 156–157, 159
Ruskin, John 16, 34
Russell, Bertrand 42
Russia 6–7, 11–13, 17, 21, 23–26, 28, 33–35, 37, 39, 42, 46, 50, 54, 61, 63, 68–69, 73, 76, 78, 89, 97, 101, 103–104, 150, 154, 171, 173–174
Russian icon 1–6, 9, 11–13, 15, 17, 20, 22–23, 26, 31, 33–35, 37–38, 42–43, 46–48, 51–56, 58, 60–66, 68, 71–72, 76, 78, 80, 82–86, 88–89, 93, 97, 99, 101–102, 104–106, 108–110,

112–117, 121, 124, 133–134, 136, 157, 161–162, 167, 170–171, 173–175

Sakharov, Ivan 33
Saldatenkov family 70
Sano di Pietro 25, 30, 50, 94
Sargent, John Singer 38
Savin, Nazarii 22
Savin, Nikifor 19, 22
Savostin, Mikhail 83–84
Schechtel, Fyodor 73
Schelling, Friedrich 172
Segna di Bonaventura 25
Serbia 58
Sergius of Radonezh, Saint 123, 126, 144, 146, 150, 157, 161
Serov, Valentin 49, 68–70, 80
Sevast'ianov, Pyotr 24
Shchekin, Mikhail Sergeevich 25, 76–77
Shchekotov, Nikolai 11, 34, 36, 38, 83, 103, 105, 108, 116, 124, 171, 174
　'Nekotorye cherty stiliia russkikh ikon XV veka' (Some Stylistic Traits of Russia's Fifteenth-century Icons) 105
Shcherbatova (Stroganov), Princess Maria 29
Shcherbatov, Prince Sergei 7, 47, 74, 109
Shchukin, Sergei 12, 49, 87–89, 112
Shevchenko, Aleksandr 126
Shpet, Gustav 125
Shuvalov family 21
Sidorov, Aleksei 124–125
Siena 30, 50, 54, 58, 79, 93–95, 99, 101, 109
　Palazzo Pubblico 79
Silin, Ivan 83
Simone di Filippo Benvenuti 25
Simone, Giuseppe 14
Smith, Mary 47–48, 96
Soloviev, Vladimir 119, 153

St Petersburg 22–23, 26–29, 31–32, 71, 73, 75, 83, 90, 96, 105–106, 130, 140, 146
　Academy of Arts' Museum of Christian Antiquities in St Petersburg 23–24, 70, 105–107
　Botkin's house-museum 26, 28, 32, 146
　Russian Museum 22, 71, 73, 78, 90–91, 128, 148, 173
　State Hermitage 23–24, 29, 31, 77–78, 87
　Theological Academy 22
Stefano di Giovanni (Sassetta) 79, 81
Stein, Gertrude 88
Stein, Leo 88
Stelletskii, Dmitrii 47
Stendhal 114
Sterbini, Giulio 80, 98–99
Sterbini, Niccolò 99
Stibbert, Frederick 26, 76
Stroganov, Count Grigorii Sergeevich 29–32, 77, 79–80, 99
Stroganov, Count Pavel Sergeevich 28–29
Stroganov, Count Sergei Grigor'evich 21–22, 28, 33
Stroganov family 19, 21, 28
　Stroganov icon 15, 19–20, 22, 54, 89, 99, 155, 173
Strzygowski, Jòzef 47, 61
Symonds, John 34
synthesis of the arts (*Gesamtkustwerk*) 124, 156–159, 161
Syria 131

Tarabukin, Nikolai 63, 138, 158
Tenisheva, Maria 80, 87
Theophanes the Greek 6, 51, 53
Titian 39, 172
Tiulin, Aleksandr 85
Tiulin, Aleksei 85
Torini, Lodovico 95
Trecento 13, 29, 35, 49–50, 52, 54, 58, 60, 62, 64–66, 78, 81, 93–95, 98, 109, 197

Tretiakov, Pavel 70
Trinity Lavra of St Sergius 119–120, 122–124, 126, 137, 142, 144, 146, 150, 154, 157, 159
  Commission for the Preservation of the Trinity Lavra of St Sergius' Monuments of Art and Antiquities 119–120, 122–124, 156
  Trinity Cathedral 120, 122–123, 142, 144, 157, 159
Trubnikov, Aleksandr 30, 77
Tsarskoe Selo 92
  Feodorovskii Icon Cathedral 92
Tuscany 15, 26, 101
  Museo Sacro di Sant'Ansano 15

Umbria 26
Ushakov, Simon 123
Uspenskii, Boris 8, 132–134
Uspenskii, Peter 170
Uspenskii, Vasilii 121
Uvarova, Countess Praskovia 80

Vasari, Giorgio 15, 21, 141
Vasnetsov, Viktor 105
Vatican 8, 13–14, 99, 141, 166
  Museo Sacro della Biblioteca Vaticana 14–15, 99
  Redemptoris Mater Chapel 8
Velázquez, Diego 12, 114
Vence
  Rosary Chapel 87
Venice 9, 72, 95, 100
Venturi, Adolfo 94, 104
Vermeer, Johannes 172
Vettori, Francesco 14–15
Viazemskii, Prince Pyotr 24
Vicenza
  Palazzo Leoni Montanari (Intesa Bank's collection of Russian icons) 9
Victoria, Queen 33

Vilnius 38
Vologda 51, 144
Volpi, Elia 26, 90, 93
Vrangel, Baron Nikolai 30, 50, 70, 77
Vrubel, Mikhail 80

Wackenroder, Wilhelm Heinrich 16
Wagner, Richard 156, 159
Whistler, James 38
Winckelmann, Johann Joachim 33
Wölfflin, Heinrich 11, 34, 36–38, 49, 52, 143
  Die Klassische Kunst (Classic Art) 37
  Einleitung in die Geisteswissenschaften (An Introduction to the Human Sciences) 37
  Kunstgeschichtliche Grundbegriffe (The Principles of Art History) 37
  Renaissance und Barock (Renaissance and Baroque) 37
Worringer, Wilhelm 36
  Abstraktion und Einfühlung (Abstraction and Empathy) 36
Wulff, Oskar 76, 82, 130–132, 134, 136, 162, 171
  'Die umgekehrte Perspektive und die Niedersicht' (Reverse Perspective and Bird's-Eye View' 132

Yale University Art Gallery 17
Yaroslavl 51, 100
Yusupov family 21

Zabelin, Ivan 18
Zaitsev, Boris 47
Zelada, Francesco Saverio de 13
Zeri, Federico 5, 24
Zhegin, Lev 126, 138, 160
Zolla, Elémire 8

About the Team

Alessandra Tosi was the managing editor for this book.

Adèle Kreager copy-edited and indexed this book.

Jeevanjot Kaur Nagpal designed the cover. The cover was produced in InDesign using the Fontin font.

Cameron Craig typeset the book in InDesign and produced the paperback and hardback editions. The text font is Tex Gyre Pagella and the heading font is Californian FB.

Cameron also produced the PDF, EPUB, XML and HTML editions. The conversion was performed with open-source software and other tools freely available on our GitHub page at https://github.com/OpenBookPublishers.

This book has been anonymously peer-reviewed by experts in their field. We thank them for their invaluable help.

This book need not end here...

Share

All our books — including the one you have just read — are free to access online so that students, researchers and members of the public who can't afford a printed edition will have access to the same ideas. This title will be accessed online by hundreds of readers each month across the globe: why not share the link so that someone you know is one of them?

This book and additional content is available at:
https://doi.org/10.11647/OBP.0378

Donate

Open Book Publishers is an award-winning, scholar-led, not-for-profit press making knowledge freely available one book at a time. We don't charge authors to publish with us: instead, our work is supported by our library members and by donations from people who believe that research shouldn't be locked behind paywalls.

Why not join them in freeing knowledge by supporting us:
https://www.openbookpublishers.com/support-us

Follow @OpenBookPublish

Read more at the Open Book Publishers BLOG

You may also be interested in:

Modernism and the Spiritual in Russian Art
New Perspectives
Louise Hardiman and Nicola Kozicharow (editors)

https://doi.org/10.11647/obp.0115

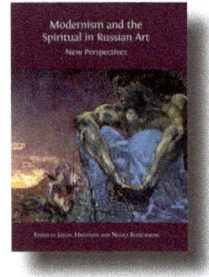

Beyond Holy Russia
The Life and Times of Stephen Graham
Michael Hughes

https://doi.org/10.11647/obp.0040

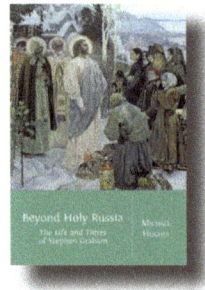

Translating Russian Literature in the Global Context
Muireann Maguire and Cathy McAteer (editors)

https://doi.org/10.11647/obp.0340

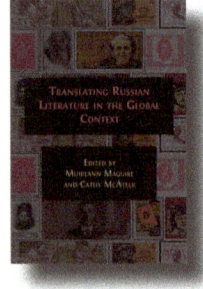